Listening to Children's Wishes and Feelings

COURSE HANDBOOK

Mary Corrigan and Joan Moore

BAAF
ADOPTION
& FOSTERING

Published by
British Association for Adoption & Fostering
(BAAF)
Saffron House
6–10 Kirby Street
London EC1N 8TS
www.baaf.org.uk

Charity registration 275689 (England and Wales) and SC039337 (Scotland)

British Library Cataloguing in Publication Data
A catalogue record for this book is available from the British Library

ISBN 978 1 907585 11 1

Project management by Miranda Davies, BAAF
Designed by Helen Joubert Design
Printed in Great Britain by The Lavenham Press

BAAF is the leading UK-wide membership organisation for all those concerned with adoption, fostering and child care issues.

To Peter and our four children, for their generous love and support over the years of my freelance career and all the children and parents I have had the pleasure to work with.

Mary Corrigan

To Graham and our two children for all their love and encouragement, and to the children and parents in foster and adoptive families with whom I have had the pleasure to work.

Joan Moore

Contents

Contents

About the authors

Mary Corrigan has a background in nursing and social work. Since 1975, she has specialised in working with children and families in transition, helping them to understand what is happening to them and supporting them to form new attachments when their placement becomes permanent. She currently works as an independent social worker, child care consultant, play therapist and trainer for several London boroughs and voluntary agencies. This includes supervising play therapists and running direct work skills supervision groups for social workers.

In addition, Mary teaches the attachment-trauma-loss interface, the development of self and the direct work/life story sequence on the Postgraduate Diploma in Advanced Social Work, Children and Families M.A. at Kingston, Royal Holloway and Brunel Universities; she also wrote an earlier version of the *Listening to Children* course in 1990, which she teaches to London boroughs, voluntary adoption agencies and children's guardians for NAGALRO and CAFCASS.

Joan Moore is a dramatherapist, play therapist, and registered adoption support agency worker with a background in social work. Currently, she provides therapy to children and families in adoptive and foster care, expert witness assessments, supervision for creative arts therapists, and teaches on in-service training for local authorities and related agencies.

Joan's Theatre of Attachment model involves adoptive and foster parents in performing their children's life history, often in fictional contexts. It developed from her research into child development, attachment, loss and trauma which examined a variety of perspectives for the purpose of helping children to reattach safely.

Joan has published several articles and has a chapter in Jennings (ed.) *Dramatherapy and Social Theatre* (Routledge, 2009). Her forthcoming books include *Stories and Drama for Children in Care: A creative approach for adoptive and foster families* (BAAF, 2012) and *Creative Problem Solving: Therapeutic story and drama for schools and families* (Hinton House, 2012).

Acknowledgements

As practitioners, we are aware that, like the group who wrote the original training pack, we have leant on the shoulders of many thoughtful and creative teachers and families. Most of all, we have learned from the children involved. Our thanks go to all those parents and children with whom our work has been incorporated in the form of pictures, stories and vignettes. We have taken care to protect their confidentiality and also ensure that our work is culturally sensitive. We hope to inspire you all to bring listening to your work via the direct/ non-directive use of stories and metaphor.

We also thank all those at BAAF for their help in putting this pack together.

Our special thanks go to Margaret Adcock and Dr David Hodgson at Kingston University; also Lisa Gordon Clark, Carole Samuels, Lynda White, Jay Vaughan, Pene Sinnot, Diane Hanlon, Fiona Peacock, Fran Taylor, Linda Hoggan, Jo Williams and Imran Rumjon, all of whom have given helpful suggestions and encouraging feedback in their peer reviewing of our work through its various stages. Our warm thanks also to the social workers, adoptive parents and foster carers who asked for the advice that prompted this work, particularly those who have read sections of it and reported the benefits with such welcome enthusiasm.

On a personal note . . .

Many other colleagues and friends have also given me valuable support and advice.

I would especially like to thank Professor Sue Jennings, and to pay tribute to the late Phillip Maddock, who demonstrated such impressive commitment in expanding therapeutic services for children in the care of Northamptonshire.

Joan Moore

I would like to add a special thank you to my supervisors, who have taught me so much over the years, and without whom I could never have taught or played with children with so much enjoyment. They include: Dolly Lush, Margaret Adcock, Jane Maltby and Jenny Kendrick, and my personal therapist, Dayle Thackray. I hold you all in the highest regard.

Mary Corrigan

Foreword

When BAAF published the original *In Touch with Children* course in 1984 there was a great deal of enthusiasm and demand for assistance in developing more practitioners' skills in working with children. Nessie Bailey, the BAAF Northwest consultant, had already encouraged many agencies to develop very good services and had introduced UK social workers and carers to Vera Fahlberg and the importance of attachment theory. Some wonderful work was done by social workers with children and families, portrayed, for example, in *Working with Children in Need: Studies in complexity and challenge* edited by Eric Sainsbury (Jessica Kingsley Publishers, 1994).

Sadly, within a few years after this levels of knowledge and skills seemed to be dwindling away. Many social service departments were restricting the time practitioners in children and families teams could spend with children. Agencies providing adoptive families often only had responsibility for supporting the carers and not the children. Even students on post-qualifying courses had difficulty finding a child with whom they could undertake direct work

Not surprisingly there is now a good deal of criticism and both public and governmental concern about the failure of social workers in relation to children. There is again a demand for better, more skilled work and this requires the provision of good quality training.

I cannot think of anyone better suited to initiate a revival of skilled direct work with children than Mary Corrigan and her co-author Joan Moore. Mary's skills in developing and presenting techniques for working with children and inspiring new practitioners are legendary, as so many former students would testify. Joan's work on the handbook will help practitioners to incorporate new theory and knowledge at the same time. I am delighted to recommend this new training course from BAAF. Its publication is timely and its content is excellent. I hope that *Listening to Children's Wishes and Feelings* will be very widely used.

Margaret Adcock
October 2011

Preface

The *Listening to Children's Wishes and Feelings* course and handbook were inspired by and have their roots in the *In Touch with Children* course, published by BAAF in 1984. The original course was devised by Nessy Bayley and Daphne Batty, who wrote and collated work given them by a group of committed and creative individuals who worked eclectically with children, using the symbolic language of play. They collaborated in order to write a training manual and course to help social workers to listen to children. In the acknowledgements, they state:

This can truly be described as a corporate exercise. Who knows, for instance, who was the originator of the pat-a-cake game that is an important step in the development of a small child?

We feel the same. Everything included in this course and book is the result of trial and error – by others or by us – with the children and families with whom we have worked. In 1984, Mary was working for Westminster Social Services with Cynthia Flood. Developing methods from the original course, they created a framework and guide for social workers doing direct work and so it was that the *Listening to Children's Wishes and Feelings* course was born.

Since then, thanks to painstaking research and practice by others in this field, Mary has been able to update and add material culminating in the creation of this new course and handbook in collaboration with Joan Moore.

Having each worked with many adoptive and foster families over the years, we realised that children need to "walk" their story in order to reattach safely, while their parents depend on help to understand and resolve their children's problems. This requires us to explain complex theory and, alongside much needed emotional support, to provide an ever-expanding set of creative skills, tools and stories. We both work in the child's home where we find that children, feeling safer, will transfer the magic of learning taking place in the "play space" to everyday life in the same setting.

This course handbook and accompanying training manual are the outcome of our work with families and all the involved professionals who support them. We draw from many strands of theory, in particular, developments in neuroscience over the past 15 years, which have contributed enormously to our understanding of child development, attachment, trauma and loss. We aim to integrate these strands in order to make them accessible and expand practitioners' and parents' confidence to use their own creativity with children. Mary Corrigan developed the training programme and guidance on assessing and supporting children through loss and transition, while Joan Moore worked mainly on the handbook, in particular, collating the theory and the chapters on play, dramatic approaches to life history and therapeutic stories. A comprehensive range of techniques with guidance is supplied on the accompanying CD.

Mary Corrigan and Joan Moore
September 2011

Introduction

It is 25 years since BAAF published the *In Touch with Children* training pack which promoted the importance of listening to children's views and feelings about what was happening to them, alongside the recognised need for high quality assessment skills (Simmonds, 2008). In the wake of several inquiries into child deaths, for which first individual workers and then the "system" were blamed, we continue to struggle to understand human relationships, even given the numerous theories on how to support children who have suffered loss, abuse and neglect. In response to the death of Victoria Climbié in 2000, the Government issued the Green Paper *Every Child Matters* (DCSF, 2003) that led to the Children Act 2004. A prime objective was to support children, parents and carers to enable children to reach their potential, highlighting the importance of listening attentively and having regard for culture and context, and continuity of care. The Papers, *Care Matters* (DfES, 2007, 2009) made further extensive proposals for monitoring and developing services for children, to ensure children in care have adequate access to advocacy, with the Department for Education and Skills (2007) recommending that 'more time be spent by social workers on relationship building with children'.

Following the recent Baby P inquiry, Lord Laming's progress report, *The Protection of Children in England* (March 2009) made a further 58 recommendations. The Government responded in May with proposals that acknowledge the need for enhanced multi-agency systems in order to reduce delays in care proceedings, as well as to improve communication and increase training in observational skills, for purposes of safeguarding children more effectively (DCSF, 2009).

Adoption legislation throughout the UK has focused on the importance of listening to children's needs, wishes and feelings; adoption and fostering regulations 2011 in England reinforce this message. Now, more than ever, it has become necessary to develop training that illuminates the issues to be grasped in complex decision-making regarding the best interests of looked after children – training that informs workers how to assess children's needs, wishes and feelings.

This handbook to help children in transition, together with the training course that accompanies it, provides practical guidance for social workers, foster carers and adoptive parents and all other professionals engaged in working with children in transition and adoption. To help guide social workers to make more accurate and effective assessments, we have brought together information on the intertwining influences of child development and attachment, the neurobiology of neglect and trauma, loss, assessment, play, communication and issues of identity for children in transition. We illustrate creative methods for undertaking life history work and guide practitioners in how to engage children in play, drama and therapeutic story-telling, while supporting the involved adults in the task of helping children to process feelings and experience, particularly of loss, with the overall aim of enhancing their self-esteem and coping mechanisms. The information is presented as an "easy-access" handbook rather than as a research study, and thus refers to the key influences and directs the reader to sources for accessing more in-depth analysis on each specialist topic.

Child development is our starting point since it is crucial for social workers and substitute parents to know how the children for whom they have responsibility are thinking, feeling and experiencing. As Lefevre (2008) reminds us, "inclusive" practice means that children have the "right" to participate in decision-making and have their views taken fully into account. Yet they can spend years in transition between family of origin, foster family and adoption, while awaiting decisions and trying to accommodate the new environments and cultures in which they find themselves, perhaps wondering when or if they will ever see their parents and/or siblings again.

All too often children are at a loss to know how to make their views heard and understood. It requires practitioners to have detailed knowledge of child development in order to understand what is "normal" development and what might give cause for concern, at the same time taking cultural expectations into account to avoid misguided assumptions. As development is sequential, neglected children can miss out key stages, which makes it more difficult for them to understand others' expectations of them. We give detailed advice on how to recognise the stages of emotional development shown and suggest ways to help children and young people to recover previously missed experiences of nurture at each of these developmental stages, so as to enable them to reach higher stages of learning.

The perspectives on attachment in Chapter 2 emphasise how dependent human infants are on parental care for their optimal development. The effects of separation and loss are of critical relevance for children removed from their primary attachment figures. We consider the impact on fearful children who, oscillating in and out of care, reveal lack of awareness or pleasure and employ various strategies against alienation that subsequently place them at risk of sabotaging their opportunities for nurturing care. To enable professionals and substitute parents to recognise and understand the differing styles, these strategies are described as they apply within each category of attachment so that interventions can be geared in the most helpful direction.

Chapter 3 focuses on neglect and trauma and draws from the last decade's impressive advances in neuroscience that reveal how the brain develops and is affected according to quality of parenting and environmental influences. From experience, children create internal models that affect the way they perceive others and communicate their feelings. For instance, aggressive, distressed behaviour that stems from fear and resultant panic invites negative responses and rejection which, in turn, further confirm a child's negative beliefs. Under stress, children find it difficult to explain disturbing thoughts and feelings they have never processed but which are readily stimulated by sensory triggers of sounds, smells and expressions that remind them of pre-verbal trauma. By explaining neurological influences and the impact of neglect and abuse that lead to difficulties, particularly from loss of an attachment figure, we hope that involved professionals, adoptive parents and foster carers will feel more confident and competent to identify and respond to the needs of these children whose complex behaviour may not be congruent to their chronological age.

In our experience, many fostered and adopted children are in shock, unable to verbally express their anxieties, perhaps too young or insecure to ask questions they need answers to. Consequently, they often "shut down". Chapter 4, on grief and loss, describes the processes of grieving and strategies to help children who have effectively lost the people (and pets) most important to them. Children in transition who struggle to trust and attach to foster (and later, to adoptive) carers are especially sensitive to criticism and rejection. Waiting for decisions about their future, these children rely on their social worker to be interested and committed to them, which includes keeping to their arrangements to see the child, and modelling genuine warmth and affection so children will learn of the possibility of quality relationships.

Chapter 5 on play and communication illustrates play as an effective bridge to communicating with children. We propose that practitioners focus on toys, puppets, pets and games as a "third object", in place of over-reliance on verbal exchanges that demand speech and eye contact. Non-directive play is an effective way of eliciting children's wishes, thoughts and feelings to inform assessment because it invites them to share their feelings in a far less threatening manner than by direct questioning. In our experience, even the increasingly popular "story stem" assessment tool can evoke threatening and distressing memories for traumatised children. To enable children and involved adults to relate more effectively, sensory play provides a valuable means of observing children's non-verbal language, as expressed through play.

Yet some children are too emotionally delayed to benefit from a non-directive approach; for these often highly traumatised children we propose a directive form of play that enables them to enjoy nurture through exploring sensory materials. Alongside our ideas are clear instructions for delivery on the accompanying CD.

Chapter 6, on assessment, illustrates the use of play to identify patterns of attachment, stages of the child's development and functioning, and the effects of loss on their sense of identity, with reference to his or her culture, ethnicity, religion, disability and gender. While the child plays, the observer uses their awareness of their own feelings and reactions to subtle and complex dynamics that may be taking place within the family and/or between siblings, which (provided they are not confused with the social worker's own issues) will help to inform their assessment and future care decisions.

Chapter 7 is about helping children in transition and explores the differing needs of children awaiting legal decisions (whereas the following chapter focuses on children in permanent placements). A prime focus of intervention is to answer the questions uppermost in their minds, such as 'Why am I here?' and 'What's happening now?' or 'Where is my mummy/daddy?'

We take the reader through the process of supporting children on their journey from arrival in care, to waiting for the outcome of assessments, until they are placed for permanence. Many of these children have no one with whom to share their worries and feelings, since traditionally mental health service professionals have asserted that it is unhelpful to provide therapy to children in transition who are not yet sufficiently safe and settled to make proper use of it. Specialised therapeutic support tends to be time-limited and subject to funding constraints, while health services usually have lengthy waiting lists. Meanwhile, social workers are being encouraged to engage in direct work so that children's wishes and feelings will be more consistently addressed. This 'shared journey' (Lucock et al, 2006) is most effectively accomplished by using play as the natural means for children to express their thoughts, wishes and feelings.

To address the chaos in a child's internal world caused by maternal separation, Bowlby (1979) and Siegel (1999) have specified that children need a coherent narrative of "what happened". The work of compiling life history books with children therefore needs to begin as a social work task when children enter statutory care. As Winnicott (1986, p.40) advised, children need social workers to 'live through the experience of the child as fully as possible, without denying the pain, and accepting the sadness, anger and depression'.

In recent decades, life history work became demoted to the province of unqualified practitioners. It has been debated as to whose task this is and whether it should, as Ryan and Walker (2007) and James (2007) maintain, be separate from therapy.

Meanwhile, opinion has differed as to the degree of intensity and control judged appropriate to apply within attachment-focused therapies. Yet, as Burnell and Vaughan (2008) explain, the memories that traumatised children carry lie very deep in their bodies, which can make them highly distressed and resistant. Chapter 8, on dramatic approaches to life history work, describes highly sensitive, therapeutic approaches and guidance for social workers and substitute parents in how to address the most difficult stories. We endorse the view held by Family Futures,[1] first, that it is not feasible to separate the task of life history work from the broader therapeutic task of enabling the child to recover memory and process their experience; second, that while children who suffer the most pervasive trauma, as defined by van der Kolk (2005), are likely to need more specialised help, they still need to "walk the story", to be able to understand the reasons behind decisions taken on their behalf if they are to access the quality of care available. Once children have processed what has happened, they can begin to explore what should have happened.

Chapter 8 explores the use of dramatic play in helping children to come to terms with their life history and make new attachments. With an emphasis on problem solving, it uses case examples to show ways for adoptive parents and foster carers to have fun with their children, in the process of addressing specific difficulties arising between them. A key influence in the development of this type of dramatherapy is Stanislavski's (1988) "method acting", which required actors to call on their sensory memory to project genuine emotion, so as to make the play's story appear as if it was real and thus engage the empathy of the audience. Another important influence was Brecht's "epic theatre" (Willett, 1977), in which he desired his audiences to be emotionally distanced from the action on stage and had his actors break out of role in order to invite members of the audience to critically reflect. Accordingly, an important aspect of the drama-therapeutic play described in this chapter is to provide sensory experience and family participation, with the aim of enhancing mutuality between child and parent.

Finally, Therapeutic Stories (Chapter 9) explains the values of storytelling, particularly of allowing children to find solutions to dilemmas by hearing how characters in stories resolve matters for themselves. Metaphor works as a form of pattern matching which stimulates communication between the right and left hemispheres of our brains, so that connection (the "as if") can be made between fiction and reality, yet the privacy of its being a story leaves children free to dismiss any metaphors that do not ring true for them. It also allows them to work at their own pace and to explore feelings that would be too painful to confront in a verbal interview. Each story is followed by an explanation of the themes arising, and questions to assist exploration and analysis of feelings and experience.

In the course of the following chapters, we hope to have demonstrated the complex interface of attachment, neurobiology of child development and the combined impact of neglect and loss on children in public care. Since emotional disturbance stems from regulatory problems that begin early in life, we hope the tools provided for non-verbal assessment will enable more effective planning and that methods for accessing unconscious processes will help practitioners and parents to improve children's capacity to self-regulate.

Appendices on listening to children and preparing for a direct work session are available at the end.

---

1   Family Futures is a registered adoption support agency offering an integrated, multi-disciplinary assessment and treatment service for children who have experienced developmental trauma and are now fostered or adopted. Both Alan Burnell and Jay Vaughan are co-directors.

Using the CD

A wide range of techniques and strategies for helping children to express their wishes and feelings are listed on the accompanying CD, linked to and arranged in broadly grouped headings that follow those in this book. A comprehensive list of materials and equipment is also included. Although these methods can be used independently, workers are strongly advised to attend the *Listening to Children's Wishes and Feelings* training course where these techniques are demonstrated in some detail.

Chapter 1
Child development and its relevance in transition

Influences

In this chapter, we examine stages of development in the specific context of children whose multiple transitions result from inadequate parenting and consequent neglect. We begin by considering how growth is affected by the external influences of cultural, legal, social and emotional experience as well as the internal influence of the child's inner world, genetics and neurobiology. Alongside varying theories, Aldgate *et al* (2006) find broad agreement: first, that children's development is orderly, with defined dimensions, leading to progressively more efficient and complex functioning; second, that interactions between children and the context in which they are raised will affect their development. This can be divided into six dimensions:

- physical growth;
- sensory development (five senses);
- cognition/intellect;
- emotional development;
- social development;
- moral/conscience development.

To become more integrated, competent and complex, it is generally acknowledged that we progress incrementally through identified stages as defined by Erikson (1967), Piaget (1952) and Vygotsky (1962). However, advances in neuroscience have demonstrated that our progression varies according to our inner world, which is not merely influenced by our external circumstances but, as Siegel (2001, p.81) explains it, the mother 'quite literally creates the mind of her baby'.

Drawing from research by Passingham (2008, pp.33, 58), we find that in having a substantially larger pre-frontal cortex than comparable primates, our brains allow us to take far more information into account. Human brains are special in the way cells connect in areas such as language and speech, enabling us to learn concepts and situations that are distant in space and time without our being given concrete examples. Using speech in conjunction with the senses lets us share our thoughts with others. Since we become aware of them via the phonological loop, Passingham speculates that sound might yet prove to be a more efficient system than visual imagery in planning for the distant future and examining causal relations.

For 99 per cent of our human existence we lived in intergenerational hunter-gatherer communities, with a ratio of four mature adults to each young child (Broomhall, 2003), a stark contrast to the contemporaneous experience of children taught in classes of 30 (at least, in much of the Western world). We humans have made remarkable progress, considering that 10,000 years ago writing and reading hardly existed, yet we have since invented thousands of languages. Perry (2008) declares memory to be the most remarkable aspect of being human but warns that by living more separate lifestyles we risk penalties of increased mental ill-health. Although growth in the womb unfolds mainly from genetically driven processes, development is affected by environmental factors, for example, nutrition and parental substance misuse. From exploring the complexity of the relationship between genetic and environmental influences, Rutter (1996) observed that, depending on how the person is raised, someone who is genetically predisposed to be a risk taker may become, say, a racing driver or a criminal. In other words, while genes provide the basic ingredients, it is the environment, 'the cooking, that matters' (Gerhardt, 2004).

While parenting programmes are effective at raising parent's self-esteem, many rely on behaviour modification approaches based on learning theory. Aldgate *et al* (2006) reflect that not all behaviour can be changed solely by such approaches. Children's temperament influences the way parents respond to them, some parents displaying lower tolerance to their child's distress, which in turn affects the child's capacity for coping with their feelings. Thus caution is required for assessing whether a child's behaviour is appropriate and related to their age and circumstances. While taking biological, cultural and social influences into account, we must bear in mind that 'the human child is all the time at all stages' (Winnicott, 1988, p.34) since the developmental stages build on one another but are never entirely completed.

Culture

During the earliest weeks of life, every infant is dependent on its mother, as witnessed through the significance of eye contact (Gerhardt, 2004). Once we begin to socialise our infants, varying patterns and attachment styles become apparent within each culture (Crittenden and Claussen, 2003; Howe, 2005). To assess a child's self-esteem, practitioners need to take into account differing expectations regarding socialising children and clients' own perceptions in relation to their culture. For instance, in the West, we tend to prize autonomy, whereas other cultural groups in Asia and Africa value the concept of belonging to the group, requiring certain obligations to be met. Children (over 9 months) who live in the West are expected to look at adults when spoken to, while in parts of Africa and Japan, they show respect by casting their eyes down or away. Children's developmental processes are affected by the influences of extended family, social networks and the wider community. Nevertheless, trauma that results from abuse and neglect disrupts developmental processes, maltreatment in any culture being detrimental, negatively affecting children's development (Aldgate *et al*, 2006). Alongside respect for cultural practice is the obligation to protect children and vulnerable adults.

Resilience

Rutter (1985) defined three main factors signifying resilience: belief in self-efficacy and one's ability to adapt; a repertoire of problem-solving approaches; and self-esteem and confidence, supported by 'a feeling of uniqueness and yet belonging to a group' (Vera Fahlberg lecture, 1994).

The speed at which young children's brains are growing, especially during the first four years, increases their vulnerability to maltreatment, which has a lasting impact. Findings in neuroscience show that children who are abused, neglected and traumatised are actually far less resilient than had been previously assumed (Perry *et al*, 2006). Yet as Gilligan (1997, 2009) and Jewett (1984) have observed, an environment that promotes self-esteem and the provision of a coherent account of their history contribute to helping even traumatised children recover and become more resilient.

Supportive relationships are, therefore, crucial to the well-being of children who need basic care, safety, an emotional sense of worth, stimulation, guidance, love and stability (Aldgate *et al*, 2006), a list to which Bettelheim (1982) added spirituality, while for Pullman (2004) 'children need the arts as much as they need fresh air'. Winnicott (1988) endorsed the view that emotionally nurtured children exercise moral judgement. Thus assessment of children's needs requires a broad, holistic approach.

The legal context

There is a focus in legislation pertaining to children and adoption throughout the UK to seek the wishes and feelings of children in legal proceedings. The Quality Protects initiative was also introduced to focus on the needs of children in public care.

In the wake of the Climbié enquiry in England (Laming, 2003), the Children Act (2004) met a demand for reform by establishing a Children's Commissioner for England to raise the interests of children. Guidance now extended requirement to seek and consider the wishes and feelings of all "children in need", defined in the Children Act 1989 as:

a) unlikely to achieve a standard of health and development without provision,

b) significantly impaired in their health or development, or

c) disabled.

This has recently been reinforced in the adoption guidance issued in England in 2011. Practitioners also need to be familiar with assessment frameworks and their intertwining influences, including the cumulative impact of adverse circumstances on health and development. We are ethically, as well as now legally, obliged to take children's views seriously and respectfully. Yet, McLeod (2008) warns that too often when children's views diverge from those of adults, it is the adult's view that prevails, stemming from attitudes whereby children are regarded as the property or appendage of adults. To obtain the views and assess the needs of younger or less verbally competent children, it is all the more incumbent on professionals to become familiar with non-verbal means of communication.

Stages of child development

When, due to neglect, children have missed stages of development, they need to repeat these stages before they can move to higher levels of learning. We find that due to the plasticity of their developing brains, recovery by older children is achievable and sensory play is the most effective means. This process requires the worker to identify levels of functioning of children who do not display the social emotions of empathy, pride, guilt, shame and embarrassment at a level commensurate with their contemporaries. To make accurate assessments depends on familiarity with healthy development as detailed in the chart that concludes this chapter. We begin by summarising the social/emotional aspects of ordinary development.

The early years: 0–5

During the first three years the emotional right brain is dominant. This enables infants to enjoy shared intense gazing with parents from being cradled at a distance of 20–30cm between their faces. At three months, healthy, nurtured infants will look for their mother across a room. At six months, their babble reveals changes in tone. The baby's eyes follow objects until they are out of sight but at ten months, by going after the object, say, under a cushion, they learn "object permanence" (Piaget, 1952). By 12 months, toddlers can stand at a window and will look for their parent. At 15 months, they feed themselves with a spoon (albeit messily). Nurtured two-year-olds hold a pencil near its tip and are busy learning the different qualities of objects such as heavy or light, sweet or sour, hot or cold. By three years, most children will know primary colours and at four years, they can generally name other colours.

Middle childhood: 6–11 years

Both hemispheres of the brain continue to fluctuate, however, the left hemisphere is mainly in charge during middle childhood, a period for increasing intellectual challenges. Children need a trusted adult to develop self-esteem and learn how the world perceives them as individuals. Vygotsky (1967) promoted targeted learning, especially for those with special needs. Rule-based games now feature strongly. Children learn to reflect on their own and others' mental life, provided they have a predictive stable emotional environment. The impact of less optimal care becomes apparent, such as less fortunate children having no concept of time (Schofield, 1998, 2005). Language provides scaffolding, thus children not spoken to are impeded from learning. Professionals need to adapt their language to the child's culture as well as their cognitive and emotional age. Schofield advises that even severely disabled children need to be enabled to express preferences at a level they can manage.

Adolescence

The main psychological task for adolescents is to separate from (parental) attachment figures in order to manage the transition to adulthood. Yet, while we value children for their obedience, dependence and lack of sexual interaction, we expect teenagers to move towards thinking independently, to take responsibility for their actions and form meaningful sexual relationships. Inevitably, they swing between being reliable and unreliable, rebellious yet at times requiring comfort like a young child. Moodiness is a sign of their preoccupation with physical and emotional changes, requirements of school, peers, parents, media pressure and own expectations. Young people focus on weight, appearance, skin, emotions and sexual health. Issues of smoking, substance misuse, eating disorders, physical inactivity and sexual risk-taking that start in adolescence are significant and may continue in adulthood (Bailey, 2006). In establishing a new identity, teenagers are concerned with questions of 'Who am I? Where do I belong? What can I do? What can I be? What do I believe in?' Some revert periodically to egocentric "magical thinking", like pre-school children, in a bid to provoke, control and reject adult dominance. Chemical changes are occurring in their brains which are maturing at increased speed. Inundated with new data, they are in a state of flux, constantly having to decide how to respond, so tend to focus on one issue at a time. Difficulties may arise when they are not ready to manage a transition or try to cope with too much at once. To emotionally separate from parents, they need their peer group to give them a secure base. Acceptance in a peer group often exceeds self-esteem needs, so while it is easy to criticise young people for letting their friends use them, it may be far harder for them to exclude themselves from the group.

Studies of parenting styles find the most beneficial to be authoritative parents who provide warmth, structure and support for autonomy. The most unhelpful are authoritarian, indifferent or over-indulgent. Nonetheless, it can be difficult to find the right moment to talk with the adolescent without provoking an argument and no one wants to argue all the time. We advise parents to be ready when their teenager is in the mood to talk. Board games or packs of cards are convenient ways to create a playful, friendly atmosphere and co-operative discussion. Of course, mismatches occur in physical and emotional development. Recognition of their potential will help adolescents express their views to greater advantage. Cleaver (2006) found many preoccupied by care of an adult with physical or mental health problems or disability.

As we move into adulthood we develop personalities, types of which are defined by a variety of psychologists, for example, Carl Jung (1953) who made sub-divisions of introversion and extroversion with "thinking", "feeling", "sensation" and "intuition". Having found variations of brain structure in the size and volume of neural tissue in specific areas that predispose us to behave in particular ways, Gardini and colleagues (2009) define four key personality types: 'novelty seeking' (impulsive), 'harm avoidance' (shy, pessimistic), 'reward dependence' (addictive personality), and 'persistence' (hard working and perfectionist). Understanding biological influence can help us to adopt strategies to obtain support and minimise risk of potential harm.

Child development chart

The chart below details the key stages of development, drawing particularly from Fahlberg (1994), Fraiberg (2008), Perry (2002), Piaget and Inhelder (1969) and Schore (2006). It begins with stages of attachment to explain how infants experience the world and learn of their effect on others. The middle column characterises average development occurring in each age group. The third column gives ways for adoptive and foster parents to provide play and nurture to older children who, due to neglect, present emotionally and socially at any of these earlier stages. These older children need to repeat the missed stages of development if they are to achieve their potential.

Child development chart: 0–2 years

Age	Characteristics (average development)	How to replicate missed nurture with the older child
0–8 months **Mirroring**	Mother reflects and amplifies her expressions; babies benefit from being held, stroked, lovingly handled; also, from experiencing their body via touch and taste, such as sucking toes and fingers; at five months, baby's eyes follow mother's finger.	Parents may attune to the child as if she or he is much younger. Mirror expressions and sounds they make such as babbling. Notice and reflect on feelings, heightening your tone. Show admiration and sincere interest. Encourage reciprocity.
8–12 months **Social referencing**	Child throws a toy or cloth to the floor to see what happens to it. When mother returns it, the child learns "cause and effect"; a favourite item with familiar smell helps child to mentally hold mother in mind when she is absent (Winnicott, 1971); at 10–12 months, the child pulls himself to his feet, climbs and walks. Reluctance at being kept still turns nappy changing into a battleground. Games of "peep bo" teach concept of object permanence (Piaget and Inhelder, 1969)	Join in child-initiated games such as "hide and seek"; on leaving a room, reassure the anxious child of where you are going, why and how long you will be; practise leaving in short 5–10 minute bursts, initially; give the child an item to keep until your return; sew item such as piece of satin into pocket for child to touch while at school. Engage in child's choice of game (throwing soft ball, bouncing on trampoline, playing drums) until she is ready to try something else.

Age	Characteristics (average development)	How to replicate missed nurture with the older child
12–18 months Socialisation	To ensure their safety and socialise them, parents issue prohibitions that shame child into submission. At the same time, nurturing parents will give reassurance and explanations that counter the otherwise caustic impact of shame.	On setting limits, give clear instructions and reassure: 'I love you, I don't want you to be hurt'. Rehearse moves and changes via play, such as by playing "shops" or "school". Crunchy foods can be used to express anger and frustration humorously.
18–24 months Internalising nurture	Children use verbal language to gain control over their impulses. Saying 'Night night!' helps the child to feel better about going to bed and being left. Child recognises own reflection in mirror (Stern, 1985), begins to interact, act coy, imitate others.	Teach simple sequences, using construction kits, push-and-pull toys, letting erected dominoes fall in a row; building sandcastles (fill cup, tip over, tap base, then lift cup); make pictures, applying glue before the glitter. Messy play acts as a metaphor for messy feelings.

Child development chart: age 2–4 years

Age	Characteristics	How to replicate missed nurture
2 years	Children explore from a "secure base" (Bowlby, 1988). When thwarted, they have tantrums and need help to contain strong feelings. Toilet training aids independence. Children enjoy repetitive play such as "sorting" and learning sequences at this sensori-motor stage. Language helps child to put feelings into words and express matters of conscience. Social emotions develop alongside use of the prefix "I". Learning self control, child represses impulses to win parents' approval but sheds blame on imaginary friends. Two-year-olds have irrational fears.	Help mastery of fear of water by allowing child to wash in sink and to wash dolls or other toys. Use an admiring tone: 'You did that all by yourself! That's clever!' By pouring from jugs to cups, children learn to control flow and discover their own proportions in relation to the doll and plughole. Playing at going to the doctors is practice for real-life experience. Older children enjoy taking apart and reconstructing old clocks, junk, jewellery, models and reclamation projects.

| 3 years | Omnipotence of "magical thinking" has children believe in their own power which can lead to prolonged anxiety and intense feelings, yet many seek non-violent solutions. Children's fear of abandonment, the dark, strange costumes, animals and of retribution makes dreams seem real. Play shows the dichotomy of good versus bad.
In this pre-operations stage, stones may be used symbolically to represent apples; children play at being Superman and ask questions frequently, such as How? and Why? | Play with puppets teaches wider social rules and views; boxes can be pretend cars, rockets or TVs; buttons can become pretend people or animals; dens (blankets over chairs) provide a neutral space for siblings to hold pretend camp fires, picnics, and so on.
Provide dressing-up clothes for role play; externalise troubling dreams by painting or acting them; tell the monster, 'Leave me alone!' Read stories of heroes overcoming fears held by the child. |
| 4 years | In this "Oedipal" stage, the child competes with same-sex parent for attention of opposite one and seeks explanations of the "facts of life", being interested in gender differences. Parental disapproval feels like withdrawal of affection. Greater distinction between thought and action develops conscience. Their elaborate fabricating is part of separating from parents. Four-year-olds fear the dark and those who look "different"; boys imitate boys but still play with dolls. | Encourage children to explore play using masks and props to help them distinguish between fact and fantasy; help them devise rules for sharing in "make-believe".
Model respect for difference through drama and stories.
Provide a pet for child to feed, nurture and play with; a goldfish may be a useful starting point for disturbed children who have no previous experience of pet care. |

Child development chart: age 5–9 years

Age	Characteristics	How to replicate missed nurture
5 years	Formal education begins in the UK. More realism in dramatic play reduces the need for props (two fingers pointed indicates gun). Language structure completes, speech sounding more "grown up". Five-year-olds play mainly with those of the same sex, ask relevant questions, enjoy brief separations and are friendly and chatty.	Encourage curiosity: show your interest in children's views and feelings; invite friends for tea, to teach social rules and culture; give support during play and respect child's need to practise! In imaginative play, explore social roles and coping with bullies.
6 years	Occupied with fairness, six-year-olds are active, bite nails, kick tables, fall off chairs, "dance or droop"; they have greater self-control, are good at starting, not finishing projects; they will argue, contradict, resist and hate apologising; thumb sucking or baby talk can resume; they fear storms, fire, deformity, death.	Provide routines to help child to stay on task; encourage special interests, e.g. trial period to play recorder. Explore child's fears, using puppets but reassure: 'You won't die from a little cut; your body is too strong.' Give plasters to make puppet "better".

Age	Characteristics	How to replicate missed nurture
7 years	This "concrete operations" stage (Piaget, 1952) has children more task-focused, keen to learn but intensely disappointed by their mistakes; they find it harder to talk about feelings. They want fairness but still cheat. Gender play is rule-bound, with hatred of being mocked, yet greater empathy and collaboration. Adopted children start asking questions about their identity.	Reassure children that it's OK to make mistakes. Help them achieve the "perfection" they aspire to. Avoid temptation to scold, or make them feel "bad" or "wrong". Explore feelings and consequences through stories to show what is fair and unfair; explain to siblings that children are treated according to their age.
8 years	Eight-year-olds show deepening interest in life's processes, connecting past, present and future, but make elaborate boasts of future goals and may detail family life in school essays. Many love horror stories about ghosts, etc, but are less aggressive, show more hurt feelings.	Introduce steps to reasoning: help children learn how to discharge emotions in a socially acceptable fashion; set limits but avoid telling off child in front of peers or siblings; read stories of heroes who conquer adversity.
9 years	Despite emotional swings, nine-year-olds are more reliable, co-operative, able to plan ahead and enjoy the social aspect of sport. They criticise others but hate making mistakes. Their aggression is mainly expressed verbally, now using sexual words for insults. They like hobbies such as collecting sets of cards.	Distinguish between major and minor values, minor being the family mores and expectations, major being limits on behaviour. Offer a wider range of activities, especially team sports, drama or dance. Horse riding teaches respect, power and autonomy.

Child development chart: age 10–12

Age	Characteristics	How to replicate missed nurture
10 years	Ten-year-olds participate in discussion of the world, social problems, values and attitudes. Adults expect them to remember equipment and homework. Friendships with peers compete with parents for child's time and interest. Boys will wrestle to show affection, while girls write notes and hold hands. Embarrassed to cry, ten-year-olds fluctuate from desire for independence to needing parents to reassure them.	Encourage your child to invite their friends home. Provide age-relevant fiction that addresses peer relationships. Set appropriate limits on time out. Alarms on children's mobile phone or knots in their bag straps will help to remind them of tasks as memory problems can last until the brain's development is completed at around 20 years of age.

11 years	Eleven-year-olds draw on different perspectives and think independently, using the core skills of reading and writing in place of just play. Though more independent, they can be quicker to anger, frustrated at the need for parental approval they still depend on. They may shun old toys yet crave a bag of sweets. Earlier fears can resurface. An age of membership and order; cyber bullying can be a problem.	Openly share values and attitudes with your child. Respect their need for friendships outside the family and make allowances; revisit the "facts of life" and discuss what makes relationships meaningful; ensure that the school is responsive to the child's individual needs. Help developmentally delayed children to improve their sense of time and understanding of past and future.
12 years	At 12, early adolescence can bring hormone changes (see age 13). Twelve-year-olds may face peer pressure to smoke, drink alcohol and have sex. They are increasingly more independent, developing their own personality and choices about friends, school, etc. It is an age when eating problems and antisocial gang behaviour can begin but also an age for developing new interests and skills, such as in sport and drama.	Invite discussion about drinking, smoking, relationships, being open and frank, yet sensitive and respectful of young person's views, showing that you are listening. Encourage physical exercise, like dance, sport, plus their help with, say, lawn mowing or dog walking. Give generous praise for efforts they make at home and in school (whatever the grade). Eat together as a family to promote healthy eating and body image. Teach safety in activities and how to handle unsafe situations at home alone.

Adolescent development: age 13–16

Age	Characteristics	Parents' task
13 years	Thirteen-year-olds have less capacity for empathy than at ten years, so are less affectionate to parents, in order to psychologically prepare for adulthood. This is due to the rapid changes in their brains and bodies, including boys' increase in testicular size and girls beginning menstruation (mostly at about this age). Self-conscious and shy, some become withdrawn and/or argumentative, worry about their body and appearance. Role models become heroes; "crushes" on teachers develop.	Teach anti-bullying strategies and ensure that the school is kept informed of incidents; encourage child to bring friends home. Provide a secure base: say you love them for who they are rather than what they do, demonstrate affection using touch and warm tone of voice. Save emotional energy for important conflicts. In minor ones, comment, 'We have a difference of opinion!' Allow differences to be acceptable, withdraw from minutiae of quarrels.

14 years	Young people of 14 are more expansive, objective and able to see both sides of an argument. They develop an ability for abstract thinking and hypothetical reasoning having grasped the concept of probabilities (Piaget, 1952). They begin to experiment with sexual roles, but too much experimenting creates problems of handling frequent break ups.	Promote particular skills; consider and discuss the young person's individual perceptions. Making the following observation: 'It's your task in life to hate your parents, so of course you resent it when we insist on knowing where you are going. Yet it's our job to ask and to worry about you. Looks like we are both doing our tasks well!' alleviates contradictory responses.
15 years	Fifteen-year-olds are in the middle of transition affecting their body, brain and relationships. Their increasing independence may cause conflict in family relationships. They need more sleep, biological programming making them more alert at night. At this stage of "post-conventional morality", they recognise conflicts between moral justice and the law, requiring a democratic way of challenging the law (Kohlberg, 1984). Young people now strive for goals to determine their future success.	Help the young person to achieve realistic self-evaluation; address low self-worth based on others' criticism. Look for moments to chat or play a game when the young person feels inclined. Ensure the young person isn't isolated (bullied or bullying). Encourage them to practise for future independence by increasing finance allowances. Suggest recycling projects, e.g. taking discarded Christmas trees to a recycling collection point, to give young people sense of autonomy.

Conclusion

There are multiple influences affecting the trajectory of children's development as our human brains continue to grow throughout our lifetime. In the first nine months, babies are entirely dependent on their mothers though cultural determinants affect the ways we relate to each other from then on. Over the first three years, young children are especially susceptible, vulnerable to abuse and less resilient following maltreatment. In play, substitute parents can replicate the early nurture that abused children miss.

Summary

- Children's development occurs sequentially through identified stages.
- We are ethically and legally obliged to take children's views seriously.
- Familiarity with non-verbal means of assessment is therefore crucial.
- Sensory play is an effective means to communicate with abused children.
- Understanding average social and emotional development will help practitioners to recognise variations in the functioning of delayed children.
- Reassuring child through favourite games replicates missed nurture.
- Adolescents' need for peer group acceptance can outweigh self-esteem needs.
- Children and young people need warmth, structure and safe limits to enable them to grow to independence.

Chapter 2
Attachment

Definitions

In attachment theory, attachment has a specific meaning. It is a tie based on the need for safety, security and protection. This need is paramount in infancy and childhood when the developing individual is immature and vulnerable.

(Prior and Glaser, 2006, p.2)

While its literal meaning is "tie" or "fastening", here we define "attachment" as the pattern of interaction that begins with infants attaching instinctively to their primary caregiver for the safety and comfort they need. Luck, of course, is arbitrary in that none of us can choose our genes, family or the country we are born into. Life is full of dangers that we cannot predict, from which we need every possible strategy to survive since our parents are not always there to protect us. Anxiety engendered by danger gives us impetus to adapt to threat (Crittenden, 2008). How well we do so while developing or maintaining a sense of self-efficacy is substantially influenced by our early experience of care. The most basic human needs are to be safe and to feel safe, to be loved and cherished, accepted and feel included, to have fun and be successful, to be heard and to be able to communicate. Some of us are lucky to have parents sufficiently balanced, sensitive and resourceful to give us an optimal start, while others are less fortunate. Understanding the histories of families that we assess can help us appreciate how they integrate experience, and enable us to plan our interventions more effectively. For a comprehensive account of core attachment concepts, and how they apply to all areas of family placement practice, see Schofield and Beek (2006).

The biological purpose of attachment

The newborn infant attaches to its mother to satisfy the basic drive for nourishment and young children seek closeness to their primary attachment figure when they suffer threat or discomfort, such as being tired, hungry, sick, cold or frightened. While fathers, siblings and grandparents are significant attachment figures, young children show a strong bias towards their mothers, evidencing that there is a hierarchy to bonding (Prior and Glaser, 2006). Babies start to discriminate in the first two months and grow especially responsive to their primary caregiver. From six months on, they begin to plan their behaviour to achieve desired goals (Schore, 2006).

The impact of separation

Bowlby (1973) observed the impact of separation on young children admitted to hospital and residential nursery to find that length of separation had an effect on attachment. Noticing three phases – *protest, withdrawal* and *detachment* – Bowlby concluded that the two factors influencing successful bonding were how swiftly the mother responds to her baby and how often she initiates positive interactions with her baby. Bowlby emphasised the significance of loss and grief often underlying anger.

The most established categories of attachment ("A", "B" and "C") were developed by Ainsworth (1978) with "D" added by Main and Goldwyn (1984) to account for behaviours that did not fit the other three:

A = insecure-anxious-avoidant

B = secure-balanced-autonomous

C = insecure-anxious-ambivalent

D = Disorganised

Crittenden (2008) expanded these into her Dynamic Maturational Model (DMM), a framework for categorising attachment and adaptation through the lifespan.

Measuring attachment

The Strange Situation procedure

To measure attachment, Ainsworth (1978) created a "Strange Situation" procedure during which infants were observed to explore the environment more freely if their parent was present; hence proximity of the parent *promotes* rather than inhibits autonomy (Prior and Glaser, 2006). We develop "internal working models" (Bowlby, 1988, p.12) from predicting how others respond to us based on our experience. Crittenden (2008) refers to these as "dispositional representations", which she views as subject to change. In our work with children in substitute families, we find that nurturing parents are able to shape the attitudes and behaviour of previously neglected children because their brains are continuing to grow and develop. From examining practice in other cultures, Rutter and Rutter's (1993) conclusion that it was the separation from the primary caregiver combined with lack of caregiving during the separation that caused the greatest upset, is especially relevant to those assessing the emotional needs of children moved back and forth between parents and foster care.

The effect of parents' behaviour

To explain why a parent might respond angrily to young babies we draw from Kelly's (1953) theory that we create "constructs" (assumptions and beliefs) according to the way we have been treated. Someone who early in life felt persecuted might view her child's cry as an intentional threat: 'My baby hates me and wants to punish me!'

When their parent is unpredictable or consistently unresponsive, infants must decide whether to cry harder or stop in case it distresses parents so much that their reaction is frightening. Ainsworth (1989) saw parents of "ambivalent" infants respond mainly to negative signals, setting a pattern whereby the child has to cry to obtain attention.

Of course, genetic influences also affect personality. Some children are more vocal, others more reflective. To distinguish signs of unmet emotional need, it is important to discover what is behind the prevalent emotional tone. Teicher and colleagues (2006) observed the devastating neural impact of verbal abuse on three-year-olds to be still evident at age 13, despite improved care in the meantime. Unsurprisingly, 'children will behave in a way that reflects their experience' (Aldgate *et al*, 2006, p.79), the brain being like a film camera, recording and remembering all it encounters.

Developing strategies against alienation

Children develop strategies when they feel uncomforted and denied any sense of belonging. Insecure children 'shrink from the world or do battle with it' (Bowlby, 1973, p.208). In a need to recover control, some identify with bullies or invite punitive responses, as 'desperate times call for desperate measures' (Schofield, 2008). Their behaviour can remind substitute parents of unhappy feelings from their own past, such as subjection to bullying, criticism or blame for unresolved loss, leaving them emotionally exhausted. Yet by recognising these feelings and seeking expert help, negative patterns can be reversed. Selwyn *et al* (2006) found that after legal proceedings, adopted children fared better than those returned to birth family. Walker (2008) advises substitute parents to look at what lies behind a child's challenging behaviour and be familiar with their own defensive behaviours.

Adult attachment

The Adult Attachment Interview (AAI) was developed from Main and Goldwyn's (1984) longitudinal research, which found close correlates of adult with childhood patterns of attachment, although adults who gave a coherent narrative of their unsatisfactory childhood could be classified as "earned secure". Secure children share the same self-esteem as their secure parents, but insecurely attached children organise their strategies according to circumstance (van IJzendoorn, 1996). Each child may, for instance, feel secure with one parent or foster carer yet insecure with another. Tools to assess attachment help us decide how capable and willing the adult is at parenting.

The adaptive nature of attachment patterns needs to be understood in their cultural context (Crittenden and Claussen, 2003); for example, research found individuals (classified as Avoidant) from a hostile, war-torn country, having lost many relatives, relied on *semantic* memory and omitted *episodic* memory (see Five Memory Systems, Chapter 3). In contrast, inhabitants from an isolated setting wherein a close, if acrimonious, group had formed, found the parents (of ambivalent children) more inclined to rely on *episodic* and *imaged* memory. The significance of this research indicates the need to base intervention on an informed view of culture and of how information is integrated.

Carers' capacity for self-reflection

Humans are inherently self-reflective but not all are able to use their insights to make required changes. Those unable to "mould" to their child require the child to mould to them. Since many children who suffer loss struggle to elicit caregiving behaviour, it becomes vital to assess and clearly evidence the states of mind of substitute parents regarding their childhood, their ability to solve problems and their capacity to adapt to the needs of the children placed with them. Fonagy and Bateman (2008) found that parents who knew their own mental states were better able to adjust their caregiving strategies. Noticing how prospective parents make us feel can provide a useful starting point to assessment.

In studying the effects of placing "disorganised" infants with "secure, balanced" foster parents, Dozier *et al* (2001) discovered that within 20 months, infants became secure. The problem is that, if they are subsequently returned to high risk-situations, the strategies they need to survive the renewed threat will have been compromised, leading them to become more confused, thus increasing the likelihood of their oscillation in and out of care (Selwyn *et al*, 2006). If we are not to lose the gains of taking children into care, we need very good reasons for returning them to potentially dangerous situations. In each situation, children need to learn how to apply strategies safely and subtly, adaptively. A vital aspect of intervention is to help children put words to feelings and help substitute parents to listen reflectively and empathically.

Identifying attachment patterns helps us to place children with substitute parents whose profiles predicate satisfactory outcomes. A complementary "fit" between (insecure) substitute carer and child has certain advantages, provided the patterns of attachment are not so extreme that carers collude or compete with the child. For example, an "ambivalent" carer may break through an "avoidant" child's defences while an "avoidant" carer might pacify an "ambivalent" child's distress and provide structure to encourage reluctant children to explore (Walker, 2008, p.55).

Tools for assessing attachment

Crittenden (2008) has developed attachment assessment tools for pre-school, school age and transition to adulthood, as well as for adults. While it is currently the only model to encompass so much of the lifespan, a drawback is that precise categorisation can make insufficient allowance for the finer distinctions between individuals, each of us being so unique. Prior and Glaser (2006) describe methods for assessing attachment profiles of children, which require in-depth skills training and supervision. We support their view that 'direct observation of the child is the most rigorous (albeit time consuming) way to assess attachment behaviour' (Prior and Glaser, 2006, p.189).

In direct work, the child's transference helps the practitioner to notice any patterns of inhibition or disinhibition. Practitioners must also be cautious of attributing concerning behaviour solely to "insecure attachment" that may stem more specifically from trauma, disability, ill health or parental alcohol misuse during pregnancy.

Planning for children who display the most maladaptive strategies

Human rights legislation clearly affirms the child's right to family life. Sadly, there are a number of children who, having witnessed or been subjected to crimes of violence, rape or suicide, suffer such severe damage that they are unable to sustain family life without specialised support, prior to being placed for permanence. These are children who were unprotected when they were too immature to protect themselves or to manage the loss of an attachment figure. Children who sexually abuse other children, seriously harm themselves or others, are cruel to animals, set fire to property and show frequent, excessive aggression present a grave risk. Crittenden (2008, p.215) details the conditions leading to severe pathology and explains how the pre-conscious memory systems for promoting safety influence behaviour that exposes children to danger. When it becomes impossible to gain any kind of caregiving response from seriously disorientated parents, children feel powerless. Since we can't "see" their fear-inducing memories, we need non-verbal means of assessment, tools and methods (see Techniques CD Sections 1 and 6).

Throughout this chapter we have shown why thorough investigation of the history of family difficulties is needed for intervention to be geared in the most useful direction. Parents being assessed during legal proceedings need to show not just that they understand that changes are needed, but prove they have the capacity to change the environmental and emotional conditions threatening their children's safety. It is vital to accurately assess how each family member copes with problems and processes information, since changing parents' way of thinking can impact on the care of their children. To conclude, we explain features and strategies associated with "secure" and "insecure" attachment, including both the organised styles of "avoidant" and "ambivalent" and that representing "disorganised" attachment.

Attachment styles

Secure/Balanced (B)

Parent

Parents respond sensitively and unconditionally to infants' expressed needs. They are able to reflect objectively on others' feelings and behaviour and adapt to dependants. Anxiety and aggressive feelings are kept under control. Secure parents apologise for misunderstandings and reassure their children when they are hurt.

Children

Infants who internalise nurture are soon discriminating towards strangers and are affectionate to parents. Recognising others' feelings and willing to share their own, they enjoy higher self-esteem, experience joy and believe they deserve attention. Motivated to explore, they are confident in parents' emotional availability. In the face of threat, their behaviour matches their affect and they recover equilibrium sooner. They communicate needs more precisely and are likely to appear clean and adequately fed.

Avoidant (A)

Parents

Avoidant parents show aversion to eye contact, are likely to wince, arch or push their child away, but can be responsive provided the child does not show emotional expression that parents find hard to tolerate. Avoidant adults idealise memories of their childhood attachments, minimise importance of hurts and make extravagant, unrealistic claims. Conveying invulnerability, they are defended and avoid sharing feelings, creating emotional distance that makes it difficult for them to share their worries.

Children

Avoidant infants rarely feel soothed, so are harder to satisfy as they grow. Avoidant children sublimate their own needs to that of their parents, but may "explode" in other settings. Some also show the "false affect" of appearing (incongruently) bright and cheerful at times when they are actually masking acute fear. They can be charming to strangers but, scared of closeness and intimacy, they appear dismissive, rejecting or wary of affection, even hostile, to keep others at bay. Solitary play is preferred to the effort of conversation while poor imagination leads to there being markedly little tension in play.

Ambivalent (C)

Parents

Ambivalent parents are inefficient and inconsistent at setting limits; for example, they may insensitively demand attention from children engrossed in play, and be responsive mainly to negative behaviour such as whining and tantrums. They can show abnormal eating patterns, due to confusing anxiety with sickness. Generational boundaries can become blurred.

Ambivalent parents reject opposing views by being coercive or threatening abandonment. As they are preoccupied with who prefers who in the family, fear of being left out being experienced as a sign of rejection, they fail to plan in advance – hence their family life typically lacks structure.

Children

Ambivalent children exaggerate negative emotion to maintain attention, suffering disproportionate anger and rejection. Due to high anxiety at separation, they will cling rather than explore. Emotions "see-saw" as children alternate between being provocative, coercive and submissive, fearful of parents' disappearance or disinterest – hence they are perceived as having a demanding and difficult temperament. Unable to stand being teased or overlooked, they "show off", not knowing when to stop. Highly distractible, they act out, blame others and try to win friendship by monopolising peers.

Disorganised (D)

Parents

Parents of disorganised children are hostile, dangerous, harmful and/or depressed, emotionally unconnected and unresponsive to child's care-seeking strategies, unable or unwilling to take responsibility for their children. Trauma interferes in their capacity to reason or plan responses. Schofield (2008) observes that for children, this threatening, coercive style of interaction arouses intense anxiety – 'fear without solution' – and means that they cannot rely on their parents for comfort, care or protection.

Children

Distressed infants thrash their bodies around; toddlers cover their faces with their hand, self-harm (bite), rock or bang their heads. The drawings of disorganised children may depict blood, monsters and weapons. Children who have not learned effective coping strategies show contradictory behaviours that "miscue". Laughing at reprimands (as a defence), or trashing things in temper, they fail to understand the impact of their behaviour or know how to resolve conflict. Highly vigilant, they desire to appear "perfect" and may be solicitous or contemptuous towards their carer, rejecting to avoid being rejected. Many find it too painful to acknowledge who failed to protect them.

Changing the pattern

Children's undesired behaviour can be viewed as at one end of a pendulum that keeps "sticking". By asking 'what is s/he trying to tell me or show me?' and appreciating the child's anger and frustration as a cry for help, parents will feel less overwhelmed by their rejecting or coercive strategies, enabling them to aim for more satisfactory balance.

Ambivalent patterns indicate high anxiety about separation from caregivers. Role play creates an opportunity to explore other ways of "being" and "doing". From trying out a range of roles and acting as "policeman", "teacher" or "doctor", children learn new perspectives. Puppets are a mechanism to talk about feelings, which gives fictional distance. Enjoying physical play experiences, such as on a trampoline or an assault course, in the parent's presence encourages insecure children to develop skills.

Avoidant individuals tend to be self-blaming. Having learned to repress their feelings they may be unfamiliar with the language of feelings affecting them. They require encouragement to talk about their past experience, put words to feelings, make connections between inner and outer experience, and recognise where feelings stem from. This process can feel like walking round with a bucket to catch drips from the sky on a cloudy day but patience reaps rewards. Experiencing a range of textures, music from different genres to evoke emotional experience or making scrapbooks of people displaying emotion will help children learn to read facial expressions.

Disorganised children particularly benefit from sensory play; for instance, with water, foam, jelly, sand, flour or clay. From playing mother/child scenarios, children can discover that the role of parents is to protect and encourage. When their self-esteem has been raised, children become less fearful and more ready to discuss their worries. Rejected children can feel resentful of never having been given a choice of parents they might live with. If they sense their feelings are being taken seriously, they will begin to reflect on the past and appreciate the advantages of their current situations.

Conclusion

Infants are entirely dependent on their parents to meet their needs for comfort and protection, yet as they grow, children organise their own strategies to ensure their survival. If needs are consistently unmet, problems continue into adulthood. The variation in memory systems used by insecurely attached people has implications for gearing interventions that are appropriate to their way of learning. Just as important as judging parent's capacity to change is assessing substitute carers' capacity for self-reflection and ability to adjust to the needs of children placed with them. Children can become "secure" when placed with securely attached parents but their new-found security may be jeopardised on returning or moving back and forth to risky contexts. In safe care, play is found to be an effective means to work towards helping insecure, neglected and traumatised children to feel safer to attach to new parents.

Summary

- We develop according to how well we are cared for.
- Attachment serves a biological purpose, ensuring survival and protection.
- Infants instinctively direct their behaviour to win their caregiver's attention.
- Parental proximity promotes autonomy, evidencing the child's need for their parent to be emotionally present to reassure them.
- Lack of emotional care in the earliest years has potentially lifelong consequences, affecting children's capacity for being in relationships.
- Substitute parents need to be able to adapt to the particular needs of their foster or adoptive children.
- Children adapt their strategies to changing circumstances and require help to learn new ways to survive and relate to others.
- Opportunity to play is of critical importance for those who miss early nurture.

Chapter 3
Neglect and trauma

To understand the impact of neglect and trauma, we will first consider how the brain develops, before looking at how neglect and trauma can affect this development and, finally, how parents and carers can help children to recover.

Early brain development

Around 83 per cent of brain development occurs after birth. Growing sequentially from the brainstem upwards, the brain triples in weight during the first year (Schore, 2006). Born with a hundred billion neurons and ten trillion glial cells connecting via synapses that grow or wither, on a "use or lose" basis, with a potentially eight-fold increase in the first eight months (Perry *et al*, 2006), the young baby is dependent on stimulating, quality care, neural pathways becoming pleasure – or stress – related (Gerhardt, 2004). Hence, the healthy brain might be viewed as like a tree in spring compared to neglected brains resembling a tree hit by a storm, left sparse and uneven. The brain is at its most plastic during the first nine months, from seven to 15 months being the critical period for limbic and attachment systems to mature (Schore, 2006). As the core of the self is non-verbal, the more loving attention they receive in the way of comforting touch, vocalising and eye contact, the better children develop.

Perry (2008) described four sequential stages to early brain development and the key functions of the brainstem, mid-brain and cerebellum, limbic system and neo-cortex.

Stages of brain development (Perry, 2008)

Stage 1:	Brainstem fully formed at birth	Controls blood pressure, heart rate and body temperature
Stage 2:	Mid-brain/diencephalons and cerebellum	Manages appetite, sleep, arousal, etc.
Stage 3:	Limbic system – the "emotional" brain	Attachment and relational behaviour
Stage 4:	Neocortex: top layer of brain	Abstract thought, affiliation, shame and guilt

The five senses

Being held lovingly is the greatest spur to development.

(Gerhardt, 2004, p.12)

In infancy, our world is recorded in our pre-verbal (implicit) memory, the earliest sources of pleasure and displeasure being smell, touch and sound. Healthy newborns placed on their mothers find their way to the breast within an hour of birth, such immediate skin to skin contact enhancing healthy development (Bergman *et al*, 2003). When senses are "switched on" by parental interaction, physically and emotionally, the baby becomes simultaneously aware of internal feeling and external body experience, and gains its first feelings of "body self". Within two weeks, infants become attentive to faces. Eye contact stimulates mirror neurons that respond in synchrony. Approving looks and interactive play generate a rush of "happy chemicals" (dopamine and opioids) that protect us against depression, while disapproving faces trigger the release of stress hormones that halt pleasure (Gerhardt, 2004). Smells and sounds connect unconsciously with early memories that cannot be deleted, which explains why early trauma has such lasting repercussions.

How memory develops

The right hemisphere of the brain integrates mainly bodily, emotional and social information – our creative side – while the left hemisphere has a rationalising and linguistic purpose, seeking cause-and-effect relationships, but both are needed to develop "coherence" (Siegel, 1999). Crittenden and Claussen (2003) explain the development of five memory systems, which we summarise as follows:

- *Procedural (implicit) memory*, unconscious and developing from birth, profoundly affects our capacity for developing sensitive responsiveness toward others.
- *Imaged memory* also develops early and is instinctive, inducing a freeze/fight/flight response from the amygdale (emotional receptor of the brain), similarly influencing capacity for responsiveness.
- *Semantic memory*, developing from the third year, is encoded verbally, allowing us to express our beliefs, rely on the approval of others, affecting conscience development.
- *Episodic (declarative) memory* developing next is event-specific, led by levels of emotional arousal; hence, comparatively few memories are easily retrieved (we may recall details of a wedding or accident from years ago but not ordinary events from last week).
- *Working memory* integrates the other memory systems, functioning mainly in the pre-frontal cortex; much is absorbed rapidly, rarely reaching consciousness, but affects how well we are able to narrate our past experience, such as whether we are rational, or dismissing (omitting data) or inclined to give lengthy, irrelevant detail.

Procedural (implicit) memory allows us to function habitually (on autopilot), as long as our routines don't alter too much. When they do, it causes mounting stress. We learn from repetition of sequences, such as the mother touching her nose while saying the word "nose". Perry (2008) estimates that it takes 400 repetitions to turn connections into a template that becomes a "memory". Later, one in 400 will maintain it. Therefore a traumatised child, long after removal from an abusive situation, may receive 399 kindly affirmations, but on hearing the 400th message as derogatory, his long-held assumption that he deserves maltreatment will be confirmed. The case of six-year-old Sam illustrates the significance of preverbal memory aroused in a child several years after his adoption.

Sam

Life history work revived Sam's memories of babyhood. In play, Sam's characters were hit on the mouth, kicked in the face and balanced on top of each other's faces.

Detailed reading of files revealed his mother had forcefully held a dummy in his mouth to stop him crying. To help Sam realise his own power, I invited him to create a painting of his head, which included a wide open mouth. We examined the purposes of a mouth and voice, i.e. to eat, drink, sing, shout and express feelings.

The painting became a portrayal of Sam as a "superhero", of which he felt proud. Devising an adventure, he enacted the role dramatically. Understanding why he had felt so oppressed removed the blocks that had impeded Sam's progress.

Emotional communication is at the heart of attachment.

(Siegel, 2001, p.81)

Consider the strength of emotion experienced at the birth of our first baby, our exultation at playing a winning shot in sport, the pleasure of warm sun after days of rain or a cool breeze on a scorching day. Emotion (the stirring of feeling) is generated unconsciously, affecting the whole brain and so, as Le Doux (1998) explains, can overwhelm rationality. Yet being conscious of pleasure or pain is indispensable to mental health since our feelings point us in the most logical direction (Damasio, 1998).

Ekman (1992) found facial expressions of fear, anger, sadness and joy to be recognised worldwide, implying universality to these core emotions. Experiencing joy, fun or pleasure gives our brains vital protection from adverse stress. Many neglected children find it difficult to recognise emotions in other people. Boys tend to have even more difficulty than girls, having not consciously connected physical to feeling states. In play, children learn to express emotion, using phrases such as 'burning with embarrassment', 'hollow', 'ready to explode' or 'sick to the stomach'. Helping them devise ways to resolve problems gives them hope and resilience.

Development of conscience

Children interpret new experience in light of previous learning, their fear, guilt and shame (held in the unconscious) being the most resistant to change. Functioning emotionally at an earlier age does not imply "learning disability", since emotion and cognition are separate processes. Many children perform cognitively within their chronological age, yet are delayed emotionally and socially. Children's ability to have conscience depends on their having first developed the social emotions of empathy, pride, shame, guilt and embarrassment.

Recovering nurture

A key goal in recovery is to revisit earlier memories within a trusting relationship, so as to reach a new preferred way of being. When children are given facts of their life history in a sensitive manner that seeks to explain rather than blame, we find they adjust remarkably. On realising that their birth parents gave them very different experiences to the present, children in a relationship with a nurturing mother invariably recover the nurture they missed, as illustrated in the example of Millie.

Millie

Six-year-old Millie had been placed for adoption 18 months previously, from a history of parental mental ill health, drug and alcohol misuse, violence and severe neglect. After two weeks in placement, her birth father died following an attack by vigilantes. Since that time, Millie, an anxious, clingy child, had suffered night terrors. Her adoptive parents were kept awake through the night; like Millie, they became exhausted and depressed.

In our sessions, Millie chose to play with dolls. She bathed and changed her "baby", applying copious amounts of baby lotion. Through acting as a nurturing "mother" to this baby, Millie began to recover the nurture she desired for herself and asked her adoptive mother to pretend to be her baby, which led Millie to realise that she wanted to be the baby. At her invitation, Millie's mother donned a fleece coat, wrapped her inside it and cradled her for some 20 minutes, an experience Millie thoroughly enjoyed and had almost certainly missed in the first six months of life.

The following week, the same pattern of play repeated but in her mother's arms, Millie, like an infant of 8–12 months, repeatedly threw a baby rattle which Mummy retrieved and returned, speaking affectionately and exaggeratedly. 'Oh, so you want your rattle? Here you are.' At the next session, Millie asked to sit in a high chair, uttering speech sounds typical of infants aged 18 months to two years. A week later, when asked where she would sit, she replied, 'I'm not a baby!' She sat on a "grown-up" chair and made play dough models. These play sessions, combined with her mother continuing to give early nurturing experiences, resulted in a cessation of Millie's night terrors. Improved sleeping gave both the children and parents more energy.

Neglect

Neglect has been defined by the then Department for Education and Skills (DfES) as:

the persistent failure to meet a child's physical and/or psychological needs, likely to result in the serious impairment of the child's health and development. Neglect may occur during pregnancy as a result of maternal substance abuse. Once a child is born, neglect may involve a parent or carer failing to:

- *provide adequate food, clothing and shelter (including exclusion or abandonment)*
- *protect a child from physical harm or danger*
- *ensure adequate supervision (including the use of inadequate caregivers)*
- *ensure access to appropriate medical care or treatment.*
  It may also involve neglect of, or unresponsiveness to, a child's basic emotional needs.

(DfES, 2006, para.1.33, p.38)

Perry (2008) defines neglect as when children do not receive the organising experiences required for at least adequate and at best, optimal functioning. Neglect is less visible than physical injury, therefore harder to "prove". Yet the earlier and more pervasive the neglect, the more devastating the effect it has on development.

The impact of neglect on the developing brain

Drawing from Perry (2002), we find that timing is critical for systems organising sequentially. As the brainstem is fully functional at birth, its sensitive period occurs during the prenatal period, making the foetus highly vulnerable to substance misuse.

Research on Romanian orphans who were rarely touched, held or spoken to, found entire "black holes" in the orbito-frontal cortex (responsible for developing awareness of self in relation to others) and severe deprivation of oxytocin, a chemical necessary for positive feelings. Hence, chronic neglect is revealed to be itself a trauma. Romanian infants adopted before six months of age had greater improvement in all domains while those removed later were at greater risk of autistic spectrum diagnosis and mental illness. Orphans adopted before the age of two had substantially higher IQs than those aged two to six years (Rutter *et al*, 2009). Late-adopted children who have too few positive interactions during infancy may take far longer to benefit from positive interactions later. Recognition of smells linked to the primary carer evokes intense distress to the child suffering loss of that carer. Carlson (1997) found that 85 per cent of abused, neglected children removed from parents had disturbed attachments. When children are neglected or abused, Stephenson (1998) observes that they suffer irrespective of whether by acts of omission (neglect) or commission (abuse) since in neither case are their needs met.

Emotional delay

Observing non-verbal behaviour helps to assess the emotional age at which children are presenting. We know it is pointless to expect an infant to stop crying on request or a two-year-old to understand someone's feelings in the way a child of six or seven would. Yet, while three-year-olds charge around a football pitch punching anyone who gets in the way, such behaviour looks strange in an eight- or nine-year-old. Acting under stress at the younger age, often from when their first trauma occurred, neglected children are less able to respond as expected of their age. They may show infant mannerisms: flapping hands, walking wide-legged, jumping on a parent excitedly, snatching, or falling over, waiting to be picked up. Those who habitually fabricate may be stuck at age four, the stage when children learn to think separately.

Physical development

Children need physical exercise to develop muscular strength, flexibility, balance and co-ordination, but neglected children often struggle to manage the feats of which their peers are capable. Being left unattended in their cots or buggies for hours or even days delays their physical development. Inadequate diet and stimulation lead to smaller skulls, the brain failing to grow (Perry *et al*, 2006). Height and weight related to skull circumference are plotted on growth charts, which are important to maintain. Rocking, head banging and excessive thumb sucking are the visible, self-comforting behaviours that can persist long after children's removal from damaging contexts.

Sensory impairment

The sights and sounds of excessive violence are extremely damaging. Abused children, hit for being messy, exploring or crying, are often given no boundaries. Many live in squalid conditions, rarely washed or taught to clean their teeth, dressed in dirty, itchy clothes, with filthy bed linen, carpets, plates and cutlery. Children who are unaware of temperature wear coats in warm weather or a summer dress in winter. Difficulty in recognising texture or taste leads them to gobble down or swallow food whole. Inability to hear can stem from ear infection and affect ability to taste subtle flavours. Many such children need to learn how to turn their heads so as to cross roads safely.

Cognitive development

The shock and fear of being with a distressed, shouting parent leaves children with no integrated maternal guide to logical thinking and reasoning. They may struggle to take in what is said or recognise social cues, and show perpetual fear of frowning faces. Yet their frustration is often misunderstood. Resistance or (perceived) attempts at control are often interpreted as deliberate naughtiness or malevolent manipulation. Such children are often accused of being lazy: 'She's not even trying!' Observing children subjected pre-birth to alcohol and/or drugs, Brocklesby *et al* (2009) found their expressive language to be more sophisticated than their receptive language, thus the full extent of their problems is masked. The emotional impact from loss of key relationships affects capacity for processing, exacerbated by having to accommodate to rapid changes in environment.

Social development

Parents' lack of emotional responsiveness is likely to stem from their own attachment history or substance misuse. Persistent denigration conveyed through actions, tone and confusing signals causes neural delay and emotional paralysis, making children struggle to develop elaborate thinking, and in need of helpful role models. It is easy to blame and shame children for the emotions they project that leave us feeling incompetent and powerless. Yet to manipulate others requires the capacity to plan ahead and to anticipate other people's thoughts and motivation, of which neglected children are less capable. To have ambition requires the sense of achievement and motivation, which are difficult for children who struggle to get from one end of the school day to the other. Play helps us to assess their difficulties and build their self-esteem.

Relating to the child's experience

If we wish to understand how and why delayed children act in ways that are hard to fathom, we are obliged to get to know them. By keeping in mind how slowly their brains may be processing, we can more patiently answer their repeated questions of 'Why? When? What?' or 'How?' as often as they need to assimilate explanations.

A vital message for parents to convey to their child is just how important the child is to them. Good-humoured intentions, asserting 'where there's a will there's a way' and 'we'll carry on trying' keep adoptive parents on track in helping children feel safer to attach.

The table below provides remedies for specific difficulties resulting from neglect.

Consequences of neglect	How parents/ teachers can help
• Patchy functioning: good in some areas, yet struggling in others	• Promote strengths; break down the more complex tasks into small steps
• Fear of novelty and failure, children assume tasks are beyond their reach	• Provide familiar procedure; kindly remind them of tasks they have achieved
• Memory difficulties: may forget names, struggle to find words for conversing	• Use the same words each time; be patient and sincerely interested
• Difficulties in sequencing, multi-tasking, planning, co-ordinating and thinking	• Give child separate instructions before rest of group, visual cues, headings
• Difficulty recognising abstract concepts so will take things literally	• Avoid phrases the child won't relate to, such as 'pull your socks up'
• Failure to convert knowledge from one situation to another; confuse internal with external experience, e.g. what s/he "wanted" with what "actually happened"	• Establish clear boundaries; some children might wish to keep a diary, record events with their own drawings; acknowledge child's expressed wishes and desires
• Difficulties measuring time, e.g. distance between weeks, months, years, therefore struggle to describe when events occurred	• Calendars, clock-time illustrations and stories that describe the four seasons can help child to develop this skill
• Easily shamed, sensitive to criticism	• Notice and praise any achievements
• Poor self-esteem results from difficulty in developing coherent thinking	• Find child's talents and help them to overcome a specific difficulty
• Tendency to predict impending doom and disaster, pessimistic outlook	• Engage children in storytelling; help them choose from two positive outcomes
• Social difficulties adjusting to personal space, recognising cues, intimacy, tone of voice or sharing activity	• Help child practise how to approach others in friendly way, using taught phrases to show their interest
• Fail to learn from experience so persist in risk taking, oblivious of consequences	• Patiently start at beginning each time you explain task
• Low stress threshold, leading to escalation/uncontrolled frustration	• Don't interrupt child as they may have to start all over again; rehearse changes
• Impulsivity: tendency to touch, fiddle, climb surfaces, be overactive	• If child can't settle, have calming place and give comfort object to fiddle with
• Does not realise how immature their actions can appear to others	• Use dominoes to show cause and effect in incremental steps (see Techniques CD)
• Forgetful, losing clothes and equipment, finding it difficult to prioritise or get anywhere on time	• Provide a "buddy" to help child find their way to the classroom; give aide memoire such as pocket lists and maps
• Dependence on ritual and routine so as to avoid the need to plan and organise, since uncertainty and choices can overwhelm	• Prepare child in advance and rehearse any change in routine, e.g. child may need to practise tying school tie, shoelaces, etc
• Delayed motor skills may present as a funny gait, clumsiness or being accident prone	• Teach routines in simplest steps slowly, one at a time, use "brain gym" exercisews
• Lacking awareness of social rules leads child to make inappropriate comments and appear over-familiar or too distant	• Use puppets to explain the unwritten social rules; practise social situations with child
• Overwhelmed by noise and large numbers of people, e.g. school assembly, sports day and shopping malls.	• Eliminate distractions and give a task, step or words to recall, to focus their concentration
• May seek to control, due to fears that their needs will not otherwise be met.	• Say, 'Thank you for reminding me but that's my job'
• Homework instructions, such as 'write about your weekend' may be misunderstood, e.g. 'I stayed home'	• Teacher/parent collaboration ensures consistency: help child to expand essay giving list of things they can describe
• Anxiety and fear can lead to irregular or disturbed sleep patterns; children may fear going to sleep so put it off	• Prepare for bedtime well in advance; relax with stories, music, massage, remind of achievements and pleasures
• Extreme sensitivity can lead to resistance to wearing certain fabrics such as school shirts or "hard" shoes	• Negotiate suitable compromise; encourage practice in touching fabrics by dressing dolls or soft toy in shirt

Trauma

Bentovim (1991, p.43) describes trauma as:

A sense of helplessness overwhelms the individual...a sense of being unprotected, of disintegration and acute mental pain. The events are often repeated, frequent, and in a context of rejection, anger, a failure to respond to the core of the child's being.

The impact of trauma on the developing brain

Trauma has an impact on every part of the brain, affecting plasticity and growth. Perry (2008) reports that in all cultures, mothers are observed to soothe their babies by rocking or jiggling them, action which ensures simultaneous sensory input on three levels, creating neural templates. If left crying persistently, babies will become either hyper aroused (maintaining a state of anxiety and discomfort) or dissociate (cut off, to avoid feeling). Either extreme will injure the brain and extensively prune growth. Perry observed acutely traumatised children to bang their heads and rock their bodies at the same speed at which mothers rock their babies to sleep, and speculates that this rhythm represents humans' need for physical closeness, comfort and engagement. EMDR (Eye Movement Desensitisation Reprogramming) is a method to treat Post Traumatic Stress Disorder (PTSD), which uses, among other methods, tapping at this rhythm, in aiming to lessen the emotional intensity of memory of the original trauma.

The impact of trauma on children in transition

Some children in public care move many times before and after entering care. When faced by frightening events invoking a "freeze", "fight" or "flight" response, humans respond instinctively, physically. (There may be no time to talk if we want to stay alive!) Exposing a child to chronic fear is like 'weakening the brakes whilst adding a more powerful engine' (Perry *et al*, 2006, p.66). Thus major problems affecting children can be summarised as: (a) difficulty with integrating positive and negative experiences; (b) poor impulse control and (c) dichotomies such as "good" versus "bad", continue to be separate, non-integrated ego states for children who have missed learning to negotiate issues of intimacy or how to play.

Referring to Perry and Pollard (1998), van der Kolk (2005) and Cairns and Fursland (2007), we now briefly explain neurological adaptation to threat.

Surviving threat

Our brain has a fast and slow response to threat. The fast response transmits what we see, hear, taste, touch or smell through the *thalamus* (processing sensory information) to the *amygdale* (emotional receptor), activating us to "freeze", "fight" or "flight" in order to survive the threat. Working as a form of control centre, the *orbito-frontal cortex (OFC)* – responsible for social relationships – receives the slower message from the *amygdale*. The OFC's task is to weigh up the scale of the threat and return a message via the *hippocampus*, which stores language to explain and rationalise the threat, so we can weigh up our options. Meanwhile, a cascade of chemicals (cortisol) is set in motion. The heart and lungs pump faster, adrenaline providing strength in fists and feet, as our temperature rises to the challenge.

When threat is repeated

Unfortunately, continual frequent repetition of frightening predicaments leads to overproduction of these stress chemicals which results in the sensory information travelling between the OFC, hippocampus and amygdale becoming patchy and stopping the brain producing the hormones necessary to cope with the stress.

The *Broca's* area, which puts words to feelings, becomes deactivated so the thinking parts shut down while the emotionally governed amygdale is "lit up" as the brain's alarm mechanism, the "thinking" and "feeling" parts being like two light bulbs that cannot shine at the same time. The brainstem acts like a generator taking over in a power failure to warn: 'It's dangerous – this has happened before!' Unable to think their way out of the trauma, the traumatised child reacts fearfully and irrationally to stimuli that appear harmless to anyone else. Repeated trauma alters the balance between hemispheres, leaving the person vulnerable to depression, phobias and panic. The consequences of living with trauma are therefore summarised by Cairns and Fursland (2007) as 'biological, psychological and social'.

Post-traumatic stress

Repeated trauma can cause symptoms to persist long after the original trauma took place. The complex form of Post Traumatic Stress Disorder (PTSD) is the maladaptive persistence of adaptive responses that began as coping mechanisms (Perry and Szalavitz, 2008, p.76).

Some of the main symptoms triggered by trauma are:
- flashbacks;
- avoiding memory of the trauma;
- hyper-arousal, poor impulse control;
- disturbed body image;
- lack of attention and focus;
- disturbance in sleeping, eating and sexual activity.

Sensation seeking

Some children are so used to the "rush" of trauma that they seek sensation and only gain relief when their heart rate is very high. As their survival instinct takes over they act first, unable to explain later why they did something. They may not even have a memory of (pre-verbal) traumatic events to know what stimuli they were reacting to (Cairns and Fursland, 2007). To avoid re-traumatising frightened children, we must be calm and work at the child's pace, using the play space as a blank canvas on which they can project their experience and feelings and direct what happens in the play.

A cautionary tale

A traumatised boy was invited to embark on play therapy at a family centre. The boy expressed resistance. He clung anxiously to his carer's side. Keen to encourage him to speak of his memories, the (untrained) worker encouraged the boy to paint pictures and decorate the playroom in the style of his homeland from where he had been trafficked. The following week, the worker constructed a dwelling from bamboo, unaware that the boy's father had beaten him with bamboo sticks. On re-entering the playroom the boy was instantly petrified. He fled and refused to return.

Dissociation

Dissociation is a mechanism for avoiding pain. Some traumatised children may appear compliant until, unconsciously distracted by certain smells, sounds or textures reminding them of their trauma, they completely forget what they've been asked to do and, unable to escape the terror, they "cut out", i.e. dissociate. In this state, they appear pale, wide-eyed with unblinking stare, robotic, numb and disengaged, yet still "go through the motions". The child wishes to shrink and be invisible. Being frequently in such (unconscious) alarm states badly affects self-esteem since it is deeply shaming to have no control over one's fear. Children may lose the capacity to recognise feelings. Some suffer such extreme anxiety it can lead to fainting or heart failure. When they identify the part of their body to react first, children begin desensitising to the paralysing effect and self-control improves. The following approaches can help to desensitise the trauma.

- Encourage children to hold in mind a reassuring attachment figure when they approach a fear-inducing situation; a soft toy may reassure younger children.
- View dissociation as a vital escape mechanism (for instance, it helps a mouse escape a marauding cat); consider which body part is strongest, most reliable.
- Invite the child to identify physical feeling in particular parts of her body that prompts her to run or freeze when she experiences mounting anxiety.
- Help the child to develop awareness of the inside of their mind and body, by observing changes in their breathing, pulse, sweat, smell, etc.
- Encourage the child to practise deep breathing while observing these changes.
- Remove stress-inducing triggers, for instance, if the child is afraid of baths, use wipes or wash at the sink; eventually, face the bath by running one for someone else.
- Create anchors: encourage the child to find a place, person or activity that helps them feel calm, relaxed, in control and able to enjoy themselves.
- Talking about this place, person or activity may serve to interrupt the child's hyperarousal in the earliest stages and thus break the pattern.
- Help the child to appreciate the role of muscle tension to create graceful movement.

Connie

Connie had been in her adoptive placement for four years, having been removed from personality-disordered parents from whom she had suffered terrifying experiences of being immersed in scalding or freezing baths and dangled from an upstairs window. In foster care, her stomach upsets had been attributed to attention seeking. On finding that Connie suffered allergies, her adoptive parents changed her diet. Yet life was a constant battle as she feared bathing, sleep, journeys and failure; she drew on walls, ripped her possessions, picked and gouged at her skin. When thwarted, Connie lost her temper, lashing out like a two-year-old. When she tripped, she lay like an infant, waiting to be picked up. On hearing her life history, Connie was immensely relieved that a sibling had suffered similarly. During enactment, she leapt to rescue the *baby* (doll) representing herself. We retold the story as if she'd been born to her adoptive family and Connie acted as *baby* at each developmental stage. Within six weeks, her concentration at school improved and parents reported five day tantrum-free stretches that gave them patience to address her longstanding problems.

To function normally, we have to be able to define our needs, plan how to meet them and consider options before acting on them. Van der Kolk (2007) advises that the task of addressing trauma is to 'tame the terror' and de-somatise ('anaesthetise') the memories. Since we only remember undergoing everyday events when something unusual happens, new experience is needed to alter the balance. As brains don't like surprises, Perry (2008) reminds us that eye contact feels dangerous when linked to danger or acute loss and, therefore, recommends sensory-based approaches to treat trauma. Cognitive Behaviour Therapy (CBT), though useful as a time-limited intervention, can only be effective when it is possible to access the child's thinking capacity, but children such as eight-year-old Connie in the example can be encouraged to process their experience by acting a story about their early development.

The importance of pleasure

Traumatised children who rarely experience pure joy will envy the sight of it in others. They benefit from being reminded of times they enjoyed when they felt relaxed and content, also from gentle touch (as long as they assent and are able to tolerate touch) in a manner that will not infantilise them, but helps them regulate their stress responses and teaches turn-taking. Once they are comfortable with touch, traumatised young people can then progress to relating to others in playful activity in which they learn to plan and make decisions on the basis of others' motivations instead of acting and reacting without thinking. Some benefit from having a doll or pet to nurture. Gaining new skills builds children's self-esteem and sense of achievement.

Understanding complex behaviour

When substitute parents are familiar with their children's traumatic history it can help them to appreciate that their child's anger is often a mask for fear and powerlessness, affecting their ability to make choices. In this handbook we explain *why* these children do not display all the social emotions, *why* they lack the self-control expected of their age and are unable to understand consequences. Surviving violence and cruelty requires courage and effort, yet in reacting to threat, traumatised children rapidly spin out of control. Acknowledging their own fears enables the adoptive parent or foster carer to place themselves "in the child's shoes" and thus protect their frightened children from taking control of them. Threats only escalate fear states, during which consequences become meaningless as the stressed child becomes mentally incapable of remembering them. Drawing in part from Forbes and Post (2006), we examine two common problems from the child's viewpoint. (Further dramatic examples addressing these issues are given in Chapter 8.)

Lying

Most of us are taught that "lying" is wrong. Yet psychological tests have revealed that everyone tells lies, consciously or unconsciously, for a substantial proportion of the time. Lying – or not telling the "whole truth" – is part of separating from parents, making relationships and in fact, surviving. Tact is necessary to enable us to pay compliments that sound sincere. We make excuses to avoid things we don't want to do. Sometimes we lie to protect others or ourselves. So, rather than condemn children for lying, let us help them analyse why people lie and for which reason, as this affects how well we are trusted and how far we can trust ourselves. Like adults, fragile children lie to protect themselves when they can't remember what they were doing. When one lie leads to another, anxiety is heightened. If children's lying seems unforgivable, parents may need to recall who else betrayed them, to avoid punishing the child for what someone else did.

Although it is important to model values, emphasising lies as "bad" will confirm the worst fears of children who, on being found imperfect – not having learned how else to act under duress – panic and draw themselves into ever-more tightening knots. Parents might regard unhelpful "lies" as mistakes made in order to survive and acknowledge how hard it is for children when they don't know how to "own up" without incurring wrath. Giving such reassurance as, *You're not going anywhere. It will be OK*, will encourage children to unravel these "knots" and organise routines differently – for instance, practise ways to ask for help if or when they haven't understood tasks (see domino game). Parents are advised to avoid responding to details of the "lie", as in defending it the child may reach a point of believing his or her version. Taking roles in play enables children to practise new ways to manage and reconstruct their survival skills as evidence of their creativity. Maintaining positive attitudes, with humour, parents and carers can notice the child's efforts.

Lewis

Lewis, 11, habitually lied to his adoptive parents about school assignments: *I haven't got any work to do this weekend* or *I've done it in my break* or *I've lost the paper I was supposed to copy out* or *Someone took it off me*. He also forged his parent's signature in his homework book.

In dramatic play, Lewis, as *hero*, gave his adoptive mother formidable tasks to carry out in her fictitious *role*. Her willingness to undertake them and work out what he required of her freed Lewis to confront and work at difficulties presenting in real life. From drawing round his left hand, Lewis wrote on each finger, the reasons why it might advantage him to co-operate with homework, such as gaining approval. On his right hand he listed possible sources of help which gave him a sense of control.

Taking without permission

Most of us at some point take more than our fair share, perhaps making personal phone calls at work, picking up other people's pens, parking where we shouldn't. We can acknowledge that it is human to err and hard to be 100 per cent honourable all of the time. No wonder then, that children who miss vital nurture early in life feel envious of those who appear to have it all, including popularity, and want a share for themselves.

Whereas a child cannot stop him or herself from having anxious thoughts, stealing is a form of self-harm that can be pre-planned. Forbes and Post (2006) explain compulsive stealing as the body's attempt at soothing dysregulation for children whose neglect can leave them feeling unsafe if over-stimulated. As their body recognises a need, their brain creates a massive chemical reaction, a rush (like that induced by cocaine) that feels good to the depressed child. As the effects wear off, the need to repeat the experience becomes even greater.

Conclusion

This chapter has focused on the effects of neglect and trauma on children's ability to attach and make satisfactory relationships. Learning to trust is essential for healthy attachment and is facilitated by sharing joy and fun in play. For children, repeated changes of care exacerbate the effects of neglect and abuse already sustained. We hope that understanding how the brain develops and functions in trauma, and thus appreciating the negative consequences of shame will help practitioners and parents make more effective interventions with children and young people in their care, and that as a result, unnecessary moves will reduce and the quality of care improve.

Summary

- We are born with billions of synapses that connect on a "use or lose" basis.
- The infant experiences his or her world through the five senses, the memory of which influences perceptions, emotions and behaviour throughout life.
- The body also has a memory for storing and expressing emotions.
- Children may be cognitively advanced but emotionally delayed.
- The more pervasive the neglect, the more lasting is the damage.
- Trauma affects the whole brain, biologically, psychologically and socially, especially the capacity to reason; children dissociate to survive absolute terror.
- Shame is especially toxic for traumatised children who need reassurance.
- Effects of trauma can be desensitised by enhanced physical awareness combined with calmly exploring the source of the trauma in a safe context.
- Children who repeat early stages of development can reinterpret past experience and adapt to new, preferred ways of being.

Chapter 4
Grief and loss

When I was a baby

When I was a baby nobody cared
When I was a baby nobody shared

When I was a baby I had no toys to play with.
When I was a baby, people shouted 'Go away!'

When I was a baby I always cried.
When I was a baby everybody lied.

When I was a baby, nobody listened to God above
When I was a baby, no one gave me love.

When I was a baby, I didn't get food.
When I was a baby, my mummy was always in a mood.

When I was a baby I had to play on my own.
When I was a baby I was left alone.

Charlie, age 8 years 6 months

Introduction

In writing this poem, Charlie tried to make sense of what had happened to her while exploring her early experience of chronic neglect and loss.

Understanding the theory of grief, loss and separation is fundamental to being able to listen to children with empathy, as it underpins much of the distress we see in working with children and families. This chapter describes the stages of loss, offering some methods for helping children through each stage of their grieving.

Loss is an acutely painful experience that 'affects children as much as adults, and psychologically, probably more so' (Perry and Szalavitz, 2006, p.38). Stern (1985) observed infants and parents to fall in love with each other in a process that starts with the "attachment dance" of mutual gazing and continues many times over. Yet, even after loss, while mourning adults sit still, children, due to their genetic make-up, will continue to run around, climb and play ball – activity that is often misinterpreted by adults as a sign that the child is not grieving and is unaffected by their loss or is simply resilient.

Children may not know "feeling words" for expressing their emotions. When their loss stems from the earliest preverbal years, they cannot tell you how they feel. Yet they have sensory and emotional memories of the pain which they hold within them, which trigger them to sudden upsets and sadness. The unexpected switch in the child confuses the adults, who may not appreciate why the child's behaviour has suddenly become anxious, sad or controlling.

The grieving process for children who are removed from their birth families is further complicated by uncertainties about their future. Children wonder if and when they will ever see their parents and other family members again. They may keep watching the door, expecting their parent to come for them at any moment. Not knowing what will happen as a result, the child may suspend the grieving process and become stuck in denial and disbelief. Many eventually accept their loss but the "not knowing" will not lessen the anxiety and pain affecting them in the meantime. This loss is real, irrespective of how the child might express it or whatever has been done to them. Grief is often masked by anger, making it hard for the child to recognise or acknowledge the source of their strong, often unmanageable feelings.

Below we look at the stages of loss and how practitioners, parents and carers can help children during each stage.

The six-stage model of bereavement

To understand how the stages of grief in a child's behaviour affect the secondary trauma in adults, below is a diagram and explanation that can be used to explain to parents or carers what is happening to them.

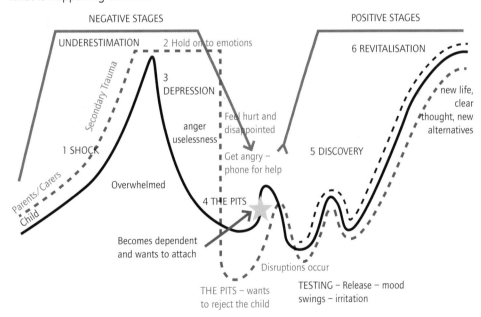

This diagram shows the six-stage model of bereavement and the effects of secondary trauma. It helps parents and young people to realise that their changing feelings and reactions to loss are normal. It charts a road to re-attachment, recovery and hope.

The dark line represents the child's grief and the dotted line is the resultant secondary trauma on the child's parents and community.

Black line

When a child experiences a shock such as loss/violence (1) the emotional effect is to spin them around so that they become euphoric (2) they may become hyperactive. Then as the loss gradually dawns on them (3) they become emotionally flat, sad, angry (perhaps breaking toys, being rude, slamming doors) and then depressed (won't play or eat.) An adolescent may alternate between not speaking or being aggressive.

When the child who has lost their caregiver finally realises the caregiver has gone (4) they become aware of their need, feel vulnerable and want to attach (see star on the diagram). This period can last for a long time through which the child's behaviour will vary, perhaps being settled for three to four weeks but then something may trigger recollection of their loss and set off upsets and confusion. Such triggers might be a return to school or a smell such as autumn leaves (if that was the time when they lost their parent) and may prompt a period of testing behaviour and mood swings.

Gradually, if children are helped to talk about their loss they can move on to stages 5 and 6 to become the "hero" of their own story, having survived these difficult times. However, many children remain stuck in stages 3 and 4 because no one helps them.

Coloured dotted line

The child's grief will have the effect of secondary trauma on carers and community which means that alongside the child is the parallel process the carer goes through.

When children initially react to their loss the parents are sympathetic but when children enter Stage 2, parents become frightened and hold onto their own emotions. As children enter the depressive and angry stage the carers feel sad, unable to help and often become exhausted. They feel hurt at being unable to help and at this point may seek help. When grief relates to loss of a primary attachment figure, children seek to make a secondary attachment to the adoptive or other parent (4). However, the substitute parent is often exhausted, unable to cope, and out of tune with the child so disruptions happen. Many carers will need extra support of both an emotional and practical type from stages 3 to 4 in order to prevent a placement disrupting.

If negative patterns of behaviour between the carer and child have become entrenched the best we can offer children is a 'secure base' (and carers who can tolerate them).

The stages of loss and the effect of secondary trauma on family and community

Stage 1: Immobility – shock and numbing

The loss of a parent, grandparent or pet, through death or any other separation, can cause children to withdraw, appear sad, with a glazed expression on their face. They don't smile "on cue". It can become hard to draw them into play. This flatness may be interrupted by outbreaks of panic when they rush around without purpose. This stage can last a few days or several weeks. Suddenly vulnerable without their familiar protector, children experience a sense of alarm. Trauma arouses bodily reactions of increased heart rate, physical tension, dry mouth, and bowel and bladder discharge (Perry, 2008). Parents can be surprised by children's sudden, unexpected bed-wetting, yet reduced motor control is common, even for adults suffering from shock. Soon after the loss, children may be sickly and have allergic reactions such as skin blemishes, runny noses, tummy upsets and sleeplessness. Fiddling with hair, clothing or skin is a common sign of raised anxiety. These symptoms may occur within hours of the loss and continue with each major anniversary until the child has been able to process their grief. They often recur when children realise that they really are about to be adopted or permanently fostered and may not be seeing their birth parent again.

In families where a child has died, brothers and sisters may experience separation anxiety and the symptoms described above. Often they reappear when triggered by the season changing, reminding the child of their lost sibling. It can affect the whole family, leading to everyone feeling suddenly very unsettled.

How can we help?

- Give the child soft, warm foods. Carers can ask, *What does Mummy give you when you're not well?* (Take into account the cultural practice of birth parents.)
- A shocked child unable to play may benefit from the carer inviting him or her to sit close, perhaps offering a teddy, reading a story or watching a film.
- A warm bed will help the child settle at night. Being tucked in or wrapped up warms peripheral body parts to help children in shock to feel contained.
- A favourite item or soft toy, by acting as a "transitional object" (see Chapters 1 and 5) can reassure the child at a sensory level, as the familiar smell and texture provide a comforting reminder of the lost person.
- Children used to hearing noise in their last house might be reassured by a recorded story or the radio being left on. Those nervous of the dark are likely to prefer a night light or to have the door left ajar with an outside light on.
- Night terrors tend to occur predictably, one to two hours after the child has gone to sleep. Children need to be reassured and may return to sleep more quickly if encouraged to remain in bed. See Techniques No. 13 on CD for further guidance.

Stage 2: Denial and disbelief

Denial is one of our earliest defences: 'If I can't see it, it can't be happening.' Children think they see the lost person and hear them on the phone. Some have dreams, day and night, in which they sense and smell the presence of their absent parent. Others appear to reject the parent they feel has rejected them, saying 'I hate Daddy', as the only means of redressing their sense of impotence. Denial involves belief that the loss is real but, at the same time, real feelings are repressed as a means of protection. Returning to the earlier preschool stage of "magical thinking", children may think 'This can't be happening,' 'I don't feel bad, so it's not real.' This gives some respite from the pain, while prompting them to repress awareness of reality that threatens to plunge them into acute grief.

To avoid pain, some children act out physically, unable to stop talking or moving. Others compulsively eat or masturbate as a means of addressing their sense of abandonment and loss. As the mouth and sexual organs contain the most nerve endings, they are the most sensitive areas of the body. Hyperactive children can find it hard to be alone and depend on the constant presence of playmates, while some adolescents resort to headphones, computer games, alcohol or drugs. If they are not helped with their grief, the undesired behaviour may continue.

Rather than apply unhelpful judgements, parents are advised to accept that feelings are largely unconscious and therefore we can't help having them. However, those trying to help the child may receive little recognition from them while they are in this stage of the grieving process. Grief lasts a long time. We can damage children by trying to hasten the process.

How can we help?

- Look through the memory box or old photos and let the child hold on to their transitional objects, a soft toy or blanket so they smell the old home or person. For example, on moving homes, Fred, who was severely neglected, sprayed his toys with urine which made the bedroom in the new house smell like that of the past. A bowl of potpourri on the play mat enabled him to experience comforting smells which helped him to give up this habit.
- Read stories about grief with the child (see Techniques CD and index of books). Just being with the child and not discounting their feelings is most helpful. Children's grief is well illustrated in books such as *Muddles, Puddles and Sunshine* by Winston's Wish (2000), a charity that helps children and families grieve when parents are about to die or have died.
- Children suspend their disbelief and talk more easily through toy telephones or a soft toy or puppet, when eye contact is not required of them.
- Young people may talk to a favourite toy or pet and will chat from the back of the car, as long as they don't feel questioned.

Stage 3: Yearning and pining – searching, anger, shame and guilt

Yearning and pining

Loss is common to all of us and has long-lasting effects. We all yearn for the person, place or thing we have lost and want to show that person our achievements, such as an award or a new baby, or we may just want to feel them close to us. Loss can feel unbearably overwhelming, and cause children to scream intensely at the pain they are desperate to forget. Sunderland (2003) cites studies by Wolpert (1990) and Goodall (1990) of chimps and monkeys, seen to die of grief within days of losing their mother. As Sunderland (2003, p.6) puts it, 'The world has a terrible bleakness and a terrible rawness, if you are a child who has just lost your Mummy or Daddy.'

Many children yearn for stories with happy endings, "sunny corners" they can escape to, or fantasies such as *The Wizard of Oz* or *Cinderella*, with satisfactory outcomes in which they can believe. Some invent their own stories with happy endings to relieve the pain or give meaning to the loss. However, children with severe trauma histories cannot imagine any such happy ending to alleviate their suffering, which is often compounded by a profound sense of rejection and abandonment, in a world that feels horrendously cold and hostile. Bowlby (1988, p.54) noticed some children defended against grief by disconnecting from it. Studies (e.g. Robertson, 1953; Heinicke and Westheimer, 1966) found that after too many changes of carer, infants aged one to three years ceased to attach to anyone and remained remote for days even after their original parents resumed care of them.

To recover from loss, children need the help of someone they trust to enable them to 'give sorrow words' (Shakespeare's *Macbeth*). Bowlby (1979, p.109) described the case of Patrick, aged four, who, on losing his mother, kept repeating that she would soon come to collect him and insisting he must put on his coat, etc. His new routine would have created a break in his pre-verbal memory, creating further anxiety from having to learn new expectations, new rules, surroundings, new relationships and so on.

How can we help?

Yearning is alleviated when the child is able to go over their story of loss as many times as they like without feeling discouraged. This takes patience. Carers and parents may reflect the feeling – 'That *was* a sad story' or 'Oh dear, the dragon was *very* fed up!' – raising the emotional tone in their voice to magnify feelings but avoiding any unhelpful emphasis on the grief feeling being "good" or "bad", even when children express it in metaphor. Children benefit from being allowed to let go a little at a time. Carers and parents can help children come to terms with the new reality by explaining the truth simply; for example:

Mum was very sick. She tried really hard to get well but sadly she died, so it's just Dad and you two in the family now. But we will keep her picture here so we can talk and think about her when you want to or look at this album.

Mum and Dad made a really strong boy [patting child's knee or shoulder] but they could not keep you safe, so you came to live with us.

Mum's head felt all muddled up and sick – she couldn't remember to give you your dinner or how to keep you safe, so you have come to live with us while the doctors look after her. [Offer the child a comforting toy or blanket with Mum's smell on it.]

When Dad had a big fight with Mum, he did not keep the rules so he had to go to a "time out" place called "prison". That's why you can only see him three times a year.

Reasons need to be short but to the point. It may be difficult to find the best words, yet children have to be able to hear them even if they don't understand their full meaning. The truth is always best, phrased to suit the child's age and developmental stage, as trust in adults is all-important at this time. The phrases become familiar to the child, so that later, they will realise they have always known the truth. Promises of happy endings are best avoided, to help children control their own hope. The difficulty with grief is the conflict between the need to let go of the lost person and a wish they were still with you – the pull between the past and the future.

Searching

Some children and young people return to the place where their parents left them and feel pulled back there time and again. It might be a park or house or the door at their nursery. In the words of Jewett (1984, p.37):

This phase draws to a close only when enough searching has taken place that the child accepts that she has mustered every effort available. Even then a conscious or unconscious contact may be made – a "bargain" where the child acknowledges her helplessness to attain part of the goal without the intervention of a more powerful other – parent or deity. The child may promise to "always be good" or to "wait forever".

How can we help?

- Demonstrate understanding and act without censure.
- On finding the place they are running to, young children can be taken home or older children told how to return or make a phone call so they can be picked up later. The child will then learn to trust their parent or carer as their sense of total abandonment begins to diminish.
- When children are in a pattern of running away, it is helpful to find them a safe place such as the bottom of the garden or a big armchair, to go to when feelings overwhelm them. This demonstrates that you care about their feelings and safety and may make it easier for them to tell you about their worries.

Anger

Falhberg (lecture, 1990) defines anger as:

A strong feeling of displeasure and usually of antagonism, suggests neither a definite degree of intensity nor a necessarily outward manifestation. It may range from irritation to murderous rage.

Many children come into care having suffered rejection, and the same pattern can be reinforced in foster and adoptive placements. Yet their angry outbursts also manifest in a system that has double standards. For instance, an adult may interrupt a child but a child may not interrupt an adult. Angry children tend to be unpopular with adults. Their behaviour disrupts the social situation with which we are most familiar and comfortable. In our culture, there is a danger that adults identify children by their behaviour. As a result, children expressing anger feel misunderstood, undervalued and may grow to feel unloved. Their acts of aggression or destruction are often signs of insecurity, anxiety, hurt and suffering from a diffused sense of self. In order to address acute grief, it is important to understand strong feelings and what may lie behind them.

Anger may be understood as:

- a consequence of the inability to tolerate inner tension which explodes in a volatile way;
- a mask for other emotions (i.e. shame, guilt, fear, jealousy, sadness, loneliness, helplessness);
- righteous strong feelings;
- stages 3–4 in the grieving process turned inward to become depression;
- a separation technique when one is feeling too dependent;
- an attempt to make physical contact;
- a learned response;
- a projection or reflection.

Strong feelings are often accompanied by high emotional energy and low coping ability. When the child is angry, reality can become distorted. It is helpful to consider how best to defuse it: Is it better to interrupt the child's discharge of tension or to facilitate it to enable him or her to regain equilibrium? For example, will separating a child from the group decrease tension (with calming influence, reduced stimulation) or will it increase fear/panic (throwing, kicking or breaking toys)?

How can we help?

- Provide a safe space such as a mat and a box of toys or drawing materials, where a child can express their strong feelings to safely act out powerful emotions which often mask deep loss or hurt.
- For young children, this stage of grieving may last only ten days (although it could last a lot longer, show in different forms, or recur at different stages of development).
- In adolescence and adulthood it takes much longer, causing people to become stuck between anger and utter despair. Children can be helped to notice they are not bystanders to their own behaviour by using the "dominoes game" (No. 24 on Techniques CD).

Shame and guilt

Shame is an extremely painful and ugly feeling that has a negative impact on interpersonal behaviour.

(Tangney and Dearing, 2002, p.3)

In their book on shame and guilt, Tangney and Dearing go on to explain that people who have been over-shamed are 'more likely to blame others as well as themselves. They can be bitter and resentful and are less able to empathise with others' (2002, p.3). New carers or adopters need to be careful not to add to the shame through their own frustration at the child's apparent resentment or lack of empathy. If they can reflect his or her feelings and help reframe perceptions, the child feels heard and can learn new ways of coping.

From being over-shamed by constant derogation or aggressive parental responses to their grieving behaviours, the self-esteem of children who are not helped to express their feelings is severely diminished, affecting their ability to manage relationships.

Tangney and Dearing (2002, p.3) advise that:

Guilt-prone individuals who appear better able to empathise with others and to accept responsibility for negative interpersonal events are relatively less prone to anger than their shame-prone peers. Guilty people seem to express anger in a more direct manner.

The implication is that shame and guilt can be very corrosive in children who have been over-chastised and not allowed to express their losses at the time. Children often feel it is embarrassing to cry; it is all too easy for adults to give the message that tears are babyish, immature or that the urge to cling to a trusted person for comfort is wrong. Children therefore depend on the involved adult to validate and encourage them to express (rather than stifle) their sad and strong feelings, and to see the unfairness of the loss from the (child's) point of view.

To summarise Bowlby's (1979) advice, chronic grief reactions result when:

a) a child loses an attachment figure with whom they had an exclusive relationship;

b) the child has no one else (such as a father) on whom to transfer affection, or who can distract the child from his pain; and

c) the child's relationship with the lost parent was ambivalent, making the depth of loss even more unbearable.

Furthermore, Bowlby reminds us that separation from an attachment figure requires us to appreciate how dangerous it feels for children who depend on their parent for protection from fear-inducing stimuli such as the approach of strangers.

How can we help?

- Children in this stage of grief tend to need swift responses to their needs, and also patience when they cling. They also need help to realise that it will take a long time to recover from loss, yet healing will happen and hurting is part of the cure.
- Children suffering shame and guilt need sensitive handling to help them see that what happened to them was the responsibility of the adults involved rather than their fault.
- A memory box can be useful for children to look at photos, pictures and objects, from the past. In this way, they can examine the feelings associated with these objects, which enable

them to come to terms with the reality of the emotions and loss through talking about happy memories of the lost person.

- Re-constructing and re-enacting memories through play helps the child process and "unblock" the trauma of their loss by trying out new, different perspectives.
- The CD offers examples of techniques and activities to use with children.

Stage 4: Despair – "the pits"

Despair can be very stressful, both to experience and to witness in children. Their distress can make them slower to speak and move. It is not uncommon for grieving children as young as five years of age to wish that they (rather than their brother or sister) had died, and for children as young as six to contemplate suicide. They may be difficult to engage in any activity. For hours or days at a time, grieving children can become chronically depressed if not helped to communicate their loneliness. Some children and young people may fill their inner sense of emptiness by grazing on food continuously.

How can we help?

- Learning to cook, paint or sculpt can help to lift children's feelings of helplessness and enable them to nurture themselves via sensory material.
- Children need involved adults to stay near, show interest and encourage them to exercise.
- When grieving children seek to eat or drink to excess, carers may say, *I wonder if you really are hungry? Let's try a hug or a backrub instead.*
- Children can be encouraged to express their feelings through creativity, such as a painting, storytelling, perhaps using a sand tray, drama, puppets or toy telephone using fictional distance to work through difficult feelings.

Stages 5 and 6: Discovery, revitalisation and re-organisation

The child may now start to invest in the future, and begin to bond to new parents, if the new parents are not in secondary trauma and thus too exhausted to bond to the child. Some days are good, some will feel grey, but gradually, feelings of sadness occur on progressively fewer days, although children will continue to seek the meaning of their loss.

Children can unexpectedly smell, feel or hear something that reminds them of the pain and shock that affected them when the loss first occurred, which can cause them to panic. Grief is easily retriggered by anniversaries of loss or by sensory reminders of pyschic pain that can cause children to slide back to past grieving behaviours.

How can we help?

- A "duvet day" can help children recover missed hours of sleep. Even if the child appears to be sleeping well, they are likely to tire quickly from using so much emotional energy, dealing with loss and handling new and stressful situations. Duvet days provide respite and a time to feel nurtured and safe.
- Sensory play (with clay, pastry, etc.) serves to "recharge the batteries", reminding the child how much their parent or carer cares about their feelings.
- Giving tasks such as puzzles, board games or easy construction kits which the child previously enjoyed will help them regain a sense of competency. Choose activities for a younger age.

Recovery becomes evident when the child regains self-esteem and acknowledges that 'the worst happened and I survived!' We now look at how practitioners, parents and carers can enhance children's resilience for dealing with grief and loss.

Resilience

Some of us are genetically resilient in the face of risk and adversity, while others gain resilience from supportive relationships. The growing child interacts with their social context and this affects their capacity to build resilience, access to supportive resources acting as a protector against adverse environments and circumstances.

A key message from research (Gilligan, 2009) is that we need to reduce negative factors and help children and young people build on their supportive relationships, networks, skills and talents. Realising they have survived the loss can help young people face their worst fears. Sometimes, when they are feeling low and not very competent in comparison to their peers, a reminder of what they have dealt with, and how well they continue to cope, helps them to realise how much they have achieved, over and above their peers, and that they are able to manage change and loss of a scale that most of their peers could not begin to comprehend.

Concepts of resilience

Resilience consists of five key concepts: responsiveness, relationships, reciprocity, ritual and routine (Gilligan, 2009). These concepts rely on having had a 'good enough parent' who can provide the four Fs (Corrigan, 1992):

- Familiar...routines, regular warm patterns to the day, food, sleep, hugs
- Fun...a sense of humour, free play to explore and use imagination
- Firm...clear boundaries with empathy
- Friendly...to be heard with emotional warmth, have hugs, cuddles and to have reassurance

The caregiver's *responsiveness* will help to build meaningful *relationships* as attention to detail wins the trust and loyalty of young people in care.

We have found that adolescents need to have their wishes met, such as food preferences, which can help them to feel emotionally nourished.

Reciprocity builds and sustains bonds of trust and commitment: 'If I do something for you, you do something for me in return. This sequence of mutual help will bring us closer and build a bond of commitment between us that will grow stronger if the cycle of helping each other continues.'

Regular *reassurance*, *routines* and *rituals* create structure and symbolism, and represent order and predictability for a child whose life may have been very chaotic and lacking any semblance of order. The structure of school routine can prove very supportive for a vulnerable child. Rituals around family, cultural, religious, school or community events may have deep meaning for those whose lives were chaotic.

Self-efficacy is an important part of resilience.

Building and encouraging self-efficacy

The most important part of building self-efficacy is encouraging the child's talents and interests. Mentor schemes are valuable for supporting adolescents. Young people benefit from opportunities to practise ways to manage life's unfolding events. "Planful competence" is a concept that refers to the capacity to plan and to avoid impulsive behaviours (Clausen, 1991, cited in Rutter, 1999), helped by:

- a positive experience in school;
- feelings of self-worth;
- a belief in being able to control what happens to them.

Encouraging positive relationships within the young person's network (relatives, friends) is important for young people in care, for a number of reasons: to support the young person day to day, and to advocate on the young person's behalf and provide a contact when they leave care, for jobs, training, leisure and accommodation. The network also serves to affirm social, cultural and genealogical identity, give reassurance through providing culturally appropriate role models and sources of mentoring, along with the opportunity to address emotional pain. Keeping in touch with their siblings also helps children and young people maintain a sense of belonging. What can carers do to promote positive ties between siblings who are living apart? See Chapter 7 and the CD for ideas.

Loss and children who wait

The impact of loss on attachment

For fostered or adopted children, their previous experiences will affect their reaction to current grief and loss in their new family. The quality of the child's attachment and relationships with their birth parents influences the way she or he is able to express feelings of loss. The present separation from birth family may trigger a previous loss (perhaps a grandparent) that was unresolved. Previous experience of loss may precipitate the child's reaction so that hopelessness and helplessness predominate. The pain and anxiety of separation causes withdrawal of the "happy" chemicals in the brain, integral to attachment and bonding. Panic triggers release of high quantities of the stress chemical, acetycholine, in high quantities to wash over the brain, leaving the child overtaken by desolation and despair (Sunderland, 2003). Abused children can find it even harder to grieve for the parent who was sometimes cruel and at other times loving, as they may have became so dependent on the sporadic good feeling, they can't bear the sense of betrayal when even that has gone. Nevertheless, anger and hostility reduce when children are comforted and able to accept comfort.

The impact of loss on identity

The intensity of coping with new surroundings and relationships in addition to the loss of their birth family can have a tremendous impact on the child, who is no longer able to take for granted many aspects of their life. For instance, a child may suddenly be unable to find her way to the bathroom or forget items that are essential to getting by in the school day. Grieving children may become emotionally stuck between stages and act younger than their chronological age, negatively affecting their self-esteem. Being unable to answer their own question 'Who am I?', can feel very frightening.

The importance of community, culture, religion, and customs

Cultural expectations affect the process of grief, for example, whether children are allowed to attend a funeral, or the way the funeral is conducted. The age, sex, temperament, intellectual stage of children and their social circumstances before and after separation need to be considered in relation to their culture and expectations. As each culture has its own way of expressing emotions, practices differing between "loud wailing" and "no tears", sensitivity is essential.

The impact of children's loss on the adult carer

When a child is placed in care after a major loss or trauma, it can stir up feelings in the carers about their previous losses. The adults' grief can run in tandem or just behind the child's, a situation which can cause adults to panic, become paralysed in their effort to meet the child's needs and find themselves unable to heal or comfort the child who inadvertently retriggers the adult's memories of loss. The adult's behaviour can then set off a chain of reactions in the child (difficult behaviours to protect themselves from fear), and the stress of coping with this can make the adult feel so desperate they are tempted to reabuse the child.

Children arriving in a family with complex attachment issues and trauma can be especially exhausting and to adults, can feel very threatening if the adult's attachment style is insecure or their history of trauma is similar to that of the child. Parents overwhelmed by sad, angry or hopeless feelings may need professional advice, to help them distinguish their own grief from the child's. In this way, they will be able to accept the child's feelings as part of his or her past, and not blame themselves as new parents.

The impact of loss on the child who waits

Loss can be a big, painful shock. Children may believe it is their fault they have lost their mum or dad. We cannot make the child feel better instantly or rescue them from sadness or anxiety but we can allow them to feel their pain while staying with them, empathically. When losing someone they love who lives somewhere else and is not dead, children often feel it must be their fault. This can make them strive to avoid all pain and fear. Children will feel relieved if they can tell someone they trust to listen and give comfort, someone who will understand how strong their feelings are and allow them to express anger that masks deep sorrow. The child may need reassurance that it is OK to cry. As Bowlby (1979, p.158) noted, following separation, it is normal to express feelings and essential to healthy recovery. Children and young people can usually tell who is good at listening. Surviving involves changing emotions and children need permission to feel "up and down". As children adjust to loss, they begin to display curiosity and absorb more of what happens around them. Children enjoy having adults to share and celebrate their ability to enjoy life and new relationships. The past can be reviewed by emphasising their achievements.

How can we help?

Empathic statements and reflections

- Listening without making judgements: saying *How sad* or *It's so hard to miss people*, heightening emotional tone of voice and reflecting the child's expression of feeling.
- *Would you like a hug from...?* Suggest someone the child feels safe with, who is kind and gentle such as their new foster carer or adoptive parent, grandparent.

- *Let's remember how special this person was to you.* Invite the child to touch and smell clothes or accessories that belong to the lost person or look at photographs that stimulate recall of special times such as what made them laugh. Make a memory jar (see Techniques CD, No. 29).
- The child can be encouraged to think of the gifts, talents and experiences gained from being with the person. Ask how the person made them feel, before and since the loss. Of course, when children have had several moves, they may not remember their birth parents. Their loss may be of an idealised memory or a more recent attachment figure, or a composite mother figure.

Thinking about strong feelings for children who wait

Consider how the child copes when angry. Does she or he manage better by being separated from the group or from a sense of closeness to others? This is especially important regarding children who have separation and attachment issues. We need to decide whether it is more helpful to facilitate discharge of tension or to interrupt the discharge.

- Does being separated from the group lead to decreased tension (having a calming influence by reducing stimulation) or reinforcement?
- Does being separated – isolated – lead to increased tension, and more out-of-control behaviour such as throwing things, kicking, or breaking toys?

After loss, young people may be hyper-vigilant to unfairness. Vera Falhberg (1994) suggested several ways to decrease tension. It is important to be open, fair and willing to respond without defensiveness. When children are angry or scared, it is helpful to be aware that anger may be active or passive.

The aim is to help the child to relax and regain equilibrium, often described as teaching the child to "self-soothe". If the child displays a "volcanic" build-up, we need to choose a helpful time to teach the child ways to release tension.

Teaching negotiation skills

We can listen to feelings, empathise with how hard it is and agree with views that are valid. If you can't agree, partial agreement will show that you are listening and taking the child's view into account, which can defuse a potential argument. (It is important to model this to your child in other relationships.) Invite the angry criticism (which may be revenge for past parents' behaviour) and reflect feeling, for example, *So, you feel really muddled or angry about all this.* Teaching negotiation skills will help the child focus on the present and the future, not just the past.

Ask, *What have you been thinking/feeling?* or, using a teddy, *I'm wondering what Teddy is thinking about this.* Your response to Teddy's reply might be, *It's so hard to miss people,* or, to young people: *If this isn't helping you, do you want to figure out another way?* or *Do you just need time to talk?* If you've parted angrily – an apology or a simple *I love you* or *Hope you have a good day at school* invites reciprocity. Allowing the child to say what they think, feel and want is often all that is needed. Some require help to reach an acceptance that we don't always get what we want. Supporting children in grief is hard work emotionally, and the parent or carer can feel unrewarded, yet listening and giving the child time will help recovery.

Conclusion

Separation from parents can feel very frightening for children. As they often display their feelings non-verbally, they depend on their carers to recognise and respond empathically to their stress, play being their most natural means of communication.

Summary

- The experience of loss is extremely painful and confusing. At each stage, the child will show their grief in different ways. When children have a stable beginning and then suffer a loss or trauma, they may recover relatively quickly, if listened to with patience and understanding.
- Those who are insecurely attached will take far longer to recover and need to be treated as if their whole being was bruised.
- Noticing, reflecting and allowing the child the opportunity to express things that indicate their internal state will help the child realise their powerful feelings have been recognised and understood without blame. Clear boundaries will help recovery.
- Explaining the truth simply, in an age-relevant, non-blaming manner, will encourage trust.
- Understanding what triggers pain and fear is essential to healing. Awareness of these triggers, appreciating the child's talents and encouraging them to build skills via rehearsal in play, will gradually ease their fear and allow recovery that will lead to new learning, resilience and sense of hope.

Chapter 5
Play and communication

The urge to play is universal and when thwarted, hampers the child's joyful path to self-discovery.

(Bettelheim, 1987)

Introduction

Why, you may wonder, is so much significance attached to play? Why should adults be involved in activity that is essentially the province of children? Play is the means by which children experience and explore their world and relationships prior to having sophisticated use of language for self-expression. Consequently, for those affected by neglect, trauma and loss, play can be a key way for the child to explain their feelings and be helped to recover.

This chapter examines the purpose, value and developmental significance of play, and its use to recover memory, missed development, work through difficulties, and to prepare for "real" life. We illustrate themes arising in play with children, and provide a framework for substitute parents and involved professionals to develop their relationship with children using sensory materials, modelling empathy and facilitating expression of feelings.

Why play is important

The word play originates from the Indo-European term – *dlegh* – meaning 'to engage, to exercise oneself' (Kane, 2004). Such engagement is for pleasure, amusement and, as defined in *Chambers Dictionary* (2001) for 'performance of acts in mimicry or rehearsal of life'. Play may include taking turns in games, directing and discharging, making sounds and enjoying freedom of movement. Landreth (2001) proposes that most importantly, the intrinsic value of play lies in its being voluntary. Throughout this century, leading exponents on child development have advised that play helps us reach our potential. Erikson (1950, p.214) observed that only in play did children's censors relax, to allow fantasy free reign, since:

Play is the natural expression of the human capacity to deal with experience by creating model situations and to master reality by experiment and planning.

Vygotskty (1967) promoted play to expand skills in problem solving, social behaviour and coping, through processing traumatic events. In play, learning about power and dominance enables children to cope better with rejection and managing feelings. For children with adverse experiences, a vital aspect of play is to allow them to reprocess and reframe their memories. Lack of emotional care during infancy results in damage to the child's developing brain (see Chapter 3). Stringer (2008) observed neglected children to use strategies of withdrawal or excessive clinging, which become "millstones" causing rejection even when nurturing care has become available. Physical exercise like running, jumping and dancing regulates mood, the brain releasing endorphins to our bodies, making us fitter and happier. It also develops bodily awareness that helps us to be comfortable in our own skin.

The purposes of play

- Play invites joy and pleasure, emotions that are essential to psychological well-being, by generating "happy" chemicals that counter stress, worries and misery (Gerhardt, 2004). It is beneficial since it is physiologically impossible to be anxious and relaxed at the same time.
- Play is a safe way to explore and validate feelings such as fear. In games of "hide and seek", a toddler might be scared but enjoy reunion on being found, while older children enjoy the frisson of being caught in more riotous games.
- Play situations serve as rehearsal for real life and relationships such as learning to more skilfully negotiate, take turns and compromise.
- Play is a means to develop imagination, useful for problem-solving.
- Play helps us develop empathy, by learning to control our feelings far more effectively than by relying on external control through disciplinary measures.

Play as practice for life

Children benefit from realising that in the course of playing they cannot make mistakes (or at least, that mistakes need not matter) since the very purpose of play is to practise and "pretend". Through play children learn to listen and negotiate meanings. In socio-dramatic play, games of "pretend" that involve taking on roles to enact narratives feature a more advanced repertoire of words and sentence construction than in any other situation. Kane defined play as vital to our adult lives, even though it is still often marginalised by the Puritan legacy defining play as 'childishness at best, deviance at worst' (Kane, 2004). Possibly, adults' resistance to play is based on fear of regression to earlier states, or of losing authority and control. Play enhances 'theory of mind' (Baron-Cohen, 1995) as the act of pretending requires the child to acknowledge what is "real" versus "unreal" and to realise that others will too. Play requires children to show their intentions and direct others in negotiation of roles, settings and sequences, since, as Schaefer (2003) noted, it gives a safe distance to explore threatening, distasteful or taboo issues, therein freeing them to express what may otherwise be denied or not identified in verbal interviews.

How children play

Children play in a variety of ways. These include:

- physical play, developing body awareness, discovery of the environment, including the properties, relationships and qualities of objects;
- constructive play, which enhances recognition and retrieval of stored memory as well as elaborate motor skills;
- make-believe play, which stimulates imagination, plus relational and problem-solving skills, and can include story-telling and reading, stimulating knowledge and intuition;
- artistic play, such as painting and modelling, which stimulates creativity and motor skills;
- games with rules, which develop abstract concepts, and the unwritten social rules, as well as turn-taking;
- practising writing and numbers, which enhances writing, mathematical and manipulative skills;
- hobbies, which help develop specific skills that build self-esteem;
- computer play, which develops technical expertise, though is mainly solitary.

Play therapy: origins and application

Play therapy as a discipline emanates from a variety of sources, too numerous to detail more than a few key influences here. Of early importance was Sigmund Freud (1925), whose observations of his son, Hans, led him to warn that repression of unconscious desires would have lasting repercussions, particularly in limiting the development of imagination. His findings led to the research of child psychoanalysis. Klein (1975) found that children's play offered unique access to their unconscious, and Anna Freud (1965) noted that children repeat in play everything that makes an impression on them in everyday life. Both promoted the process of "working through" conflicts to bring unconscious issues into conscious awareness, although they had ideological differences on the interpretation of verbal and non-verbal communication. Winnicott (1971) saw play as the way in which children manage transition between their inner and outer worlds, with toys, etc. being the "object" that symbolises comfort and serves to project the child's thoughts and feelings. Winnicott used many methods such as the scribble game (see Techniques CD, No. 30). He also worked with mothers to explain their children's signals, yet his unique style proved hard for his followers to emulate.

Axline (1967) contributed to the development of non-directive play therapy with her case study of a six-year-old boy who achieved mastery of his fears. The resulting book, *Dibs in Search of Self* (originally published in 1946), inspired a vast readership. Influenced by Carl Rogers's (1961) person-centred counselling, Axline (1987, pp.73–4) developed eight principles of practice for non-directive play therapy listed below. Oaklander (1978) provided imaginative ideas for practitioners to adapt in play with children, to enable focus on specific problems, already identified by the adults caring for them.

Principles of play therapy

1. The therapist must develop a warm, friendly relationship with the child, in which good rapport is established as soon as possible.

2. The therapist accepts the child exactly as he or she is.

3. The therapist establishes a feeling of permissiveness in the relationship so that the child feels free to express feelings completely.

4. The therapist is alert to recognise the feelings the child is expressing and reflects them back in such a manner that the child gains insight into his/her behaviour.

5. The therapist maintains a deep respect for the child's ability to solve problems if given the opportunity. The responsibility to make choices and institute change is the child's.

6. The therapist does not attempt to direct the child's actions or conversation in any manner. The child leads the way; the therapist follows.

7. The therapist does not attempt to hurry the therapy along. It is a gradual process, recognised as such by the therapist.

8. The therapist establishes only those limitations necessary to anchor the therapy to the world of reality and to make the child aware of his or her responsibility in the relationship.

Developmental significance of play

Play and drama therapies have been proven to help neglected and/or traumatised children by increasing their competence in social and language skills. Russ (2004) examined a wide body of research, including Fisher's study (1992), who found that play assisted cognitive development, improved flexible social problem-solving skills and verbal fluency. It also encourages insight and divergent thinking by permitting the expression of positive and negative feelings, spontaneity and joy, among other characteristics of quality pretend play (Fein, 1987). Fein observed that in such play emotional themes are processed, even though the sequences of events may not follow the actual or conventional, and that children observe themselves acting as someone else in another time or space, allowing transformation to take place.

Embodiment-projection-role

The concept of play as a process incorporating the three components of embodiment, projection and role (EPR) was developed by Jennings (1992). She viewed play as central to our development of self: ideally, it continues throughout life to give practice and opportunity to try things out, in order that we realise our potential.

Embodiment play begins in infancy when we play with our body, suck toes, fingers, etc.; as we grow, we learn to skip, dance, swim and play team games; as adults, we keep fit and socialise through activity such as dance, sport and martial arts.

Projective play starts from around the age of 12 to 18 months, when the child plays with objects (outside his or her body) such as toys, sand, water and play dough. As adults, we project our personalities through our choice of career, tastes and style.

Role play begins with pretend games, for instance, talking for "teddy" on a toy phone, as soon as children discover that they exist separately to their mother. Role play becomes more socially interactive from about three years of age. By five, children dispense with real-life props and use their imagination to create backdrops for their dramas.

In play we prepare for the many roles we take on in adulthood, in our family, work and social groups. Providing children with the range of opportunities encourages experimentation and problem-resolution towards fulfillment of life goals.

The following case study illustrates how a child progressed through embodiment, projection and role play in exploring her abusive experience, until she was able to play safely, trusting herself and the adults in her new adoptive family.

Fiona

Fiona, aged nine, had suffered sexual abuse from infancy. In play therapy, she began playing with rattles. She loved to sway on a rocking chair as if on a fairground ride and experimented with a variety of hard and soft toys to see what comfort each brought (embodiment). With clay and play dough she created shapes that were metaphors for bodily substances (projection). From clapping games, books for infants, games of hide and seek and "grandma's footsteps", Fiona progressed to (role) play in scenes of "servant and master" and "mother and child", in which roles were exchanged. Mirroring Fiona's actions served to reflect her anxieties about safety and reframed her expectations of adults as unreliable and dangerous. She learned to play co-operatively and enjoy peer friendship.

Understanding the internal world of traumatised children

Children's mode of play reflects their internal world. Unusually violent play is likely to mirror the child's earlier experience of violence. Characteristics of the play of neglected and traumatised children are:

- lack of use of imagination;
- the child may not know how to play, or how to use toys/equipment;
- the child may play violently, such as hitting a doll to make it go to "sleep";
- themes of aggression, death and catastrophe predominate;
- bizarre content such as snakes spilling from ears, heads chopped off;
- story endings are invariably negative.

When children are playing, parents often leave them to it, yet self-esteem is built more effectively when parents give their full attention and play alongside them, following the child's lead, stimulating their imagination and celebrating achievements.

Processing experience in transition

Moving from family of origin to foster care, then on to adoptive or kinship care involves processes of separation and loss, transition and reincorporation similar to those identified by the anthropologist van Gennep (1987), who explored how it feels to be marginalised and not own a proper identity. For children, unresolved loss makes the task of transition to new families especially traumatic (see Chapter 4). In play, we can help children to express painful feelings resulting from loss.

To supplement missed nurture, it is especially beneficial to incorporate "messy" materials such as sand, water, clay, paint, play-dough, shaving foam, jelly, pastry, cornflour and water. Caution is necessary for creating a balance that encourages the child without "overloading" those who are unused to sensory experience or re-traumatising a child for whom particular substances are reminders of intrusive memories.

Neil

Neil, aged three, was in foster care, having been abandoned by his mother and raised by his mentally ill father. On seeing the toy knives and cooker, Neil declared the (play) kitchen to be a 'dangerous place'. He enacted the story of a *fire* that could not be *extinguished*. Neil then covered himself in layer upon layer of clothes, buried all his toys in the sand and layered sticky plastic over his paintings, revealing his need for protection from (previously unacknowledged) fears. His *characters* (hand puppets) repeatedly remonstrated: 'I've had enough of you!' Neil told me his brother had often said this to him. By giving Neil the opportunity to safely express his rage and frustration, the play facilitated his successful transition to his adoptive placement.

Accessing the five senses

Neglected children tend to be unaware of their senses. Play that accesses sensory materials enables children to access experience which leads to development of imagination and problem-solving skills, inviting hope for desired change. A useful tool is a "feelings bag", from which the child is invited to select items, construct a story or arrange in a "sculpt". Finger and glove puppets, clay, sand, water or candles also provide sensory experiences.

Touch and smell

Many young children like to give their dolls the nurture they crave for themselves. Children may apply lotions to dolls or to their own limbs. Teenagers enjoy exploring a variety of scents, make-up or nail painting. Trips to the woods can yield collections of conkers, leaves, etc. Scraps of fabric are useful to make pictures and invite discussion about textures, e.g. rough, smooth, soft, etc. Try printing fabrics, hand/foot painting and finger paints.

Taste

Children can be encouraged to expand their experience by tasting a variety of fruit and vegetables. Crunchy raw vegetables such as carrot and celery can also be used to represent sounds. Compare hard, loud sounds of "noisy" foods to soft, "quiet" food.

Sound

Soft mood music such as ocean sounds (reminding of sound in the womb) can be effective to calm anxious children; some love to hear music associated with previous memories and experiences, such as pop songs to which they learned dance moves in previous placements; others find emotional connection to the words of particular songs. Young children enjoy making shakers and learning preschool nursery songs.

Sight

Pictures and stories are invaluable resources to enable recovery of missed nurture. For young children there are increasing numbers of cleverly designed pre-school books, embellished with fabrics that are woven into the story.

Themes of play

In play, children explore their memories and, with encouragement, seek new outcomes. Damaging experiences make it difficult for some to imagine a positive outcome and when they find it hard to explain their fears, we struggle to know what is worrying them most. Yet when allowed to process their loss, most children will reach the stage of being ready to attach to new carers. To illustrate how children work through experiences, we give a few examples of themes commonly arising in child-led play.

Abuse

This case example, entitled *The Magician*, illustrates work with three girls who had been sexually abused by a neighbour. Their mother, also abused in childhood, felt depressed and powerless. The children had few friends and rarely attended school.

> **The Magician**
>
> Three girls, aged seven, eight and nine years, created a collage of their street that led to enacting a carnival scene. Along came a magician who 'performed the worst tricks in the world'. The drama led the girls to recalling past sexual abuse. They created stories of spiders that illustrated the sickening horror of their experience. As a result of processing and rewriting memories, the girls felt more secure. They began to attend school regularly, made friends and their mother accessed counselling for depression.

Powerlessness

Having experienced his parents as too "hostile" or "helpless" to rely on, four-year-old Tom was determined to maintain his independence. Dramatising his story allowed him to discover the potential reliability of a "friend" who recognised and empathised with the depth of his pirate's shame and despair, feelings that belonged to Tom himself.

> **Tom**
>
> Tom's pirate "killed" sharks, whales and all the pirates in the land, except himself. Acting as the pirate, Tom felt powerful, asserting that he didn't need anyone. As a fellow (almost dead) pirate, I reflected my sadness at his being all alone, wondering how he would cope if he cut his knee, as no one could cook him nice dinners or play with him if everyone was dead. Tom created a magic spell to retrieve his "friend" but in the final scene, as pirate, he went into hiding, declaring he was buried 'too deep' and 'smelled too bad'. Eventually, agreeing to be rescued, he enjoyed a ceremonial barbecue to celebrate his safe return.

Rescue

The most rewarding part of therapy occurs when the child feels empowered to choose the outcome, as did Jimmy, adopted at age nine, having suffered neglect by parents who had learning difficulties. Rather than suggesting what we would do in the circumstances, it proves helpful to allow the child in his role as "superhero" to discover what he would do, if capable, in such a situation. From a starting point of feeling powerless, Jimmy came to view himself as brave and capable. He realised that his birth parents had made unfortunate choices and could have acted more protectively.

Jimmy

The Princess married the Pirate and had three babies. Then Super Hero found another baby in the street. He brought the baby home so that made four. The Pirate thumped the Princess so hard she went to hospital. Super Hero fought the Pirate. No one else knew about the fights. They didn't believe in fairy tales and they didn't think there was such a thing as a Super Hero but there was! Afterwards, Jimmy explained that the moral of his story was: 'If you're good and do the right thing you'll feel like a Super Hero!'

Identity

Dominic, aged eight, and adopted in infancy, fantasised that he had been removed from a rich family who would have him back if they knew where he was. Drawing from the animated story series, *George and the Jungle,* he explored issues of identity and belonging. His adoptive mother took part in this process, but later asked, 'What's the relevance? He's not using his imagination – he's just telling you stories he already knows.' Yet children's *choice* of story is illuminating and also, in Dominic's case, especially relevant.

Dominic

Leaving the jungle to search for his brother, George (played by Dominic) learned that his brother (like Dominic's) had been in trouble. On his return home, George discovers the jungle is under threat of excavation (representing life history work, in digging up the past). By the end of the story as he explained it, George had decided to settle for a wife, revealing Dominic's own craving to feel more bonded with his adoptive mother.

Parents often need help to understand the significance of themes in their children's stories. Explaining the content helps to protect the parent from feeling persecuted, and instead, to realise the child needs their understanding and compassion.

"Good" versus "evil"

Emotionally delayed children can be stuck in "magical thinking" causing them to believe that what they wish for (including bad thoughts) will happen. Nine-year-old Harry had been abused and abandoned by his family and been through several foster placements. Harry loved drama and took the role of a "villain" to gain power. The reaction of others helped him to realise choices he could make, including the kind of person he wanted to be and to accept good and bad parts of himself.

Harry

Harry's story of Ali G opened with the line: 'In the beginning, Ali G turned evil!' He shouted insults at his guards (foster carers) and rudely refused food they brought. They cowered before his anger. A Viking servant (worker), entering with Ali G's latest order, expressed a desire to be treated politely. Ali G began to reveal his courage and generosity. Challenged by the arrival of skeletons (ghosts from the past), a fight ensued. Harry then took the role of Superman in order to rescue his friends.

Friendship

Neglected children often show impressive determination yet have limited awareness of the effect of their behaviour on others they seek to control. Dramatic play gives them practice at making friends. Leading the play allowed eight-year-old Mark to explore his fears until he felt ready to attach to permanent carers.

Mark

Mark presented a pattern of avoidant attachment (see Chapter 2). Highly anxious about his prospective move to permanence, he positioned himself as far away from me as possible. As he loved football and was fascinated by its rules, we began by making a clay football pitch. Various superheroes took part in his football matches conducted in miniature. Mark then fashioned a clay chessboard to play out battles. His victorious soldier shouted 'No one can get me!' These self-imposed structures gave him scope to negotiate rules of play and explore which strategies were effective. Within six weeks, Mark began to build reciprocal relationships and make friends.

Transformation

Johnnie, aged 10, constructed various personas in dramas during which he changed from a two-year-old boy into a monkey, then into a masked magician. The magician turned his parents into animals. Through this process, Johnnie came to realise he had always felt like a monkey forced to perform tricks, but now felt more secure, entitled to be a person in his own right. He began to seek affection from his carer.

Johnny

The Amazing Monkey, called Vicious, was a performing monkey. One day his heart stopped beating. They took him to hospital. The surgeon was surprised to find a human heart in him. When he was mended, the monkey returned to the zoo. There, in the midst of performing his tricks, the person who was inside the suit took off the monkey suit and became a human being!

Exploring difference: two case studies

Tania

Tania, of African-Caribbean heritage, was in foster care following many and frequent moves between her birth relatives and short-term foster placements, due to her mother's mental ill health. Tania was due to move to live with her maternal relatives. My task was to help Tania process her experience of physical and emotional abuse. In an early session, I wondered who had chosen Tania's (real) name and what it meant. Tania did not know but thought her name might be African. We shared feelings about names and this opened a window for us to speak of difference. Tania's main preoccupation proved to be coping with feelings about her mother who had belittled her, possibly as a projection of her own sense of inadequacy.

Initially, Tania focused on the theme of survival. She painted, then told a story about a hungry sheep and hen who relied on children to feed them. These creatures had to find new sources of nourishment to avoid dependence on passing strangers. In her drama, *The Frog that Couldn't Keep Still*, the Wizard's (worker) magic took a while to work as the 'frog never stopped jumping around'. We reflected on how frustrating it feels when we try to help people who can't adapt. In play, Tania prepared for moving by planning what to take and leave behind and how to stay in touch with friends.

Her painting of the Crucifixion led to her examining her confusion about who is "good" or "bad" and how to make these judgements. The emerging story featured a 'dirty, black sea' visited by 'poor people' and 'good water' that made the people 'rich' when they performed for 'audiences who paid well'. In exploring attitudes and issues of social status, Tania appeared to appreciate the worker not challenging or correcting her views, instead, enabling her to work these out for herself.

In her drama on the theme of betrayal, the shopkeeper revealed herself to be a witch who turned the Princess into a frog. Tania decided the Princess was really a witch too. The Princess said, *I'm a person, I don't eat frog food!* The Prince responded, *You've been nasty – it's what you deserve!* They travelled from the UK to Jamaica then to Kenya, encountering new habits and expectations. In Kenya, the Wizard of Oz reversed the spell but when the witch tried to cheat him, the Wizard turned her back into a frog whereupon she was destroyed. Tania realised she too had often felt tricked. Destroying the witch gave her power over this experience.

The Viking Princess and Queen sailed to many lands, holding duels with ill-tempered pirates and making friends with slaves. A witch tried to be nasty but her spell failed to work. In exploring the nice and nasty side to her own nature, Tania declared that the moral to this story was *there is no point in being nasty or pretending to be someone you're not because when people keep changing and pretending, it just gets them into trouble.* Many of her stories were concerned with poverty versus wealth. In one play, 'poor people' made music to earn money but were accused of stealing.

A girl met a new mother who gave her daughter chores and became cross when she played first. Tania told me this mother was like a previous foster carer who bullied her to do household chores.

Tania was a bright, articulate child, sometimes reserved yet with a lively imagination. Recalling difficult feelings and discussing how to judge who is or isn't trustworthy, how to survive and make the best of her situation empowered her. Having always lived with people of her own ethnicity, Tania did not feel disadvantaged by her heritage. Though it had influenced her mother's treatment of her, it was just one aspect of the complex prism of experiences which Tania chose to share through the privacy of metaphor. She may have retreated if connections had been made explicit. Tania gained in self-esteem to view herself as a great storyteller, proudly acknowledging her courage, skills at making friends and impressive artwork.

Raymond

Raymond, aged six and of mixed heritage, was in foster care, awaiting court decisions. His white British mother, angry with his black African-Caribbean father for having left, had used Raymond as a scapegoat. He also experienced racist attitudes at school. Though an attractive child, Raymond had grown so used to being victimised that he scraped at his skin to make it look whiter like his fair-skinned sister, action which prompted his referral for play therapy.

Choosing to play with the sand tray and animals, Raymond enacted battles between opposing forces of dinosaurs. The larger army of green dinosaurs would always beat others of different hue, a blue dinosaur being particularly targeted by the green ones. When the worker commented on this, Raymond said the green dinosaurs 'hated' the blue one, explaining, *It's the wrong colour* (expressing exasperation that she hadn't already guessed). *That's unfair*, protested the worker. Together they compared the dinosaurs. *See how many different shades of blue this one has. It's prettier than the green ones*, said the worker, wondering if the green dinosaurs might be jealous of the blue one and asking how the blue one might escape. *He moves fast*, said Raymond. *I bet they wish they could move as fast as him*, responded the worker. Raymond grinned. From this point on, the battle lines were more evenly distributed.

Training parents in therapeutic play

In the course of work in adoptive and foster care, practitioners are often concerned with enabling parents to continue the process after conclusion of an intervention in order to sustain and enhance attachment. Work in this specialised area requires time with the family and managers need to ensure that sufficient hours are made available. For example, one session would rarely suffice to put across many messages. Regular reviews and appropriate supervision are necessary and reports need to be shared with parents.

Transference and counter-transference

Transference is a psychoanalytic term that describes the (often unconscious) transfer of feelings from one person to another. How the child makes the adult feel can guide them to realise how the child feels. For example, annoyance may spring from the child seeking attention in a manner indicating that she or he is also feeling irritable. People can feel very hurt when they sense that despite their best efforts, the child wants revenge for their past hurt, rejection and abandonment. Yet the feelings children leave us with can also relate to the way others have treated us in the past. Responding with attitudes that are a legacy of our past is called counter-transference. When parents and professionals are aware of how the child is affecting them and how their reaction impacts on their child, they will be better able to see what is happening for the child.

How can we help?

As we have seen, children are greatly helped by knowing that their feelings are being noticed, listened to and understood. In play, a good way of helping to ensure that the child feels heard is through "tracking". This means simply noticing what the "child" is saying and doing; she or he will tell you or show you their meaning if they can. The adult then reflects the feeling expressed by the child, saying, for example, *So, you were really sad about that!* All children need their feelings to be accepted. The aim is to observe patterns from what we see and hear, without imposing our values or judgements.

The following tracking techniques can be effective (also see 'Open-ended questions and reflective listening skills', Chapter 6):

- Notice, reflect, show curiosity, see the child's perspective. Make positive statements such as: 'I'm so proud of you. You did that all by yourself! Well done! Very impressive!'
- Allow disaster to occur in the story. Avoid trying to rescue immediately but notice how it might feel for the character(s) to be on the receiving end.
- Enjoy being part of child's thought process; resist the temptation to concentrate on teaching him/her rules of how to play; and resist temptation to take over the story, laugh or be scornful towards the child.
- Represent the child's thoughts, fears and aspirations by taking one or several roles in a story or drama of the child's choosing, following child's direction.
- After a while, if the child seems stuck, perhaps ask, *I wonder if anyone can help this person/ car/animal)?* But try not to insist on an answer.
- Rescue vehicles such as fire engines, ambulances, police or superheroes may be introduced, but allow for the possibility that they can't help.
- Play on the child's physical level (usually on the floor). Admire the capacity of *heroes* who survive. Give praise but allow expression of rage within play.
- Model how the child wants you to be, but if uncomfortable be ready to respond in role: *It's hard being horrid – no one likes me! It feels lonely.*
- Allow the child to recover early missed nurture; explain to older children that this is a special space when it is safe to play like a younger child.

Measuring progress

How do we know when children have gained from the experience of play?

We need to take into account their functioning, confidence in adults' availability, ability to engage in play and to use materials provided appropriately. Over an agreed period, observe adjustments in presenting issues, which may include the following:

- capacity to control expression of feelings;
- ability to be in a group, rather than be solitary;
- ability to make and keep friends;
- health issues: sleep, eating, toileting, complaints of feeling unwell;
- hygiene issues, influenced by and affecting self-esteem;
- patterns of self-harm, worrying, low mood, cheating or stealing;
- traumatised children's ability to cope with fear-inducing stimuli;
- restless, fidgeting, frequent tantrums or fights with other children;
- inability to tolerate sibling(s).

We can observe the quality of the child's play, such as:

- capacity to take on imaginative roles;
- ability to tell a story with a sequence: a beginning, middle and end;
- ability to find outcome with which the child is satisfied;
- willingness to explore a wider variety of play opportunities;
- ability to use toys and materials appropriately and creatively;
- able to identify and communicate feelings affecting characters in play.

We can measure the child's progress at home and school for capacity to:

- sustain concentration, to complete tasks;
- take pleasure in school work;
- pride in appearance (stature, smiles, tidy presentation, etc.);
- generally be kinder, affectionate and more aware of others;
- relax and think before acting on impulse;
- show desire to be helpful, co-operative;
- share attention, fewer arguments with siblings.

We can also observe changes in the way parents talk about and relate to their child.

Children who employ fantasy and imagination are able to think of more things to do in stressful situations that require control of aggression (Russ, 2004). Drawing from the affective processes (impact on child's feelings) occurring in play, as defined by Russ, change can be measured using the chart below.

Processes in play	Signs of progress
Adult labels feelings arising in play.	Child is able to name feelings.
Adult validates feelings exhibited by child in role as another character.	Child displays increased tolerance of feelings; better able to sustain friendships.
Child's involvement in the play task may depend on adult's patience and interest.	Improved concentration; accelerated progress in managing cognitive tasks.
Adult models tolerance of child's anxiety.	Child is calmer, less fractious.
Adult is deeply interested in and sensitive to character's predicaments.	Child gains greater insight into self and others.
Adult accepts adaptive regression and invites choice, in helpful manner.	Child exercises his choice to be "little" or to act more maturely.
Adults help children understand the meaning trauma has for the child.	Child organises fragments of experience into meaningful narratives.
Child is permitted to control the play to gain power over oppressive experience.	Child talks more freely about previously inhibiting experience.
Through modelling, the adult displays alternative views and coping strategies, e.g. finding friends and sources of help.	Child tries out new ways of being, from internalising a nurturing parent. Capacity for story resolution expands.
Adult displays empathy and warmth towards the child.	Child expresses hope, expectation of desired change and appears less lonely.
Adult invites and encourages child to take new risks, try out new skills.	Child is now willing to join club or special interest group.
Practicing physical stance, e.g. standing more erect when assuming authority role.	Child shows improved posture and self-awareness.

Conclusion

Play has many purposes, both developmental and social, its intrinsic value lying in its being voluntary. The generating of "happy chemicals" in play protects against stress and anxiety. In allowing access to the five senses, play enables children to recover nurture and confront complex and difficult feelings, which may otherwise be unacknowledged. The privacy of "fictional distance" allows children to explore experience of difference. Model situations are created, which children learn to deal with by experimenting and planning, leading to greater verbal competence and communication skills, helping them to reach their potential. In play, children learn to manage the transition between their inner and outer worlds, and their trajectory from dependence to independence. There is a range of directive and non-directive styles of intervention, most being principally child led, encouraging children to create new outcomes to old dilemmas. When parents are helped to recognise how their anxieties mirror those of the child and to model empathy, children are reassured, which results in enhanced reciprocity. It is vital for abused children to feel understood, have their despair acknowledged, be encouraged to access sources of support, and to learn that adults can be reliable. Children often struggle with polarities. When involved adults engage in play, and are authentic in sharing their own feelings and reactions, children are helped to integrate (otherwise fragmented) aspects of self.

Summary

- Play promotes the development of "theory of mind".
- Themes and content of play reflect children's preoccupations, such as with loss, exhaustion, oppression, invasion, kidnap, desire for transformation.
- Play is an important means of enabling children to explore feelings and experience without fear of reprisal or of making mistakes.
- Children need "permission" to own negative feelings which becomes compromised when the expression of them is experienced by parents as hurtful. They require adults to be playful and model self-control and empathy.
- Acting as rescuing heroes empowers children to realise choices and new outcomes, thus begin to "rewrite" their past as helpless victims.
- Explaining to children that in story "anything can happen", the outcome being the author's choice, frees them to change previously unhelpful patterns and to realise new strengths, the availability of friends and possibilities for change.
- Children often connect with and admire characteristics of animals in stories which can help them own and confront difficult experiences.
- Useful resources include familiar stories such as *The Ugly Duckling* that incorporate transformation, thus illustrating capacity for change.
- Performing enables us to externalise the contents of our unconscious so that they are seen by others. Reflecting on feelings expressed by characters in their story will help children become aware of your strong interest in them and your understanding of the scale of their courage and strength.

Chapter 6
Assessing children's needs, wishes and feelings

Untitled

Look for the child
Trapped inside
Look for the child
Trying to hide

Watch for the child
As she cowers away
Watch the child
Who never learned to play

Listen for the child
For her desperate cries
Listen for the child
Don't hear their lies

Reach for the child
Take her by the hand
Reach for the child
Take her new land

Live for the child
After what she lived through
Survive for the child
She survived for you

Author unknown (in McIntee, 1992)

Introduction

The previous chapter on play demonstrates that children use objects to project their understanding of the world. We now focus on the child's language of play to explore and ascertain their wishes and feelings. Play, fun and exploration are used to guide practitioners involved in the safeguarding process, including court proceedings and the task of helping children into future placements, with particular advice for those who need help with unresolved loss and trauma.

When we listen to children we are not solving their problems but allowing them to explore their strong feelings through the play and in this way, to discover their own voice for expressing needs, wishes and feelings. In due course, they will process their grief and begin to heal, which will enable them to problem-solve and gain resilience. Children who have suffered neglect or abuse during their first three years have no words to explain what happened to them as their memories are encoded at a sensory and emotional level, so play is a way to communicate these experiences and feelings. When starting this work, it can be useful to use a third object with some sensory component to enable the children to express feelings. As they gain recognition of body, self, emotions and senses, they learn words for feelings and are able to ask for their needs to be met. Before undertaking assessment, it is important to read the previous chapter to understand how, through play, children explore and express their experience and feelings, as well as Appendix 1 on listening skills. For help on preparing a direct work session see Appendix 2.

Note that the normal confidentiality rules don't apply in assessment to the extent that they do in long-term therapeutic work or in permanent placement, since when assessing children in transition we do not know what the child might disclose or if they are safe.

Making an assessment

The task of assessing children requires the worker to be familiar with patterns of attachment and how these can be recognised, alongside having comprehensive knowledge of child development, in particular, how it is affected by neglect and trauma. It is important for practitioners to be able to distinguish attachment difficulties from other complex problems, including those stemming from parental substance dependency affecting children pre and post birth, the full impact of which can last a lifetime.

Cultural sensitivity is a prerequisite for assessment. Black adoptive parents have described encountering racist attitudes, which put them off applying for or accepting post-placement support, as reflected in the difficulties encountered by Rushton *et al* (2009) in recruiting participants for their research.

To ascertain the needs of children and families, it is important to demonstrate an open, enquiring, yet respectful attitude while ensuring the protection of vulnerable children.

We now look at the questions that our assessments aim to answer.

Assessing children in transition: What are we looking for?

- Children's needs, wishes and feelings
- History of parents and grandparents
- Identity: ethnicity, religion, culture, sex, disability, interests
- Child's current profile, skills and presenting attachment profile
- Significant losses/trauma: stage of grieving as currently expressed
- Development: age and stages of functioning in six strands of growth, particularly sensory, social, cognitive and emotional; genetic issues
- Specific physical difficulties which may be affecting child's capacity to hear, see, use senses, balance their bodies and ability to learn
- Capacity for self-expression, speak clearly; experience of school
- Ability to play with and relate to peers and substitute carers
- Themes and patterns in play that give insight into the child's views

Assessing attachment

It is important to find out which attachment style children appear to present, with whom and how their strategies affect their relationships, behaviour and ability to accept intimacy with a protector or within a peer group. The full history of how children came to (or might) be removed is needed to inform the plan for longer-term care needs. Examining their relationship with existing carers and noting the impact the child has on the assessor will help to identify the child's attachment style, while bearing in mind that different attachment strategies are used with different people.

Parents' influence on attachment

Children depend on their parents to explain matters until they are old enough, from about four years of age, to reflect on their own and others' behaviour. Until then, they rely on parents' version of events. Parents' mental states inevitably influence the child's recall of events so it is useful to observe how they organise their responses to stressful situations. Crittenden (2009) cites cases in which troubled parents' intentions to protect their children differed from the outcome of their actions. Understanding parents' motives can help us to work more effectively in the interests of safeguarding their children.

To have memory of the past is essential in order to make predictions. Our memories are modified each time neural networks storing past experience are reactivated. This capacity for adjustment enables us to process the past and plan for the future. When given full information on sources of problems influencing children's relationships, foster and adoptive parents appreciate that it can take two or three years for older children to safely reattach. Rushton and Monck (2009, p.62) found that 65 per cent of adoptive parents had not been helped to develop the parenting skills they needed to re-parent their adoptive children, evidencing the necessity for detailed information to be given prior to placement as well as strategies to cope with children's loss and trauma.

Ethnicity and culture

Children and young people's attachment style needs to be viewed in the context of the family's ethnicity, culture and where they live. The primary interaction between mothers and babies across nations may be almost the same up to nine months of age but from then on, cultural and social norms influence behaviours. Sensitivity and cultural awareness are necessary to explore such differences. For example, unaccompanied children from stable families may have come to the UK to seek asylum for safety reasons. Although their attachment style is secure, they may show signs of disturbed behaviour due to loss or trauma so will need time to adjust. They need to be placed in a family from their own ethnicity and culture wherever possible.

Attachment: recognising the signals

There is a 30-second "window" after babies start crying before increased arousal further distresses the baby and mother, each in turn affecting the other's response. By 11 months, infants learn to predict their parents' responses to their cries.

The letters ABCD, used below, refer to Ainsworth and Main and Goldwyn's categories of attachment outlined in Chapter 2. However, avoidant and ambivalent children may claim personality traits opposite to the category more accurately matching them, hence "A" children describe themselves as having "C" profiles and vice versa, which is confusing and may indicate the child's dependence on others to evaluate their performance owing to their lacking a sense of identity. Problems related to attachment are often misunderstood, which may partly account for substantial increases in autism diagnoses. Traumatised children become very controlling as a way of keeping themselves safe, but once they have been helped to process their experience, their style of attachment may adjust. Social workers are advised to arrange a psychiatric assessment for severely traumatised children who are at risk of developing the more severe mental health problems.

Attachment: the role of foster carers

Foster carers need to be aware of the effect on children of having to talk to so many other professionals. Children may be feeling very confused and are likely to be grieving. They require parental control until they are able to self-soothe and calm their own feelings. At the beginning of a placement, their behaviour may be fearful, chaotic or controlling. Frightened children may act far younger or older than their real age. Some make complaints about their previous parents or carers and tell new carers, 'I want to be with you!' Very early in placement, this attempt by the child to win approval is likely to be a survival mechanism to avoid further rejection. Carers are advised to keep a diary to inform the involved professionals making decisions about the child's future. Carers are advised to take careful notes and inform the involved professionals who are assessing the child. It is frightening for children to feel abandoned and out of control. When traumatised children fear physical closeness, the foster carer can best support them by remaining nearby and by speaking calmly. An effective means for sharing feelings is to listen empathically by inviting children to talk through the medium of puppets or soft toys. Say 'It's so hard for you to feel this way but I'm not leaving until you feel OK' or 'It's really hard to miss...' reflecting the feeling without trying to make it better.

Using play to assess attachment and developmental delay

To translate the child's sensory experience into cognitive language, we need to:

- assess the developmental stage of functioning and ability to process information;
- understand meanings and the child's recognition of "cause and effect";
- examine the parent–child relationship and from this, observe our own feelings of transference and counter-transference in order to appreciate how this child has experienced previous relationships.

The child's attachment pattern is a predictor to the quality of care likely to be needed in the future (Moore and Peacock, 2007).

In the following chart, the left column lists key areas of children's sensory skill development; the middle column gives activities to assess capacities while the third column lists questions about how children engage, to inform assessment.

Development	Activity	Observation
Physicality	Keep a balloon in the air, off the floor; throw and catch (soft) ball; tug of war (Scarf); Tub of Bubbles; "Simon Says" game; dramatic play with costumes.	How confidently and competently does the child move? Slowly, rapidly, freely or clumsily? Can the child catch the ball? How does he or she react to tug of war? Can they blow bubbles, name body parts, follow instructions, dress themselves, with zips, buttons?
Fine motor skills	Cutting and sticking; threading beads; playing with small objects; drawing, colouring	How well does the child grasp and handle objects, e.g. scissors, spoon, buttons, zips, etc.? Can they thread beads? (usually achieved at approximately three years)
Senses	Sand, water, paint, play dough, clay, "slime", food, fabrics; "Silly Senses" game	Observe reactions to substances. Does the child use separate colours or mix them all to sludge? Do they clean the paint brush in water, add water to make sand malleable, draw people? Is the child pleased with her or his effort or do they rubbish it? Can they say which food they like, list familiar meals, describe taste or textures?
Sequencing	Cutting and sticking to make collage, cards, pictures, etc.	Can the child recognise and follow a sequence such as spreading glue *before* sprinkling glitter. How far can she or he count without help or mistakes. How well does the child structure narrative, with a beginning, middle and end?
Expression of feelings	Make a scrapbook, e.g. of TV stars, footballers and different facial expressions; use percussion to create sounds that match emotions	Can the child name and accurately recognise facial expressions and/or do they misinterpret them? Identify feelings in pictures of expressive faces. Encourage the child to name, and explain their own or others' feelings.

Stages of development are revealed in children's drawings. For example, stick legs drawn straight from the head and large "cauliflower" hands are characteristic of children around four years of age. In dramatic play, assessors can note feelings projected into *characters* represented by the child's choice of toys and can observe:

- how the toys are handled, e.g. thrown, spun or treated cautiously;
- the spatial relationships between each character and object;
- whether children seek approval, attention? Are they hyperalert?
- do they bite, scratch, pinch, smile or sing (masking confusion or pain)?
- is the play ritualistic or does it display mainly "risk"?
- what the prevailing themes are;
- whether characters in the play able to seek or accept help (Check story is the child's before attributing emotion entirely as their own wishes and feelings.);
- if there is a "happily ever after" solution or is the story doom laden;

- how the child uses their power and makes you, the interviewer, feel.

(The child may transfer how she or he has been made to feel.) Be aware of counter-transference. (See Chapter 5 for further explanation.)

From the above observations, we can assess children's developmental level in the six strands of growth to observe the displayed social functioning and behaviours as compared with the developmental age at which these would normally be expected.

Observing children's play will guide assessment of the way in which children communicate, helping us understand what she or he needs and to feel listened to. At the end of this chapter and in the chapter on play are descriptions of the themes common in play, for your report.

Developmental delay

There are many reasons why children may be performing behind their peers. Findings from observations of play interaction can be related to characteristics given of each stage of development, as in the chart in Chapter 1. There may be discrepancies between the child's expressive and receptive language that are less apparent if the child presents as articulate, superficially having learned to cover up how little they actually understand. Often, neglected children who are slow to progress emotionally, socially or educationally are rejected by peers due to their social immaturity, yet regarded by teachers as too "borderline" to access the specialised provision they need.

Specific learning difficulties

These might include dyslexia, dyspraxia and auditory processing problems. Signs include: mirror writing, letters missing from words, the child seeing writing as like rivers running down the page, inability to read, clumsiness (being often left strapped in a buggy can lead to weak legs and balance problems) or poor fine motor skills, affecting the child's ability to control a pen. Children may also have poor sequencing and coding skills affecting memory, such as inability to recall a list of things they should be doing. It is important to seek expert professional assessment when necessary, while avoiding unhelpful and unnecessary labelling.

Attention Deficit Disorder (ADHD), Asperger's Syndrome and Autism

Before thinking about these labels, it is necessary to consider the impact of loss and trauma on attachment as a possible underlying cause of problems. ADHD can run in families as a pattern of behaviour whereby the child physically finds it difficult to stay still. A full professional assessment is recommended for children who appear especially fearful and/or chaotic. In general, such children show poor recognition of social emotions and awareness of others around them.

The effect of sexual abuse

Children who are over-aroused as a result of early stimulation of their sexual organs may continue to self-stimulate in order to gain the arousal their body has learned to need. They should be supervised to ensure the protection of other children, and require specialised help to understand what happened and to learn how to protect themselves from further harm. (Chapter 7 on transition offers further information and advice.)

Effects of drug and alcohol misuse

The effects of drug and alcohol misuse on the unborn child include Foetal Alcohol Syndrome, caused by prenatal exposure to alcohol. This can lead to frontal lobe damage and disorder of the central nervous system, resulting in small stature, impaired logic, borderline IQ, seizures, facial abnormalities, learning disabilities and behavioural difficulties. Foetal Alcohol Effect is a subtler, less visually apparent variant that nonetheless has long-lasting and pervasive effects on the developing brain. Brocklesby and colleagues (2009) found local authorities reporting up to 70 per cent of children in need of substitute care to have drug and alcohol misuse in their background, including exposure to these substances during pregnancy. They summarise the processing problems of these children's difficulties in linking cause and effect:

They can suffer from hyperactivity, impulsiveness, short memory spans, concentration difficulties, poor planning and organisational skills, motor difficulties, perceptual problems and specific learning difficulties. As they grow older they can have social difficulties in relating to their peer group and often face a traumatic path through adolescence and beyond.

(Brocklesby *et al*, 2009, p.22)

Obtaining accurate information of the scale and type of substance used by mothers during pregnancy is of critical importance for diagnosis and future prognosis. This requires social workers to check the information given by parents (likely to minimise their intake) with other involved adults and professionals, such as GPs.

Inherited genetic disorders, such as schizophrenia and bipolar disorder

Children whose parents suffer from mental illness may be terrified of inheriting it. The propensity to inherit illness decreases with age, especially when the environment supplements nurture that was previously missed. The local authority medical adviser will advise prospective adopters and refer them to specialists.

Accessing specialist assessment

In order to access help and funding, prior to specialist assessment becoming available, social workers might preface their findings in reports with phrases such as 'This child is showing patterns similar to...' Though not qualified to diagnose disorders, in this way they can bring to notice the serious nature of some behaviour to enable the child to get appropriate help.

Loss and trauma

Chapter 4 describes the six stages of loss. It will be important to find out which people (and pets) have been significant losses for the child, the age at which the loss occurred, and its impact. Assessing the stage of loss is the key to understanding children's behaviour and underpins all work with children in transition. It involves a thorough reading of the history and discussion with birth parents or relatives.

The following are key questions to explore:

- What stage of grief is the child at now?
- How many moves and changes has the child had?
- Does this child have a history of trauma (physical, sexual or neglect)?
- What are the likely triggers and/or dates of anniversaries?

- Does she or he have a sense of time, including past and future?
- Has anyone helped the child to understand his or her past losses or trauma?
- Are there any reports, relatives or previous workers who could help?

Evidencing neglect

If babies are not given bodily and sensory experience, they are unable to release endocrines to digest calories so may fail to thrive (Perry, 2008). The chapter on neglect and trauma explains why children's brains are so vulnerable. Neglected children find it hard to negotiate issues of intimacy, or to play and compete with their contemporaries, and have difficulty enjoying positive experiences. Often stuck at the stage of "magical thinking" (Piaget, 1952), their play may continue to reveal dichotomies, which for them remain as separate, non-integrated ego states.

In our assessments we can observe patterns in children's play which reveal their experience of care being fear-inducing or nurturing. Cairns and Fursland (2007) advise adults to notice the child's reactions to sensory stimuli, for example:

- Are children more stressed by silence or a noisy environment?
- Do they react to particular textures in clothing, animals, furniture?
- Do they react to any particular smells or sprays, deodorants, perfume?
- Is fear of bathing or swimming related to water temperature or noise?
- Is the child who delays getting ready for journeys, afraid of what will happen in transit?
- Are journeys associated with abandonment and unforeseen change?

Traumatised children can be helped to prepare themselves in advance of expected triggers by becoming familiar with the physical, bodily experience at the first sign of anxiety and rehearsing their survival. Calming them depends on the adult being calm, and having a clear, gentle presence, as well as using calming language.

Assessment: identity, ethnicity, religion and culture

When assessing a child, it is also important to find out how well she or he knows and understands their ethnicity, religion, culture or who is in their birth family.

Issues to consider are:

- The child's first language: do they speak the same language as the carer?
- What needs does the child have in connection to their ethnicity, for example, health issues requiring sensitive enquiry?
- Can the child find his or her place of birth on a map? Does she or he know from which part of the world their birth parents came?
- Does the child know the family's cultural customs and traditions and how do they feel about them?
- How does the child feel about his or her body? Are they aware of body sensations? If of a suitable age, does the child know the facts of life?
- How appropriate is it to tell these to him or her in the context of the religion or culture which they or their parents may practise? If so, who should undertake this task?

The transition chapter gives ideas for sensitively exploring these important questions. Assessors are advised to be aware of the ways in which their relationship with a child may be affected by their ethnicity, religion, culture and value system, so as to avoid feeling inhibited in reporting the child's wishes and feelings.

Assessment: disability, physical, mental and emotional health

Assessments need to consider possible physical and mental health, learning difficulty and∕ or medical problems including ear, nose or throat problems that may affect how well children can hear and speak. Consider how the child performs in school and functions in groups. How happy is he or she at school and home? Play needs to be carefully planned to take account of disability, for example, providing a small sand tray to fit on a wheelchair or a board with roads painted on, rather than a play mat which can wrinkle up. We urge social workers to be creative and have fun.

We now consider ways of assessing the impact of developmental delay, using play interventions that are adjusted to the child's presenting needs.

Assessment: using direct work and non-direct work approaches

We have clarified that the assessment task is to ascertain how children perceive their world and make relationships in the light of the trauma and or loss they may have experienced. The purpose is to ascertain their wishes and feelings while considering the impact of developmental delay. There are many methods of assessment, but in this model, we propose combining the non-directive approach of child-led play with toys and projective materials such as sand, clay or objects with directive interventions when necessary. Direct interventions include interactive storytelling, employing specific pictures, drawings, materials and games that enable the child to play out their life experiences via metaphor. Delayed children who do not know how to play or use materials for the purpose of play are often bewildered by too much choice and can be intimidated by equipment they have not learned to use. We find it is more helpful to assess their capacity to use their imagination and the available materials. Generally, the more a child is able to develop their imagination, the greater their capacity to access a wider range of materials and, in this way, express their needs.

As a social worker, foster carer or adoptive parent, your observations and interaction within the relationship is all important. Techniques provide signposts on which children can find their way, often using fictional contexts to show you "what happened". 'Change the context, not the child!' is the advice from Crittenden (2008) and Aldgate *et al* (2006), who promote attendance to feelings as the prime source of information.

Responding to and reporting disclosures of abuse

If a child discloses abuse and is in danger of significant harm, the adult to whom the child disclosed has to report it immediately to the safeguarding team of the local authority in which the child resides. The worker must tell the child that she or he heard what they said and should explain, *No one is allowed to hurt a child in this way*, ideally, heightening their emotional tone. Being heard is all important to a child. If ignored, they may never be able to trust an adult to talk about it again, which can eventually lead to mental health difficulties. Adults to whom children disclose abuse need to reassure the child that they will try hard from then on to keep them safe.

Direct work tools for assessment

Direct work tools and methods are useful to explore children's wishes and feelings, and how safe they feel. A non-directive free play session is a most useful way to start. (For instructions in direct work tools see Techniques CD.)

Assessing the content of the play

After at least three sessions with the child, the assessor can examine the emerging themes and patterns, reflecting on issues raised throughout this chapter. The worker can compare her own observations of children's perspectives expressed in the context of play with what children have said they want to happen. It is important to avoid making assumptions about meanings in a child's play without checking with the child what it meant for them. For example, in taking the part of a lion, a child might display aggression, but his intention may be to defend another, rather than to harm or destroy. See Chapter 5 for further guidance.

Themes and patterns

The stories of maltreated children tend to end in disaster because they have not learned how to resolve conflict. Some rely on magic. Their story might progress from a disaster to having a wonderful time with the parent who actually abused them. In play, children often regress to the age and developmental level when they lost the primary caregiver. They may prefer games of "peek-a-boo" to telling stories. Many who are desperate for nurture enjoy making "food" with playdough, which they may be unwilling to share, say, with a doll or puppet. Some shut down. Noticing the feelings the child transfers to the adult and how you find yourself compelled to respond will inform you how any new carer will experience the child during the 24 hours of caring for them, feelings that could be overwhelming for carers who have insufficient support or have had a poor attachment themselves.

Some typical themes and patterns in the play of maltreated children:

- good versus evil
- kidnap and rescue
- overwhelmed/loss/near death experiences
- place of safety/survival and recovery
- deserving/undeserving
- fear of inadequacy (shame after a telling off)
- aggression/power/oppression
- trickery/telling the truth
- rehearsal for living, re-nurturing and practising for growing up

Assessment report

- Using the *Framework of Assessment of Children in Need and their Families* (DH, 2000), incorporate the above themes and patterns that you have observed and any other observations you have made and provide evidence from play interviews.
- Use the child's verbal statements and pictures to clarify his or her experience of life. Explain the context in which children gave these pieces of evidence.
  It is useful to begin with a brief "pen picture", i.e. a balanced short description of the child that includes physical appearance, talents, skills, and emotional and behavioural state, to provide a clear image of who this report is about. The child's wishes and feelings need to

be stated in the way she or he intended. Most reports have guidelines for the information required. Social workers are advised to consult with others involved with the child, on their thoughts about the child's attachments, development and future needs. Their views may not coincide with what children say they need. However, the task is primarily to keep children safe and give them an opportunity to grow up and heal during the period of childhood they have left. The social worker's report needs to reflect on the children's capacity to cope with change, make appropriate choices, engage in satisfactory relationships, to feel joy and have sufficient self-esteem to be able to deal with the ups and downs of life.

It is essential that social workers tell children what they are going to tell the judge and why they and the team have come to this view. An explanation might be:

I know how much you love your mum or dad and they were really good at making strong healthy children [giving a gentle pat on their back to reassure].

Or

I told the judge that you told me how much you loved your mum or dad but that you also told me you were scared. I told him I didn't think it was safe for you to stay with Mum and Dad because they really couldn't remember not to fight. So they forgot to feed you sometimes and at other times you weren't at all safe.

It is the adult's responsibility to make decisions on behalf of children. (See Chapters 7 and 8 for more ways to explain decisions.)

When the hearing is over, children should be told about the decision and what it means for them, in age-appropriate language and in a way that they can understand. If they are unable to take it in, a story could be told to help them comprehend what is happening. Honesty is reassuring for children because they know deep down what is right but often have loyalty to their parents, whom they may feel they cannot betray. In the words of one child:

I'm glad you told the court what you thought and not what I thought I wanted. I was really cross with you at the time but I couldn't tell you that Mum was never there, so I'm glad you noticed.

Conclusion

When starting work with a child an assessment is essential. This is the means by which we check that a child is safe, living in a nurturing environment (however temporary) that promotes good health and emotional care, with carers who can cope with the trauma the child may have been through. Legal proceedings can be long drawn out, leaving children in a state of limbo in which they are perpetually anxious, stuck in feelings of grief and loss, with little sense of hope. A good assessment acts as a guide for carers to support the children through this transition. It also helps integrate the plans made for the child to achieve her or his maximum potential.

Owing to complex legal situations, children may be assessed repeatedly. The need for therapy is often recognised but not easy to access. Children benefit from having someone to "hold" them through transition to a new placement or return home. It is helpful for the child to have a professional who will support their carer while getting to know their wishes and feelings, to ensure they can talk about worries and yet flourish. In this way, he or she can gain resilience, build their skills and talents, and begin to understand their own story. Talents especially provide the internal bedrock from which the child will build a sense of their own self-worth and discover the sense of hope needed to recover from loss. Listening with empathy is particularly therapeutic, as it addresses the child's primary need to be heard and paves the way for in-depth therapeutic work once she or he is in a permanent placement. (To help this next phase, see Chapters 4, 7, 8 and 9 for ideas.)

Summary

- The assessment of children's wishes and feelings is effectively achieved through playing with them in a regular series of sessions.
- It is also important to consider attachment, loss, ethnicity, religion, culture, relational, health, genetic and developmental issues.
- Parents' influence on the child's attachment style needs to be observed. Children can show different behaviours with different caregivers.
- Foster carers are advised to keep a diary and maintain a protective role.
- Play helps us to assess the child's attachment and possible developmental delay. In play, we can observe competence in physical movement, fine motor skills, sequencing, expression of feelings and reactions to sensory experience.
- Children's communication through play can guide the assessor to recognise particular areas that may need further support, such as for learning disability, autistic spectrum disorders, sexual abuse, effects of foetal alcohol or drugs, trauma, neglect and acute loss.
- The assessor can explore the child's understanding of their personal identity and knowledge about their family of origin and decisions about their future through interactive play and storytelling, keeping the child's safety in mind.
- Typical themes and patterns in the play of traumatised children for inclusion in the assessment report may reveal feelings of powerlessness *versus* over powerful, kidnap and rescue, good *versus* evil, betrayal *versus* trust, and the need to practise for coping in real life.
- Guidelines are given for report writing and explaining to the child how you intend to deliver their wishes and feelings alongside your views to the court.

Chapter 7
Helping children in transition

The Child

An object passed from here to there
A bundle of feelings
I have memories of places in me
Facts, fears, fantasies, illusions, hopes and dreams
Secrets
Sensory experiences
Mum, Dad, siblings and relatives.
Race, culture and religion
Skills
Friendships
Treasures, my very own

(Mary Corrigan, 1989)

Introduction

In this chapter we explain how to help children after assessment, when they may be moving to a new caregiver or returning to birth parents. Having established a framework for supporting children in transition, we briefly outline the importance of building children's identity and self-esteem, managing the moves between birth and substitute families, and helping children to understand what has happened and why. We provide guidance for social workers planning for the needs of children, divided into three parts, each denoting a different stage of transition:

1. awaiting court decisions;

2. after the court case – preparing to move, whether returning home to birth parents or waiting for a permanent placement to be identified;

3. moving to a permanent family.

Framework

The framework (Corrigan, 1990) outlined below aims to help social workers to formulate a plan on completion of the necessary case history research, to address the needs of children waiting for legal decisions. This is to help parents and social workers know where to focus their efforts at each stage so as to prevent having children repeatedly re-address painful experiences.

A framework for children in transition

Assessment	Focus on needs, wishes and feelings.
Transitional support	Prior to court, orientate the child in the present situation and basic life history. Support the grieving process, building identity skills and resilience.
Repair	After the court hearing, explain the decision and help the child to own their life history. Continue to support children during the grieving process and help them to understand the facts, fears and fantasies of their lives in order to continue building identity skills and resilience.
Moving without trauma	Focus on moving, using rehearsal to help children to re-attach with their birth or substitute parents.
Repair, in new placement	Focus on sharing their life history to help children process their grief, and attach safely.
Return home	Involve the child's birth parents, foster, adoptive or kinship carers to establish trust and sense of belonging alongside contact. Maintain safe relationships.

Children who are taken into care will require help to understand and explore what has happened to them. Although this is often referred to as "life story work", as described in Chapter 8, we use the term "life history". This is to ensure that children realise we are exploring their history and will not dismiss it as just a "story" or assume it is about someone else. All work with children, especially regarding how they feel about decisions taken on their behalf, needs to be recorded for inclusion in the child's book about their life, which will accompany them to their next placement or home to parents or relatives. Copies need to be held for children rehabilitated home, in the event that they return to care and the book has to be replaced.

Having addressed the "core assessment", we now focus on helping children and young people to find their voice to express their grief. Our task is to listen, reflect feelings and guide children through their bewildering changes. When given explanations and emotional support to explore their feelings and fantasies, children will take ownership of their "story" so that, rather than feel that the information has been imposed on them, they will actually want answers to the questions: Who am I? Where do I belong? Whom and what have I lost? Why am I here? Where am I going?

We enable this process by allowing children to lead the play, using their natural playfulness and curiosity while offering the non-directive communication tools of play therapy, art, drama, music, as well as directive interventions when necessary. During play children need clear boundaries, in a safe consistent space (see Chapter 6). The relationship that social workers build with children is an important influence towards change, as it provides the model for the child to explore future relationships with trusted adults. Erikson (cited in Cole and Cole, 1996, p.402) found transition and life history work to be a continual process for all of us:

'Throughout their lives people ask themselves, "Who am I?" And at each stage they arrive at a different answer.'

In short, it is the processing we do in order to find the answers that helps us to come to terms with fears or panic states, which can interfere with letting go and finding the contentment to just "be", without having to "do" or control everything in our lives because of fear.

Preparation

This transitional and preparation work is often not undertaken because adults worry they won't know how to answer children's difficult questions: *I don't want to uncover a lot of pain because I don't know what to say or do with it; if I say the wrong thing it will just cause the behaviour to get worse!*

It is easy to put off the task on the (often realistic) basis that 'I haven't a lot of time.' Yet having an adult giving even ten minutes of their undivided attention and conveying their belief in the child's innate skills, is of immense value to that child. In experiencing the value of their own feelings and views, the child gains a glimpse of a future they might hope for. We all feel more appreciated when listened to. This therapeutic type of listening is something we do in our everyday lives. It is a skill that makes us human and is a warm experience that enables children to imagine hopes and dreams for themselves. Ultimately, it serves as a model for the growing adolescent when they are seeking partners who can repeat that underlying message of being valued.

Change is very frightening and brings on many muddled and confusing feelings. Waiting for a legal decision on their fate places children in a state of anxiety and, sometimes, shock. They do not usually understand what a court is and meanwhile are grieving for their parents, friends, relatives, culture, places and pets. Helping children to articulate their feelings in a way they find comfortable and supporting them to grieve is one of the most important and empowering things a parent, carer or social worker can do. Giving children the opportunity to be heard in the way they wish to express themselves is imperative if they are to heal.

It can feel very unfair to children if they have to wait for a permanent home before they can tell anyone what really happened, or is happening to them. It is often argued that children need a permanent safe place in order to benefit from therapy. However, permanent homes can take a long time to find. This predicament has led to development of new creative ways of working with children in care, many with special needs. To deny them the opportunity to tell a safe person like the social worker or carer about what is making them feel sad or angry, is to keep them "shut down" emotionally, which affects their understanding of their world and can lead to the child becoming increasingly "fixed". It is human to feel grief and normal for children who are separated from loved ones to talk or play about it. Many traumatised children also benefit from therapeutic intervention with trained therapists once they have been placed for permanence.

Identity

Having a sense of self-worth is a significant advantage for coping with the challenge of managing change. In order to explore this, we examine the development of identity and the effect of transition on the way children in foster or adoptive care feel about themselves.

At this stage of the process we aim to:

- help the child to become aware of his or her own senses and bodily feelings, by encouraging him or her to find words to describe feelings;
- orient them to the changes in their lives – rehearsal helps to manage change;
- encourage children to build their skills and gain competence and resilience to recover from loss and develop more positive feelings about themselves.

We begin by summarising some key theories on developing identity and self-esteem that children, particularly those showing developmental delay, may be struggling with.

Hughes's (2002) stages in the development of self illuminate just how unrealistic it is to expect traumatised, neglected children to engage in narrative play when they are functioning emotionally and socially at a far earlier stage of development:

- 0–2 months: *emerging self* The infant is, as yet, totally dependent on parental care and does not know that she or he is a separate being.
- 2–9 months: *core self* Infants begin to recognise their internal and external bodily feelings and that their non-verbal expression and vocalising can be effective to get parents to meet their needs.
- 9–18 months: *subjective self* Now the child has learned that she or he is psychologically separate from parent and has a sense of ego; he or she begins to crawl away and play the "peek-a-boo" game.
- 2 years: *verbal self* The child is using single word statements such as 'drink', 'no', 'mine'.
- Beyond 2 years: *development of narrative self* The three-year-old child may now say, 'My name is Jane. I am three, my brother is six.'

In our observations of children's functioning and behaviour, child development theories help us to identify at which age and stage the child is operating, to inform our planning (see Chapter 1). Once children have recovered missed stages of development, their sense of self begins to increase as they recognise their ability to make independent, informed choices.

Developing a personal narrative

The process of creating identity is, inevitably, ongoing but the ability to create a personal narrative does not develop until children discover a sense of self from realising they are psychologically separate from their mothers, mainly in tandem with acquiring language. Children gain a unique sense of self from the experiences they have and the stories they weave about themselves, which connects them to their past, present and future, and gives meaning and coherence to their lives.

Personal narratives give us a "personal theory" of who we are, both to ourselves and others. However, though strongly influenced by those who care for us during our first three years, it is possible to change our personal narrative since we relate in different ways to different people, depending on how they respond to us. As we grow and make relationships outside our family, our horizons expand, altering our perception of our surroundings and ourselves. By telling and processing our personal narratives, we can change their outcome. Attaining a balanced sense of self helps children who have suffered unwelcome disruption to accept the facts of their life histories and come to terms with their fantasies and feelings, despite losses and traumas. Children are not bystanders in their development except when they have been severely damaged *very* early on.

Safeguarding children within the care system requires giving the children with whom we work what Hughes refers to as an 'integrated self', which is a balanced sense of security, and identity. When children have been repeatedly threatened and traumatised, their "self" becomes fragmented (Hughes, 2002).

Security versus threat*

Safety	Threat
● Integrated self	● Fragmented self
● Flexible behaviour	● Reactive affect
● Resonating affect	● Impulsive behaviour
● Reflective thought	● Rigid thought
● Coherent narrative	● Disorganised narrative
● Presence	● Dissociation

* From Hughes (2002) 'Road to recovery', a course, p. 2 in course notes

Many of the people reading this book will be re-parenting or helping children and young people with a "fragmented self", resulting from painful losses and multiple traumas early in their lives. Traumatised and neglected children self-diminish by constantly asserting: 'I am rubbish at this.' They tend to give up when they have hardly started. Some children act in a superior way as a defence, for instance, declaring 'I am a really good gymnast' after seeing the sport on TV but wishing they were the star turn, being desperate to measure up to their own or parents' expectations. Such attitudes become a self-fulfilling prophecy. Prompted by internal negative "voices", children can be quick to defend their fragile, over-shamed self which can result in excessively controlling behaviour.

Unable to confront their pain and too immature to understand the impact of their behaviour, they build a fantasy self. Neglected children often have poor judgement of their body senses, such as being unable to taste finer flavours or notice changes in body temperature. Having no words to explain feelings, they perceive themselves as mainly at the mercy of others. It is not until they are assisted to use their senses through sensory and embodiment play that they can begin to express and verbalise feelings about their loss and trauma.

How does self-esteem develop?

The child's developing brain is like a computer, which can only work properly if it has been adequately programmed to make the necessary connections. In the early years, parents or carers are the "programmers" of children's brains. Everything that primary attachment figures say and do is recorded by the child's brain, rather like a film. The amount recorded and accessed depends on a combination of the child's genetic capacity for growth and parents' responsiveness in regulating their child's emotions and providing stimulation. When children grow within a meaningful, reciprocal relationship with a parent, they discover that they are a separate person, with their own 'unique identity, yet a sense of belonging to family or group' (Fahlberg lecture, 1990).

As Virginia Satir (1972, p.24) has explained:

An infant coming into the world has no past, no experience in handling himself, no scale on which to judge his own worth. He must rely on the experience he has with the people around him and the messages they give him about his worth as a person.

The ability to communicate and accurately interpret verbal and non-verbal messages is essential to building self-esteem. Studies of emotional meaning in face-to-face interactions (Marsh, 1968, p.47) found 55 per cent were conveyed through facial expression, posture and gesture, while 38 per cent were transmitted through tone of voice.

When we talk, we talk with the whole of us. 'A child will tend to believe the body language rather than the spoken words' (Plummer, 2004, p.16).

A child who has been given mostly positive messages will have internalised a sense of self-worth and become progressively less reliant on others for approval. Those remaining dependent on constant praise (from external sources) to maintain their self-esteem find it hard to cope with life's traumas, show less resilience and are more likely succumb to mental illness (Shore, 2006). Insecure children depend on adults' reassurance of their capabilities and need confirmation that what they do or say gives pleasure. So, rather than telling a child, *You're clever*, with undertones of expectation that the child may worry about fulfilling, parents could say, *You worked so hard at that. Nice job! I am really proud of you!*. Plummer (2004, p.21) categorises the elements necessary to have a sense of self-worth as 'self-knowledge, respect and tolerance for self and others, self-acceptance, self-reliance, self-expression, self-confidence and self-awareness'.

It can be easy to confuse signs of low self-esteem in children with the stages of loss. Paying attention to the child's feelings is therefore essential.

Common signs of low self-esteem include:

- hunched shoulders, poor posture;
- picking at sleeves, biting finger nails, avoiding eye contact;
- a whiny high-pitched voice, very needy, constantly by your side;
- can be easily influenced by peer group;
- can't join in group activities but if they do, they often have to be first;
- appears depressed and tearful, emotionally flat, or aggressive and unpredictable;
- emotional pain expressed physically, complains of tummy ache and headache;
- may tease, diminish or bully others, or be a victim and easily bullied;
- at school the child can't concentrate and may act as the class clown.

Part 1: Awaiting court decisions

Working with children in transition while awaiting court decisions can pose problems, as they see or speak to birth parents who may be unable to stay "on message". Naturally, the parents are fighting to get their children back, so will make promises they cannot always keep or ask the children to tell social workers and foster carers a certain story. However badly they are neglected or abused, children love and desperately want to measure up to their birth parents' expectations and not be abandoned by them. This can result in their staying faithful to the parental message, denying their real feelings and the abuse they have experienced, even refuting medical evidence. As a result, some develop a fantasy view of parents' love and care that prevents them from remembering or learning from the danger they actually experienced (see 'Type A' profile, Chapter 2 on attachment). Being stuck in a fantasy can lead to the child or young person making poor choices throughout life.

Working as a team

During legal proceedings, the children's guardians will also be seeking children's wishes and feelings. With so much at stake, children become especially anxious, withdrawn or over-controlling, depending on their earlier experience of parenting. It can be difficult for foster carers and social workers to help while waiting for the legal process to be completed. Each person who has contact with the child should listen, reflect their feelings, answer questions honestly and reinforce the message that at the moment we are trying to keep them safe and are all thinking together to assess what they really need.

We can be blind to reality for years if our needs and feelings are not met. When they are, we are able to make better choices. In this challenging transitional period, before legal decisions, many children remain entrenched in this state of seeming blindness until, like Rosie below, they are given the opportunity to express their wishes and feelings through play.

> **Rosie**
>
> Rosie was asked about her wishes and feelings. Having put on a white wedding dress from the fancy dress bag, she said, 'I want to marry a pop star, have a swimming pool and live in America; my mum can come and stay with us.' After the court case, when the worker had nearly finished their sessions, Rosie reminded her of their earlier conversation: 'You remember what I said? Well, I don't think I will live in America but I think I want a flat in London, a job and I don't think my mum is safe, so she better stay in a hotel!' Rosie was acknowledging her mother's failure to protect her from gross abuse.

The social worker's task

The role of social workers has changed a great deal in recent years, moving towards case management and co-ordination of services. The task of meeting the needs of children who have suffered trauma and numerous changes of care is complex and social workers may worry that they are insufficiently trained or find their time too limited. However, their job is to supportively "bridge" the child, from the past to their future. Social workers hold a lot of power, knowledge and access to relevant information and history. Since the Children Act 1989, young people have had the legal right to be heard. McLeod (2008, p.30) argues that people who work with children are therefore 'legally (and ethically) obliged to take children's views seriously'. Listening sensitively and reflectively does not require advanced training and is the least children have the right to expect. Reflecting on their thoughts and feelings (rather than trying to find solutions) helps them to find their own answers.

Undertaking this transitional bridging work with grieving children is often painful for the adults involved and preparation is essential. Children need a supportive team to meet regularly and clarify who is undertaking which part of the work, to help ensure completion and minimise misunderstandings. It also helps avoid the kind of snap decisions, such as suddenly moving the child, that can cause well-made plans to go awry.

Telling the truth

Giving children truthful explanations from the beginning is essential. Whatever has happened, it needs to be explained according to the child's age and developmental stage. Children may not always understand the words used, but recognising sincerity will help them learn to trust that person. Before court cases, social workers cannot promise children that everything they (the children) tell them is confidential. The social worker's job is to keep children safe. It is helpful to begin by explaining the role:

My job is to keep you safe. I cannot keep secrets that won't keep you safe or are making you very sad. So, only tell me what you feel comfortable sharing. I will tell the judge (or your children's guardian) your wishes and feelings, but I will also tell the court what I think would keep you safe so you can grow into a strong and healthy person. You might not always agree with me but I will always try to tell you the truth as far as I know it.

When plans are still uncertain

The following framework will enable social workers to plan their work, starting with the questions the child is likely to be struggling with: 'Who am I? What's happening?' By setting aside regular time and giving short, honest answers, social workers can demonstrate their commitment to helping the child build skills and gain a stronger sense of identity, with the reassurance that they are in a safe place – at least for the time being.

Preparation framework

- Complete assessment of children's needs, wishes and feelings.
- Find out if children know and understand why they are living in care or being helped. (See River of happy, sad and lonely feelings, No. 65 on the CD.)
- Gather facts from files and, if possible, interview parents or past carers.
- Make a timeline adding the impact of any changes.
- Think about the hierarchy of attachments and who else children are missing.
- Give the child a sense of hope by showing your commitment in their process.
- Make sure their skills are being enhanced by carers.

Foster carers/ adoptive parents

Prior to the conclusion of legal proceedings, foster carers can undertake self-esteem work and skill building. Children may arrive at the foster home with a sack of belongings that appear messy, with clothes and toys they have grown out of. Carers might be strongly tempted to dispose of these items but the child's belongings have a familiar smell, which provides a sense of comfort and allows the recovery of memories that help them process loss and recall happy and sad events. The child's belongings need to be kept where they can access them. Exploration of memories may be kept brief, if a child's behaviour is volatile, due to anxieties about the future. Children benefit from being allowed to lead their play while parents or carers listen. If the adult is controlling the play by insisting on organising it, the child may shut down or destroy treasured objects.

Social workers can support foster carers by giving them information about the child and praising children, admiring their achievements and adding to the memory box from trips out together. Foster carers depend on social workers to model empathy and support them in setting clear boundaries with children when they are especially challenging. Carers also feel better supported when social workers are reliable with arrangements. If they are late or fail to arrive, the child's feelings can rapidly escalate. Failing to keep appointments merely reinforces the negative working model previously set.

Identity work: Stage 1

In undertaking the assessment of a child in transition, the social worker will hope to have built a level of trust with the child, who needs explanations regarding their current situation. A visit to the court and/or a re-enactment of the court procedure in the style of a play (see Chapter 8) helps the child to understand how decisions are made and, if they want to know, inform them of what their birth parents are likely to say or have said.

Who am I?

It is vitally important for children to be able to make factual and emotional links between past, present and future, so living in the same foster home and having the same social worker is especially helpful in providing a sense of continuity and containment.

Why am I living here?

The child can be given one of the following explanations:

Your mum and dad knew how to make a healthy child, but unfortunately their behaviour stopped them from being able to keep you safe, so you are staying with us while we see if anyone can help them change/until we work out what's best for you.

...because your mum/dad was mentally ill (and/or drank too much alcohol/took too many drugs), their mind became muddled so they did not remember to feed or care for you as a young child should be cared for. This is why the people at court are thinking about where you should live at the moment.

Techniques for answering children's questions can be found on the CD.

Life orientation maps (No. 58), River of happy, sad and lonely feelings (No. 65) also, for young children, brick wall (No. 57) and film story boards (No. 66) will help to explain children's journeys in a way which reduces the pain. Use listening skills to allow strong feelings, see under grief and loss chapter and on the CD.

Life history books

These books can be divided into two parts. Work needs to focus on 'who the child is now' until legal decisions about the child's future have been made. Foster carers can help by starting photograph albums of family events while the child is living with them. Social workers may need to decide who undertakes which part of the work.

- A ring binder or display book can be chosen by the child, and card provided to draw on, placed in plastic sleeves so that the child can change their ideas about what they want to record. These books need to be both accessible and robust.
- It is useful to provide fun items such as coloured pens, sequins and stickers with which to decorate the folder and card.
- Suggest that the child decorate their folder.
- Find out if the children would like to display an up-to-date portrait photo on the first page with their date of birth. As a way of building up a sense of self, help the child to frame this

picture with decorations. Show interest in colours and patterns. Any standard of decoration is acceptable. It's not a school lesson!

- On the next page could be a collage of all the child/young person's interests such as sports, pop stars and favourite food, an activity they can find very satisfying. The child may use a disposable or digital camera to take photos of favourite items. Magazines (culturally appropriate) are useful sources for illustrations of food, life style, and heroes/role models. Children may wish to include pictures of their pet or favourite band – actually playing their music communicates acceptance of their ideas and feelings.

Identity work: stage 2

For the second stage of identity work we suggest ways to help the child process their feelings concerning each piece of information.

Birth certificate

Birth certificates may not be available before court decisions. Prior to giving a copy to the child it is important to check that they know who their parent is, and that the birth date on the certificate is the one he or she has been celebrating! So often, the facts differ from the child's knowledge. When discussing absent birth parents of whom little is known, the child will need to gain a sense of their inheritance in a way that will not dent their self-esteem. Even if the parent(s) made irretrievable mistakes, it is important to distinguish between their decisions/actions and attributes that their child has inherited.

Examples of how to explain this:

Whatever mistakes your mum and dad made, they got some things right. I can see they were really good at making a beautiful girl [or boy]. You have strong legs/lovely eyes.

Or, if the parents' history is missing, you might say:

I can tell from your talents that your dad's/mum's family must have been good at running [or gym, music, drawing, etc.] like you!

In this way they build a positive construct of a missing parent of whom little is known.

Using play

Learning about senses and bodies through play is crucial to emotional and social progress for neglected children. Chapters 1 and 5 describe ways to engage children's senses (so often shut down) and help children to process traumatic events. Also see the CD. Younger children often love playing "babies" using a "baby basket" and doll, or being the baby themselves, to experience nurture (see Millie case study, Chapter 3); older children can regain missed nurture through model-making with clay, sand or painting. In addition, young people can benefit from playing with a much younger child which gives them licence to play with toys they had little opportunity to experiment with in their early years.

Keeping to boundaries

By leading the play, children retrieve the power taken from them (when they were deprived or abused). For example, carers might allow the child to use a whole bottle of lotion, as long as the activity remains on the boundaries of a plastic mat and counts as "special play time". Adopted or fostered children who are regularly offered nurture play soon recover missed stages and move on to more age-appropriate games, unless there is an organic reason or excessive trauma keeping them at a younger age. When foster carers encourage children to attach, their sense of security can transfer to new parents.

Talking about bodies and difference

A way to help the child own their body is to start with measuring their height, weight and shoe size. Children may like to count their teeth while facing a mirror. (Caution is advised since touching the child's teeth might trigger memories of a previous abuse.) The "egg drawing" (Falhberg, 1990) shows which part comes from each side of the family, while silhouettes using body-coloured pastels help children accept their body and heritage, and are especially beneficial for those with poor body image.

It is important to talk about difference and commonalities. To introduce the subject, comparisons can be made that enhance the child/young person's self-esteem, for example, comparing the shape and colour of bodies (using safe touching), especially if the adult is of very different appearance to the child. Being open about difference in a way that celebrates it will break down barriers so that relationships are more open and equal. Children need a sense of pride and belonging. Appropriate heritage matching helps but has to be balanced with the child's timescale, particular needs and personality.

Many children have a different ethnic heritage to others in their new family, where each person may have a different skin tone and hair texture. Children need foster carers and adoptive parents to provide skin creams or body products suitable for hair and skin type, and to take them to hairdressers who know how to deal with their hair. Books, music and magazines reflecting cultural difference serve to convey the importance of heritage. Knowledge of the history of other ethnic groups will make it easier for parents and social workers to listen and respond wisely to a young person's complex question about "race" and discrimination. It is especially important for young people in care to have role models who can help them see their lives and relationships in a positive light. Men can show young people how to take safe risks, whereas women (as protective mothers in a child's early life) may try to over-protect. Young people benefit from meeting people from their own and other ethnic backgrounds. By inviting adults and children of diverse ethnicities into their home, foster carers can give children a greater sense of belonging to a group and to our multicultural society.

How we can help

- If we show warmth and respect, in time the young person will return it, so knowing about their origins will give them a sense of belonging.
- Prepare or help them cook recipes they remember as well as yours.
- Familiarise children with their birth parents' faith.
- Festivals frequently mark the rhythm and seasons of particular cultures.
- Playing music from their heritage conveys cultural acceptance.
- Visiting the school and photographing the area the child came from (as long as the child is safe from relatives who may place them at risk) can boost self-esteem.
- Memories can be both healing and painful. Encourage children to explore funny as well as sad memories, including sounds and smells.

Sexual abuse and bodies

When neglect or abuse is suspected, children need ways to tell trustworthy adults "what happened". Sometimes children want to show the adult where they were hurt physically or sexually, which can be painful to hear. Children require adults to attune to their feelings so that, in their acute pain, they feel held and accepted, despite their self-blame. When young children have been groomed, their private parts can hurt or may have been over-stimulated in a sexual way. Playing with an ordinary doll, a doctor's set, lots of newborn nappies, baby cream and talcum powder is the most useful way of helping them process and recover. Children lead the play while adults reflect how "dolly" might feel.

> **Case example**
>
> A child used crayons to show bruises all over the "private parts" on her picture. She asked her worker, 'Will you come back next week so I can colour in my back and show you where all the other bumps are?' At six years of age, she understood her gender's body shape and wanted someone to listen to her horrific story. To convey appreciation of the child's distress, the worker raised her emotional tone, saying: 'No grown-up should hurt a child this way,' and waited quietly, showing acceptance of the child's story and pain. She returned to hear about the rest of the child's experience.

Sexually abused children may reveal distortion in their understanding of relationships. This can lead to their developing unconscious self-persecutory drives that invite new adults to continue to abuse. These vulnerable children need clear explanations about "the facts of life" and how to be safe. Answers to children's questions need to be general, honest and brief but clear enough to help them realise that they have control of their body parts that are private. Social workers need to be aware of the child's cultural and religious practices but ensure these do not prevent children from having this discussion and check that children's knowledge is not just from school, because abused children often shut down in such lessons.

A helpful way for children to process their damaging experience is to use the water game (CD, No. 81), to show them that (in most cases) they were born out of love that can be shared, gained and lost. The child discovers how feelings are transferred, the metaphor of water as representative of love providing privacy to explore powerful and upsetting feelings.

When it is apparent that a child needs to know how babies are made, the foster carer can explain simply: 'When a mummy and daddy love each other they can share their eggs. These two eggs get together and make a baby.' The child may ask how the eggs get into mummy's tummy. Babette Cole's *Mummy Laid an Egg* (see booklist), aptly and amusingly explains all and can help in focusing eye contact on amusing drawings. Children whose bodies have been over-stimulated by sexual abuse at an early age need to learn safer choices for themselves. The following explanation may help:

When you were born your body worked very well as you were a strong and healthy baby. Unfortunately X switched your private parts on too soon. Now it is safer to switch them off and not use them until you are in a grown-up, loving relationship to help you care for the baby you might have.

Foster carers can talk to children over ten about being in control of their own sexual health, so they are aware of their right to say no to sex and learn to protect themselves from unwanted pregnancy and/or sexually transmitted diseases. The emphasis needs to be on making trusting relationships in which mutual respect is of utmost value.

Bullying

Knowing what bullying relationships involve and how to say no firmly is essential for children to keep themselves safe and maintain self-respect. They easily become vulnerable through fear. Whether children are bullies or being bullied, they are usually victims of poor relationships. If bullying occurs at school, children should ask staff for help. Being part of a team comprising their social worker, special needs co-ordinator and parent or carer gives the child courage to follow the programme in place. Sometimes bullying is so endemic, the child may need to move to another school. There are some excellent books on bullying for all ages (see booklist). The charity Kidscape and many schools have "No bullying" programmes.

John

John said, *I had a big bruise on my foot.* When the worker asked, *How did that happen?* he replied, *My dad dropped the telly on it!* Heightening her emotional tone, the worker responded: *Oh, that must have really hurt! How does it feel now?* John said, *It still hurts.* The worker replied, *I'm sure you can really feel it!* She displayed empathy by not discounting the child's feelings, even though the event had happened a long time ago.

Disabilities

It is important to provide appropriate care and support for children who have a disability or specific needs for educational support, and to ensure continuity of support services when the child moves to a new school. These children may not find it easy to express how they feel or may feel misunderstood by teachers but may want to discuss their gains and losses, including talking about their bodies. The social worker's task is to encourage this discussion and ensure that disabled children are enabled to take part in lots of activities. It can help to say, *Other children have talked to me about how sad/great they feel about X,* since including the words 'other children' can help to make them feel a sense of belonging. Reflective listening techniques, perhaps with music, help to enhance children's feelings.

Using toy figures, beds and hospital sets can help young people with physical disabilities and/or learning difficulties reveal what they want or have experienced. A doctor's set, with bandages and plasters, enables them to show their hurts and related fears. Children with disabilities have often experienced medical interventions as very abusive. In taking a child to the dentist or doctor, parents are advised to rehearse this event through play, to acknowledge and reduce the child's fears. Rehearsal of medical procedures is found to bring healthier outcomes and reduce pain. To help children feel competent, however complex their needs, parents can be creative, perhaps with a computer or by providing a small tray on the child's wheelchair on which they can play. Drama, dance, music and swimming encourage children to develop self-confidence and co-ordination.

General health

Children can learn self-care from reading books with adoptive parents or foster carers which invite discussion about varying body shapes, skin and hair types, to realise that the way to self-respect is to take care of their bodies. They can say no to the wrong foods and make positive choices, such as following a healthy diet, keeping physically fit and having respect for their body as a private space. This helps them feel good about themselves and their attitude. Daily exercise is essential to health and needs to be fun and playful to ensure that young people carry on making it part of their routine into adulthood.

Building skills to help a child recover lost competence

By caring for an animal, or a plant or by making a meal, children gain nurture for themselves. Activities such as horse riding, gardening and cooking also help them to build skills, competence, self-esteem and a sense of inner control. They will develop a sense of trust in self and respect for others. Horse riding is especially valuable for sexually abused children, as they learn to control their bodies while gaining power over a strong creature (the horse). Participation in clubs, music, sailing, sport or self-defence like judo and karate help to make friends in a new environment as well as learning new skills.

Being in a team is a skill and it is often hard for traumatised children to integrate into such a group. Willing perfection, they often demand to be first and cannot understand the necessity of relying on the team because it requires trust they have not learned. Less competitive groups include Scouts, Girl Guides, Woodcraft Folk and Sea Cadets. Children may need parents in attendance until they are settled in. Adolescents may need another teenager to go with so they are less self-conscious and more likely to feel they belong. When parents attend displays and tournaments, they demonstrate respect for the child. Sometimes there are jobs involved with the club that parents can undertake to show support and earn the child's respect. Having fun with adults helps children to discover that it is fun to learn new skills and encourages them to develop a sense of humour.

Kevin

Kevin, aged eight, was having huge problems at school playtime. He fought with every child who challenged him. His adoptive mother realised that he had not internalised any self-control as a toddler and was unable to self-calm, so she decided to hide behind the playground fence at break time. When she saw him lift his fist in readiness to drop a punch on some unsuspecting child, she called out in a firm but warm tone, 'Kevin!' He immediately dropped his fist and looked around. Seeing his mum smiling, he felt supported. She continued to go to school at break time for about three weeks and with her prompt Kevin began controlling himself a little better.

To help children make friends, other children can be invited to play, with supervision and planned activity so the child does not need to be in control. When the child is tolerant of one playmate, two can be invited (although this can cause difficulties if one feels left out). For children and young people who find school difficult, it can help them settle in if parents are involved in a voluntary capacity at the school. Working with a child to achieve very small goals can make life generally more manageable. Incentives help but, for the child, the greatest reward is one-to-one time with their parent.

Part 2: After the court case – preparing to move

Returning home to birth parents

When the decision is to return children to their birth parents and the child has been told of the plan by the social worker, photos can be added to their life history book to enable children to show their parents what they have been doing while in foster care. Children will have had self-esteem building experiences and memories they can share without any embarrassment. On return home after long periods away, for example, when parents were in hospital or prison, children often punish their parents. Sharing positive memories is a way to show how it felt when they didn't see their parents or saw them only in weekly contact, and can be healing, as it reduces the guilt in the child and parent.

Helping children understand moves

Explaining reasons for the next move does not always abate children's anxieties. Social workers can help the attachment figure give the child their unconditional permission, which helps children accept decisions more readily: *It's because I love or care about you that I want you to have a keeping or forever family.* Some birth mothers courageously make their own story books. They may not always be "on message" but can be incorporated into the life history book, with a new understanding of facts that children have discovered for themselves, which can deepen their relationship with adoptive parents or kinship carers as well as help them to learn acceptance of their birth parents' situation. Foster carers can meanwhile give an unconditional message: *Because I care about you, I want you to have a forever mum and dad or a "keeping" mum and dad.*

Waiting for a permanent placement to be identified

It can take some time for a new family to be found, so what can we do in the meantime? Children have numerous questions they are often too scared to ask. If the court plan is that the child is to be adopted or live long term with foster or kinship carers, life history work can help to prepare the child for a move.

The main questions to ask are:

- Where do I belong?
- What happened to me?
- Where was I born?
- What happened when I lived at home with Mum and Dad?
- What was fun/sad when I lived there?
- Why did I come into care? What did the judge say?
- What happened to me since I came into care?
- Who did I live with and what did I do or learn when with them?
- How many places have I lived at (i.e. foster placements and relatives)?
- Who were my friends?
- What schools did I go to?
- What is a foster family, compared to an adoptive family?

●   Where do my grandparents live?

Life history work ideally includes visits, taking photos and meeting people from the past to hear memories of their early childhood, perhaps including meeting siblings they didn't know about (although this would be at the proviso that the child's safety is not at risk). (See Techniques CD under transition and life history for contents to cover in life history books, canvas life maps and games to help record and process the history.)

Below, we suggest how workers and parents can answer children's questions. This section contains general information about supporting a child in life history work. Methods for the more experienced worker or trained therapist can be found in the next chapter.

Planning

The need for supervision

As well as gathering the facts, social workers have to consider who else could support this often emotionally painful journey, since it may well bring up feelings from their own past, especially when the child (and/or foster carer) has experienced a multitude of traumas.

Foster carers and adoptive parents should be able to obtain support from their link worker or a therapist. Social workers need to obtain support and supervision with the agreement of their manager. Life history work is not just about collating information; it is a journey that begins when the social worker first meets the child and lasts throughout their life in care and/or in their adoptive family. Social workers need the support of someone who can help them reflect what is happening for the child. A co-worker, or in more difficult cases a professional clinical supervisor, is most helpful as they enable the worker to gain insights into helping stuck children, while providing essential emotional support. Untrained workers may be skilled at collecting information or taking photos, and often have a positive relationship with the child from being the escort in contact. However, they too need professional support in order to know how to reflect feelings. A therapist is likely to be the more appropriate choice to support the most traumatised child's emotional life history journey. Facts need to be part of a repair process the child can own, rather than being left in a cupboard because it is upsetting to think about them, which tends to lead to serious problems later on.

> **Grant**
>
> Grant, aged 22, looked up his old social worker. She had worked through his life history with him when he was eight years old and had given him a little Disney album with photos of the play, poetry and music they had made together. When they met again, Grant brought this album, bulging with new poems and songs that he read out. They enjoyed sharing the past. However, on being asked what had happened to his life history book, Grant said, *My foster mum put it in the loft. Playing with you was the happiest time I had in care, but I never saw the book again.* Grant had many troubles but his skills at music and poetry, of which he was proud, gave him hope for the future and respite from his pain.

The reader will appreciate from this story why we recommend this work to be undertaken by a trained, supervised social worker or a child's permanent parent, who will listen to feelings appropriately and not reject the child as a result of hearing such fear and pain. When the court hearing is over, revisiting the River of Happy, Sad and Lonely Feelings is a helpful way to explain the agreed plan and answer the question, 'Why have I come into care?' (To address worries see the brick wall game, No. 57 in Techniques CD.)

Saying goodbye to birth parents

To help children process their loss it is useful to find out where the child really wants to be. They may be stuck in grief or the fantasy created by parents, hoping to win the court case. After many assessments and rehabilitation programmes, the child may have experienced repeated let-downs. This is very sad but if managed well, the birth parents and the long-term parents can often eventually find a way to let each other know how the child is getting on via direct or letterbox contact, ideally, amicably. Clearly, the outcome will be more positive if the adult is focused on the child's best interests.

"Goodbye" visits to birth parents need to be managed carefully. Advance rehearsal helps parents to think of ways to explain to their children why they can no longer care for them. It is especially valuable for social workers to take photos of final contacts, both for the life history book and to give the birth parents. As these farewell sessions may plunge children back into grief, they will need to talk to their social worker afterwards and be allowed to express rage. A drum can be useful for the child to express strong feelings.

Fred

Fred, aged six, had several traumatic, scary times with his birth mother. In play, he was prepared by his social worker for his final goodbye visit to Mum. The birth mother had already received some counselling from the same social worker and had thought about how she would answer his questions. They had written a card to say goodbye, to place in Fred's life history book.

At this last contact, Fred asked, *Mummy, why are you nice now and why did you used to be so horrid?* Mum replied, *My mind was all muddled up. I have an illness that makes me seem horrid sometimes so I can't promise to be nice all the time, that's why I want you to have a forever mummy and daddy.*

Obviously this was very hard for her, but Fred accepted this as fact and went on to play "hide and seek" (an unconscious metaphor for their relationship) with his birth mother, who was later collected by her worker and supported, as was Fred. It took Fred a long time to fully understand what mental illness does to people, but he settled well in his adoptive family. His letterbox contact with his birth mother included videos.

Preparing to move

Having already experienced change, children generally want to stay where they are. When a family has already been identified, the child will have barely said goodbye to their birth parents before they are saying goodbye to the "bridging" foster carers and being placed for adoption or kinship care. In this situation, unsuspecting adopters or carers find they have taken a child who has shut down and may seem compliant (known as the "honeymoon" period), but later becomes unmanageably distraught, with unresolved loss of all the people she or he has ever known. Even if a family has been identified, time should be taken to allow the child to come to terms with the knowledge that they won't be living with their birth parents. They need to have rehearsed their life history and learned words to express their feelings. (See life orientation maps, No. 58 on the CD).

The in-depth therapeutic life history work and memories can begin when the child is in their permanent substitute home, with attachment work alongside, so that the new parents and the child can share their different histories with each other. From this process, the child learns to trust their new parents because they realise that they have been accepted, despite their difficult history. It is this experience of sharing that leads to enhanced mutual understanding and trust.

To enable children to come to terms with their complex history and planned move, a story that uses a character or animal with parallel experience can help children process their feelings and address fears before facing more changes. Encouraging children to add their own stories and illustrate them enhances their ability to own their history and builds self-esteem. In play, children can rehearse the change, ensuring it is less of a shock when it happens. Stories of equivalent situations are especially helpful for children who refuse to listen to the facts of their own history. Creative and effective ways to play out impending moves and changes with younger children include painting a film strip, making a card book and scenery with houses.

Some children fail to understand why they need to be parented. The brick wall of needs (No. 57 on the CD) helps them to explore their experience of parenting. Alternatively, a non-directive approach can involve providing toys and items that a baby or young child might have and allowing the child to play out at their own pace what they needed when they were very young. Photos of their play can be added to the life history book, with a caption such as 'All children need these things to grow', adding their requests; for example, 'Can I have the whole pot of cream and eight bottles of milk please?'

Having new parents to meet their needs helps most children feel safer to attach, although more emotionally fragile children will need to play these games many times over before accepting the reality of their losses. Keep explanations simple and truthful:

Your parents loved you but were not able to keep you safe or care for you. At times, they forgot to feed you and take you to school every day. Sometimes their behaviour and your behaviour got muddled up and it was very scary.

We can have happy and scary memories. No one can take away the basic love you and your mum or dad had for each other. That love remains within us always and it warms us when we feel sad. The good thing is that we can learn to love other people, which is what makes us feel lovable.

It was the grown-ups' responsibility to keep the children safe, and the children's to make good choices for themselves. Children can choose, say, to wear red socks or green socks. But it is a mum's responsibility to have plenty of dinner on the table and share it equally.

Children do not need to carry the behavioural ghosts of a parent who failed to care for them; they can acknowledge and understand the facts, but need to shelve the burden of responsibility to understand that it is their positive behaviour which will give them hope, and that they do not have to repeat patterns from the past but can make better choices. Owning their own behaviour is an important part of healing, as is learning to forgive themselves and others, to gain a sense of self-worth. Stories help to illustrate these facts.

There are many books on life history work published by BAAF (e.g. Camis, 2001; Shah and Argent, 2006; Ryan and Walker, 2007) – useful for parents and professionals as prompts for questions to be addressed, and as guides to make a history with a beginning, middle and end. However, for neglected children, writing in ready-made books about feelings can feel far too onerous. The resulting response may be of frustration, confusion or disinterest. They prefer to play out their life history and have their version of the story recorded adjacent to the facts. Children tend to prefer multi-sensory and creative activity, having fun and seeing how the facts sit with the fantasies and dreams. Creative and playful approaches give them a sense of a hoped-for future as well as respite from pain or fear, so are usually by far the best way to engage them.

Inheritance and the family trees

It is important to have an accurate record of the child's family tree. Advances in technology such as inheritance websites have made it easy to research family history and add more cultural information to the details on file. Online maps and tourist offices give historical and cultural information, though researching this can be laborious work for children. When introduced to the written account of their life history, they benefit from time to play out feelings through stories or drama and usually prefer to allow the adults to do the recording. On finding it hard to make sense of past chaos, they may cross out their work angrily. A scribble picture saying 'there was a mess' will be enough to show that their feelings are accepted and they own their history. Their comments can be added to life history books with dialogue and pictures.

Jessica

A foster carer was given a smelly, old, worn blanket which most people would have thrown out without thinking, but she noticed it had a yellow ribbon and a couple of patches that could be saved. To show her appreciation of the value of this object she cut out the two patches, rebound them with yellow ribbon and gave them to Jessica, then nine years old. It may not have still smelt of Mum, having been washed, but Jessica used one as a 'transitional object' (Winnicott, 1971) to cuddle, and the other patch as a dolly blanket, gaining comfort from these items during her move to adopters.

First memory

The child is invited to paint a picture of their earliest memory. The adult can also draw theirs and talk about it. This exercise leads spontaneously from one memory to another, pictures of which can be photographed and added to the life history book.

Life history maps

Life history maps (Corrigan, 1986), drawn on lightweight canvas cloth, using fabric pens to depict the houses and places significant to the child's history, are far more useful than paper maps as they can be played on over and over, as in the following case study.

Tina

Tina, who drew her life map, took three sessions to complete it. The ideas and memories came tumbling out, of an extremely neglectful early life with very rejecting experiences. On the third session, her worker suggested she could play on it with the houses and people figures. Tina put a fence around her foster home saying, *I don't want to go!* After acknowledging how scared she was about moving, and worried that the new family might reject her, she placed a fence round the adoptive family house declaring, *No one can get me here.* The worker observed, *You really need to feel it's safe! I do,* asserted Tina. She later went on to hold a candle ceremony that enabled her to say goodbye to the past people in her life.

A month into placement, her anxiety reappeared. She was worried that this family might not keep her. However, with the help of games Tina understood that her new family had really claimed her and wanted her to stay. Because her adoptive family was so accepting, warm and containing, she settled surprisingly quickly.

Canvas maps are a particularly useful aid to help a child explore and play out their history, bringing up all kinds of memories (see Techniques CD No. 61). Once found, a new home is easily added. The names and places of siblings not living with the child can also be recorded on the map, giving them a sense of place or country and how locations are connected by road, air or sea. The map helps children to practise and rehearse moves, thus assisting them to manage fear of the unknown or of a previous frightening experience, so they can regain control and process fears. Alternatively, timelines can be drawn to illustrate key events and allow the child to see the proportion of their life that lies ahead.

Supportive messages from people in the child's past

It may be helpful for the social worker to visit an adult who was important to the child, to talk to them about the history. If the person gives permission, the interview could be taped, enabling supportive messages to be delivered to the child, even if not in person, thus helping to provide a sense of belonging and inheritance.

Other useful techniques are moving calendars, the empty chair game and telephones for dialogues, role plays of 'life before I came into care' or 'the supermarket' role play game. (Also see Techniques CD under life history.)

Lucy

On making an adoption order for Lucy, the judge drew a picture of a boat, saying, *This boat is called Lucy and it has been bobbing about in and out of different harbours all its life.* The little girl nodded in agreement. He continued, *Today I tied the little boat up with this big rope, in this harbour to keep her safe and only when the little boat wants to go on a trip do Lucy and her parents leave, but this is the harbour they always return to.* His explanation won a big smile from Lucy and her new adoptive parents.

Life history with complex children

Social workers will need to consider the impact of loss, change and attachment on the child and their developmental age when key loss and change occurred. Using play techniques applicable to the age when the child lost their parent enables them to grieve and move on. Children over six (provided they are able to resist playing with fire) will respond to a candle ceremony to say goodbye to people who are no longer available and can be used in many ways, over and over again to help children process all the emotions of loss (see No. 26 on the CD).

Questions to consider:

- Does the child have sufficient experience of attachment to be able to grieve?
- Has the child capacity for empathy, pride, guilt, shame and embracement? If not, the child will find it hard to express emotions and may, at this stage, be unable to grieve sufficiently, to move on emotionally and safely attach to a new parent .
- Is the child consumed by guilt and shame?
- Does the child have a conscience?

Very damaged children need to know why decisions were made and be involved in life history work. Traumatised children may need someone experienced at therapeutic life history work to support them and manage the impact of their arising feelings, possibly alongside their social worker writing the account for the life history book.

In preparation for a move to permanency, I once spent two years working with a damaged child just using different types of balls as a "third object". The balls spun round and round but eventually settled next to a football pitch. The new parents had their own football pitch! Although he had been badly neglected and abused, this work helped the child to settle well and he continued to use sport to soothe and self-calm.

Neglected children who have serious attachment issues and whose personality has been damaged by severe trauma can be helped by learning 'as if' they knew how to feel the social emotions through drama, in which they are given roles and a costume to wear (Jewett, 1984). They can act the role and, in time, their learned roles of sociability become part of their persona. For example, at a family gathering, you could ask your children to look after the visitors, perhaps take coats and hand out drinks so they learn how to be hospitable. These principles can be applied with imagination to all ages and tend to be very helpful through adolescence.

Part 3: Moving to a permanent family

Before placement it is good practice to have a Child Appreciation Day (also called a Life Appreciation Day). At this event, the new family hears from everyone who has cared for the child (though not usually birth parents). They all share as much as they know, bringing with them photos, certificates or school work from teachers. The meeting is recorded, to retain information. It is often the little memories that come up at these meetings, which aid understanding and healing for children. (For detailed information about Child Appreciation Days, see Sayers and Roach, 2011.)

It also helps for the adopters to meet with the birth parents, if possible, to share information, ideas about their lifestyle and special moments in the child's early life. It is a huge relief for a child to know that their adoptive parents can describe meeting their birth parents and say it was helpful, as it shows their acceptance of them and willingness to be able to talk openly.

Preparation for adoption

However well settled children have been in foster care, moving to a new family causes them to act out previously learned behaviours. They still may not have had any life history work so may be anxious that they are going to move back into the pain and grief of the past (see Chapter 4). The social worker's job is to help the child understand what is going to happen and who is responsible for each task; for example, that the social worker and family finder are responsible for finding the right family, not the child. Children need to be able to tell everyone their feelings and what they want, including their fantasy about a new family, but also need to know they can't always get all they want. However, it is helpful to find a family whom the child will perceive as having the criteria to offer a safe environment and be less likely to have so many of the triggers that make the child feel unsafe.

Using a range of techniques and play materials, such as a dolls' house, helps children to express feelings about moving. It takes a child at least three (weekly) sessions to express their particular anxieties, for instance, to feel able to tell their foster carer that they don't want to go, knowing that the carer and social worker/adopters are communicating. These anxieties need to be shared with the adopters or kinship carers in front of the child, so there are no secrets and they all understand how the child feels. This will help to give the move the best chance of success.

A calendar can display visit times or telephone calls from the new parents. Adding a sticker each day and a special one for the day of the visit allows young and neglected children with a poor sense of time to check what is going to happen. Children depend on adults to join in their happiness at feeling "chosen" and can rehearse their move with dolls and puppets. Stories about moving provide fictional distance that help the child get used to the feelings. They can also be reminded of the successes in their present placement. If their shows of anxiety and resentment lead to children being isolated, for example, sent to their bedroom, it can reinforce their sense of abandonment: 'I moved because I was naughty.' Feeling over-shamed and guilty reawakens their sense of poor self-esteem.

Withdrawn children may need reassurance that there will be food, a cosy bed and a night-light. Foster carers can, for example, wash bed linen belonging to the new family in their own washing powder so their new bed will smell the same; the child can sleep in these sheets the night before leaving and transfer them to their bed in the new parents' home on the day of the move. Adoptive parents should provide babies and young children with teats and dummies of a shape they are used to.

Transitional objects such as blankets, puppets or teddy bears can accompany the child on the journey back and forth. Foster carers or the new parents need to do the escorting, as they can help the child process their feelings on the journey. Once the mid-term meeting is over and the placement completely agreed, a small number of belongings could be taken with the child on each visit so that the new home gradually feels like home.

Thinking about contact before placement

Contact is a crucial part of planning permanent placements whether adoption, long-term fostering or kinship care.

> **Jerry**
>
> Jerry, aged 17, said, *I didn't realise my mum was so young – she's not much older than me. I couldn't look after a boy now.* Jerry's visit to his mum put things into perspective for him. He sees his mum and new siblings because times have changed for her now but he couldn't go back home because the damage to him was too great. At the same time, he knows them all and is happy to have two families.
>
> In direct face-to-face, telephone or indirect letterbox contact, it is important to agree what is going to work best for the child on the basis of whether the birth parents and relatives can stay "on message", saying *I am glad you are with this mum and dad.*

The main issues to consider in planning contact are:

- What are the losses and gains for the child, of face-to-face contact with parents, siblings and relatives or letterbox contact?
- Babies and young children miss parents and siblings but can't tell you how they feel. If reunification appears viable, they may benefit from frequent contact. However, the benefit and frequency of direct contact with parents and siblings have to be carefully weighed against the possibly distressing effects it can have on babies whose parents or siblings are uninterested, emotionally unresponsive, frightened or frightening.
- Who is supervising the contact? This job is usually the responsibility of the post-adoption team, especially in abuse cases.
- If the child has face-to-face contact, which venue will provide adequate space for siblings to play – perhaps a ball park or "jungle gym" with a café? One hour 30 minutes is about as much as most children can manage without upsets and fears being reignited. If these contacts are with birth parents, a support person for each family is helpful, to talk to during and after the contact.
- How frequently should direct contact take place? In our view, the maximum for school-age is three times a year; otherwise the child does not get a chance to be themselves without interference from the unhelpful pattern in the past.
- In very large sibling groups it is helpful to write a newsletter (each parent contributing a photo and a little bit about the child), for the siblings to read. It is often hard to get large groups together more than once a year.

- Contact needs to be reviewed as children's views and their understanding of the world change over time. Their behaviour may change as a result of contact. When adults' behaviour is inappropriate (e.g. if drunk) or unhelpful messages are being passed to the child, contact should be reviewed and possibly ceased.
- Letterbox contact can work very well if the situation is too stressful or risky for face-to-face contact. Post-adoption workers can help birth parents to write letters with healing messages and there is less chance of confusion regarding gifts.

Introducing the new family

Adoptive parents are encouraged to make a book about their family, home, relatives and pets. After the matching meeting, this book can be shown to the child by their social worker, to help them become familiar prior to the new parents making their first brief visit to meet them. Introductions usually take a week for a baby under one year and from two to three weeks for older children; teenagers usually vote with their feet and if they are happy, move in sooner than will allow them time to feel! The adopters, foster or kinship carers should make a point of welcoming the child and saying that they want her or him to be part of their family before actually having the child move in permanently. The parents also need to repeat this frequently, as it can be healing for the child. Before moving in, children should have the opportunity to say, 'I think they are right for me'.

Foster carers also need to be allowed to express their own view about whether the match feels right. Sometimes the bond between child and foster carer is extremely strong and they often have very intuitive feelings. Foster carers will also be grieving for the loss of the child. Although this may seem daunting for a new parent, it actually demonstrates the child's ability to form strong bonds, which bodes well for their future. However, in some situations, splitting and conflict can occur and the professionals need to help to keep communication open. While adoptive parents can feel quite jealous of the child's bond with previous carers, if handled well by the supporting team, the child will eventually transfer the bond to the new family. Children who have had many placements may talk about missing a 'mummy and daddy', not having actually lived with any parent for more than a few months. Their perception is of composite mother or father figures, leaving them unsure of who is who. A sequence of photos will help to address this confusion.

During introductions and early in a permanent placement, adoptive parents should expect challenging behaviour from the child and it is advisable to rehearse new situations such as going on holiday or to a new school.

Mid-introduction meetings

A useful suggestion is for all parties to meet halfway through introductions to decide whether the adoptive family is right for the child. Research on disruption shows that those attending such a meeting may feel unable to say how they felt at the time because they were rushed or their partner was unable to attend. Careful and sensitive handling of the adopters' and foster carers' emotions is important. Feelings can be the barometer, predicting how this placement is going to go, and need to be expressed in order to sustain the placement.

Endings

It is advisable for the foster carer to let go slowly, explaining: *These are your new mum and dad and I have now got to get on with my job and foster two new children,* making their role clear to the child in a kindly way. Foster carers can help the child practise saying goodbye and arrange a goodbye party just after the mid-term meeting. Teachers can tell the child's class that she or he is leaving in advance of the event. Carers can send a box of sweets to the school with the child and an autograph or address book, so that over a few days, classmates say their goodbyes and sign the book, helping them to get used to the idea of the child leaving. Friends are so important and they can all mourn each other. Family goodbye parties can be held a few days ahead to give the child a day or two with just their carer before the final move. The child can say goodbye to pets by giving them a treat and take a photo for their book. Foster carers should avoid giving big goodbye presents that make it too hard for the adopters or kinship carers to match. The new parents usually collect the child from the foster carers and make a phone call on arrival at the new home to reassure them. Social workers might visit the foster carers after a few days, to thank them for looking after that child; goodbyes are hard work, often leaving carers emotionally drained.

The adoptive parent, long-term foster or kinship carer will eventually, in the child's mind, become the parent who nurtures them and keeps them safe. After the move, the new family and child should meet with the foster carers in neutral venues, gradually leaving longer gaps between contact. The child needs to be able to think of them like aunt and uncle figures whom they don't see often. If separation is too sudden it can feel like death, leaving the child stuck in grief and unable to attach to their new family.

Telling the child about being adopted

Being open and honest in adoption, or in other forms of substitute care, helps positive attachment, even though it seems hard at the time. The adoptive parent, while cuddling or changing the nappy of their adopted child, can practise saying, *You are my beautiful adopted [name]. You were born in my heart and in your birth mum's tummy*, pointing to those parts of your body and then give him or her a smile or tickle. Gradually, the child will get used to this message which will grow to feel natural, as will a sense that they had always known they were adopted. In repeating this message to older children, the parent can hold the child under a coat close to them. Two children can have a place each, on each side of their parent, to hear the same message. When the parent shows the child their life history book later on, he or she won't feel the shock of not knowing they were adopted. Several BAAF books focus on talking to adopted children about their origins – see Morrison (2007) and Wolfs (2008).

Telling very difficult stories

Many children's backgrounds are so complex and horrific that adults feel unable to explain the truth. It helps to tell the truth gradually, as children develop, using words they understand and making the facts short and to the point. Children accept these facts within their present developmental understanding and are then less disturbed by the full account later on. It is essential to start early in order that the child never feels they didn't know or that they were lied to. If not explained before adolescence, these truths can come as a terrible shock, as well as leading the young person to feel they cannot trust you with other important facts. Two examples are given below.

Explaining rape

Show via the water game (see No. 81 on the CD) how the child was conceived:

Your mum and dad got together, shared their seeds and eggs and made a beautiful child with lots of talents.

Remind the child of their talents and speculate as to which parent might have given them these genes, before explaining:

Your dad broke the rules when he shared his seeds with mummy but he still gave you a great body and lots of talents.

This gives the child a positive construct of his or her inheritance. When the child is old enough to understand the word "rape", ask if they remember you telling them about their dad and explain the act is called "rape". This is less of a shock as the child has already learned the facts.

Explaining murder

Using toy figures, tell the story about Mummy's death, making sure that the child understands the word "death". Books about nature can show how leaves, insects or animals die. You can then explain in a matter-of-fact tone that Daddy killed Mummy in a fight. Hearing the explanation will help the young child gradually realise facts she or he has always known. This means they will be less shocked when learning the concept of murder (usually at around eight years of age). The child will then begin to trust you to tell difficult truths.

Forming new attachments

Generally, adoptive parents and foster carers are advised that in making new attachments – provided the child is not too traumatised and afraid of adults coming anywhere near – he or she can be encouraged to practise getting physically close with physical games, reading stories together, building dens, blowing bubbles, going swimming, sharing food such as hot chocolate and biscuits before bed, and cosy chat times. New parents/carers might massage the child's hands and feet and watch a favourite film together (see Techniques CD for ideas.)

Parents are encouraged to sit and talk with children when they feel sad. If the child can't say how she or he feels, using a toy or puppet as an intermediary can be helpful. The parent can pick up a puppet, look directly at it and say something like: *Mr Tortoise, Jane is worrying about something. Do you think she could talk to you about it?* Direct the toy at the child and speak as Mr Tortoise: *What's up Jane?* Children will usually start speaking to the toy as long as the parent's eyes are also focused on it. Alternatively, parents and children could make a play of the child's life history, as if in a theatre (see Chapter 8).

Adults need to model trust and recognise that any transition is scary for children who often don't want to go to school or leave the bedroom, these being trigger times that bring up unconscious fears from previous moves. Rehearsing situations playfully, for instance, games of trust and rescue in the swimming pool, can help children to trust their new parent to understand their fears, thus learn to self-calm, and a deeper bond will form.

Here we draw from Fahlberg's (1994, p.149) guide to helping children to understand the difference between types of parents:

- *Birth parents give you*: life itself, gender, physical looks, intellectual potential, basic personality, special talents, pre-disposition for diseases. The child can be told, 'No one can take this away from you.'

- *Legal parents give you*: material and financial care, safety and security, decide where you live and where you go to school; they sign for early marriage, operations and give permission to travel.
- *Parenting parents give you*: love, food, toys and clothes, hugs and kisses; discipline; and care when you are sick.

The following guidelines for positive parenting will help children to attach:

- Enjoy emotional nurturing and play with the children.
- Encourage a basic sense of acceptance for each individual and be tolerant of your own ambivalence about the child.
- Be prepared to have times of unconditional love, modelling refusal to be rejected; try your best to stay committed in tough times, which will pass.
- Check on new ideas of appropriate limit setting – see *Managing Difficult Behaviour* (Pallett *et al*, 2008).
- Arrange for positive role models to be part of your family circle.
- Review past achievements as it encourages growth and change.
- Teach responsibility.
- Teach appropriate expression of emotions.
- Encourage reciprocal interactions (see Techniques CD, under child development and attachment, for ideas).
- Try to achieve a balance between dependence and independence.
- Use discipline rather than punishment.
- Use fun and humour to teach life and relationship skills for survival.
- To be a parent you need a long-term perspective; when you look back you can see growth. You can only tolerate this if you have time for yourself.

These characteristics modelled by the child's new parents should encourage a deep relationship to be formed and will ultimately help the child to become more self-confident, provided our expectations intuitively match the talents of the child. Encouraging new and varied experiences helps these talents come to the fore (see child development chart, Chapter 1).

Conclusion

What helps children most in transition is the worker's'/parents' style of relationship, which reflects complete acceptance of the child and a clarity and warmth in the overall tone. If at all possible, the same person should work with the child until they are settled and safe.

As a result of the work undertaken, children will be able to articulate or show their wishes and feelings through their play, grow in self-confidence and make choices for themselves. They should be enabled to accept their mistakes and become resilient because within trusting relationships, they can understand the facts and feelings about what has happened to them and thereby gain the confidence to let go of inappropriate fantasies. This will enable their imagination and resilience to increase, allowing them to envisage a future with hope, giving them rest from the pain and uncertainty of change, helping them let go of the past and invest in the future.

New parents of all kinds aim to give a child the opportunity to live well. Looking after troubled children who are very rejecting of help can be a lonely business. Social workers and substitute parents need all the support they can get. Foster carers and adoptive parents can benefit from support groups; professional help is available from adoption support teams, although in some areas this can be patchy. Developing the child's innate skills can help. Foster carers and adoptive parents may benefit from "filial play" training with a play therapist who can teach how to have special play times that aid attachment. If the child is emotionally and behaviourally stuck, it may help to find a therapy that fits their particular talents and skills such as art, music, dance, play, drama or psychotherapy: 'See success as things getting better, not perfect' (Katz *et al*, 1994).

Summary

- The framework for children in transition is a guide to when to approach different parts of work.
- Children need boundaries, time limits of sessions and confidentiality to feel safe.
- Social workers are advised to explain their role, why they are coming to visit; also to explain the court's decisions to children.
- Reports need to include evidence from the child's play themes and their views, wishes and feelings as stated, e.g. their hope to return home, even if you are recommending something different.
- Social workers need to be aware that all children will be somewhere in the six stages of grief (see Chapter 4) at any time, or may be stuck in fear, shame or guilt, and need help to get in touch with their senses, to help express strong feeling.
- Children need time to process grief and get used to their new situations for a positive sense of self to emerge. Unhelpful labelling needs to be avoided.
- To help process identity and life history, the child can be given a folder for their history, with pictures and a memory box for all of their trinkets and treasures, to keep belongings from the past together; these can also be used as memory aids.
- Throughout the work, children need to be given answers to their questions: 'Who am I?, Where do I belong? Where am I going?' as simply and honestly and as early as possible to enable the child to trust their social worker and caregivers.
- Dramatising and rehearsal help reduce fear states about moves and changes.

Introduction

The previous chapter discussed the importance of explaining to children in transition why they are in care. We now focus on the use of drama to address the needs of children already placed for permanence, who need help to come to terms with their life history and make new attachments. The first part of this chapter explores the importance of life history work and the basis for undertaking it with children through drama, including how to handle difficult truths. We then describe the type of props and techniques commonly used in the practice of dramatic play, before looking at how these can be applied to broaching specific issues associated with traumatised behaviour such as intimidation, lying and taking without permission. We also discuss ways of addressing feelings. Techniques are amply illustrated with case examples to encourage parents and practitioners to engage and have fun with children in ways that enable them to process their experiences and recover missed nurture.

Some key questions

Why life history work?

The purpose of life history work is to invite children to "walk the story", to enable them to process significant events of their life, so that they feel safer and more ready to attach to their substitute parents. Some children, on being introduced to "the story of what happened to you" appear to assume that it is just a story, a fictional account that didn't really happen or was actually about someone else. This is why, here, we refer to life 'history' rather than life 'story'.

When should it be done?

Children need to know the reasons for decisions taken on their behalf. However, to embark on life history work during the course of legal proceedings can place them in an invidious position, as during contact children may ask questions which their birth parents are ill-equipped to answer. In-depth life history work is better left until after the plan has been ratified for children not to return to their birth parents' care and contact has been reduced, in preparation for permanence. Many adopted children will also benefit from revisiting their life history at key stages of development.

Who should take part?

Children more readily accommodate explanations from someone outside their family, such as their social worker. The difficulty for adoptive parents is that they can be heard as judgemental by children who think, 'My birth parents were violent so I will grow up to be the same'. Nonetheless, it is important for adoptive parents to obtain the history and if the appropriate resources are not available, to find suitable ways to explain to children why they came to live with and be adopted by them. Adoptive placements under intense pressure may benefit from the more specialised support of therapists to address problems that families find especially testing.

In work of this nature there are huge benefits to the inclusion of adoptive parents or foster carers as sharing the history with the child, first, facilitates bonding, and second, helps children feel safer to attach to adults who know their history and demonstrate willingness to declare their full commitment to them (Moore, 2006, 2009). Children are sometimes identified as the "problem" by adoptive parents or foster carers who in fact need attention for themselves (Adcock and White, 1998). Some require separate time to learn about the significance of their child's play and understand what she or he requires of them. Older children may prefer privacy and siblings generally benefit from separate attention but may be seen collectively for activities such as closure ceremonies. On realising that, in play, mistakes really don't matter, insecure children keep trying, encouraged to experiment, to "get it right".

How do we balance accuracy with sensitivity?

As each person is likely to have a different memory of the same event, when a child's view is at variance with recorded information it is important to include both accounts, for example, 'The teacher told the social worker this...yet Johnny remembers that...' Sensitivity is required in balancing the child's age and developmental stage with explaining details such as conveying how violence was expressed in the family and avoiding over-blaming one party. Clarifying *Your dad took drugs that made his mind sick so, unable to control his temper, he hit Mum and broke her nose*, makes it easier for the child to recognise "cause and effect", whereas saying, *Your parents took drugs, which led to domestic violence between them* fails to explain who was responsible for which act. At the same time, a distinction needs to be made between "honesty" and the kind of "truth" that is unhelpful when it causes the child to feel blamed and shamed. For instance, telling a child, *Your carer wasn't able to keep you safe* is far less condemnatory than *Your placement broke down because of your behaviour*.

It is important to include the positive aspects of children's birth parents, such as their interests, tastes and talents, in order to lend balance to the account. Alongside prompting children's own memories, careful investigation of their lifestyle, such as where the family shopped, their favourite takeaway, taste in music, clothes, jobs, talents, the church/mosque or football team they supported, and so on, is especially valuable for those who are unaware of their heritage, due to having moved too often to know much about where their family originally came from.

Aren't they too young for sordid facts?

Fostered and adopted young people are legally entitled at 18 years of age to information held in their files about their early life in previous families, although some third-party reports may be removed. From the moment they are taken into care, they need explanations of the reasons for these decisions, in language appropriate to their age and stage. Often, adults worry about upsetting children yet the children often know more than we realise. Our advice is that the sooner they are told what happened the less shocking it will be later on. For example, explaining *The baby growing inside Mummy wasn't strong enough to live* will have less emotional impact on a young child than it will on adults. The longer information is withheld, the less trust children will have in adults. The child may worry: *What else have they not told me? How do I know what to believe?* Children also depend on their carers to remind them that abuse was not their fault.

What if the child doesn't want to talk about it?

Usually children's resistance to life history work is rooted in abject shame and fear, feelings that are important to address prior to giving them complex explanations. When you acknowledge how worried they are and explain that you want to show them how they became brave heroes, children generally become keener to co-operate. However, some children survive by retaining an idealised view of their birth parents. Although it is a dangerous misconception to believe that when children are adopted their past can be simply banished or forgotten, it is not always appropriate to force them to hear another's account of their history, unless the child's idealisation is causing significant problems and impeding new relationships.

How do we go about telling difficult truths?

Most children in the UK are placed in public care as the consequence of neglect and abuse. Patterns of domestic violence, parental substance misuse and mental illness tend to repeat through generations. On recognising how limited the available options were, children realise that their parents survived in the only way they knew how. It helps if substitute parents admit that 'If I had been in your parents' situation, I expect I'd also have struggled to make the best decisions!'

Parents with histories of severe neglect

The way we view our world and relationships is hugely influenced by the context in which we are raised. Consider the child who became learning disabled owing to severe head injury, neglect and violence, and grows to adulthood so persistently threatened that he believes everyone is out to "get" him. Having no positive model of parenting, and assuming his crying children hate him and want to hurt or anger him, he locks them away for hours. To explain to children why this happened we can say:

Mum/Dad locked you in your room because s/he felt distressed and frightened and couldn't think of other ways to stop things getting out of control. Mum/Dad didn't plan to harm you, but never knew why young children cry or how much you were depending on them.

Explaining parental drug/alcohol misuse

We all need stimulation and nurture. Addiction to drugs, alcohol, tobacco or food can stem from care giving being so unreliable and unpredictable, that for comfort and stimulation, children grow to rely on substances instead of people (Sunderland, 2007). We can explain to children:

Your parents found alcohol/drugs gave them more comfort than people did, because their mummy and daddy kept letting them down when they were little.

Explaining suicide

When parents have committed suicide, we can explain: *Your mum/dad found their sadness too much to cope with. Living became too painful for them. To end the pain, they made sure they would stop breathing. They were so stuck in their own sadness, they didn't know how it would affect you.* Explaining how it happened must relate to children's age and how much they know.

Explaining crimes of violence

Acts of violence are often the outcome of stress suffered by emotionally fragile individuals who have inadequate control of their rage. Premeditated violence linked with "voided emotion" also emanates from early trauma. To children whose parents committed violent crimes, we can explain: *Your mum/dad was too scared to realise what they were doing or to appreciate what you most needed from them.* Discussing the purpose of rules in the foster/adoptive home, and what happens when they are broken, helps children to realise the necessity and value of safety and order. When parents are in prison, explain that *Laws are rules made by grown-ups. Your parents broke the rules so they were punished in a way that adults are.* Birth parents may have made unwise decisions but children can realise they do not have to repeat their parents' mistakes.

Parents who sexually abuse children

Adults who sexually abuse children have usually been the victim of emotional and/or sexual abuse in childhood and, in some cases, had their bodies aroused and stimulated long before they were psychologically or physically ready. These adults may confuse their sexual drives with childhood attachment needs for comfort and safety. Some are so emotionally immature that physical closeness is a way to gain the emotional closeness they crave and distortedly regard as "love". We can explain that: *In his head, your daddy was like a little child – he wanted comfort from you in a grown-up way. It stopped him remembering the rules and how wrong it was for you.*

Or, if the parent was learning disabled: *He didn't understand.* This helps children recognise why the abuse occurred and feel less ashamed to have disclosed it. It is especially important that children do not see adults recoil at memories of abuse, as they can clam up on sensing that the adult is too badly affected by the content. Children can show remarkable insight when adults are honest with them.

Why use drama to enact life history?

Stemming from the Greek word meaning 'to do', drama is defined as 'a story showing life and action' (Chambers Dictionary, 2001). As play engages our emotions, dramatic play is thus a physical and an emotional experience that enables us to learn at a far deeper level than from just reading and cognitively processing facts.

During the 1930s, Susan Isaacs (1930) found that by inviting children to explore their feelings and emotions in relation to others, dramatic play was an important way of enabling them to achieve their potential. The advantage of using dramatic play in life history work is that during the course of enactment, children become actors in their own lives and gain a heightened sense of motivation and control. As Ryan and Walker (2007, p.4) comment in relation to life history work, 'It is the process rather than just the product which will reveal the most benefits for the children and young people involved.' This view is supported by earlier research on child drama by Slade (1954), who found that of 32,000 school children (under 14 years), only three preferred scripted play to their own drama. This led him to conclude that children need to be allowed to develop their own play, not have adult ideas foisted on them. Nevertheless, we find that neglected children, who haven't learned how to play, benefit from help to develop their play skills and to use their imagination to process their experience.

Practising role is integral to dramatic play and helps foster carers and adoptive parents to "step into their children's shoes" and so appreciate their continual state of fear. Infants depend on their mothers to reflect and exaggerate their expression of feeling, from which they gain a sense of their entitlement to loving attention. Drama also provides a natural way to replicate this 'mirroring' relationship (Winnicott, 1971). Not least, experiencing fun and pure joy in dramatic play activates the neural chemicals that protect our brains from the effects of stress (Sunderland, 2007). As Seligman (1995) asserts, 'the happier we are, the more likely we will achieve'.

Enacting life history plays

Just as some adults readily take to drama, some children are natural thespians who respond enthusiastically to revisiting their history dramatically, which involves enacting brief snapshots of past events. A list of scenes can be prepared, ready to improvise on the day, but the amount of advance preparation required, such as writing a script, will depend on the family involved since preparation can heighten as well as reduce anxiety. It is just as important to prepare the child. Having already heard the main facts of their history, children can be helped to think about what costumes and props are needed to enact the story. They often love to dress up and see their parents in costume such as a police helmet, nurses' cap, judge's wig, scarves or shawls. Dolls can be used to represent the children or other absent people.

To set the "stage" children are encouraged to write tickets for the "audience". There may be black bin liners spilling with clothes, the floor strewn with paper nappies coloured brown on the insides. Children can make "pills" (from playdough) or "spliffs" (strips of paper rolled up to look like cigarettes). (Of course, it is important not to make assumptions about squalid conditions without knowing the full facts.) Music of the period creates atmosphere and helps to stimulate memories. The therapist or social worker taking the role of birth mother makes it easier for the child to express anger at the "parent" who let them down. The social worker or therapist should have the information and insight to be able to (in role) answer the child's questions at the end of the play. They should also be prepared for the child interrupting with flashbacks, such as 'This is when she threw me in the freezer!' Other participants, such as foster carers or adoptive parents, grandparents and the children if they so choose, can take roles such as of relatives, judge, teachers, social workers, neighbour, foster carers and police officers (see case examples later in this chapter).

Engaging in fantasy play

Some children will find it too difficult to address the facts presented as the "reality" but will respond to the opportunity to enact their experience in contest of a fantasy. This imaginative play can help parents and children to identify the underlying source of problems and reasons for fearful reactions Children are given control within the boundaries of play. Practising social cues helps them to recognise the purpose of rules. For instance, as "teacher", the child can deal with "silly" behaviour of "pupils" played by adults. Children learn to appreciate praise for well-earned efforts and adults recognise the effects of transferred feelings in a fictional, thus safe, context.

Setting the scene

Scenery can consist of old cloths of varying colour and texture to serve as landscape, blue fabric denoting the sea, while a draped chair becomes a throne. Useful props include assorted bags, coins, rope and weapons such as handcuffs and plastic swords.

Costume and props

Children love to dress up in hats and old clothes (charity shops being an inexpensive source), also as characters such as Jack Sparrow from *Pirates of the Caribbean* or Snow White. Dressing up serves several purposes.

1. First, it is fun to dress up and pretend to be someone else.

2. Second, wearing the costume helps us to assume a different persona, inviting us to practice new poses, different ways of walking, moving and talking.

3. Third, entering the "skin" of another being is a step towards empathy.

4. Fourth, the smell and texture of fabrics can trigger reminders of earlier states. Such sensory arousal propels us into trying out something exciting that perhaps feels unpredictable and risky, yet invites transformation and change.

Masks can be useful to explore desired and undesired aspects of character, but caution is needed as while some children love masks, others find them quite frightening. Masks can be bought or made using a variety of materials, such as papier mâché (pasted over a balloon and once dry, cut in half), air-drying clay, paper plates with a stick attached, boxes, or a piece of card decorated with collage materials.

Puppets, so often used for communicating with vulnerable children, are another valuable dramatic tool. Children who have lost people important to them often find puppets easier to explain their feelings to than people. By dramatising situations such as bullying or teasing, parents can show how to solve problems and access help.

How to begin

Parents can create a special time in which children are allowed to lead the play, so long as everyone is safe and comfortable. Children in sibling groups tend to benefit from separate individual playtime with parents. If this is not possible they can be encouraged to take turns. For children with poor self-control, certain rules like no hitting or hurting of people, property or furnishings should be agreed in advance.

Invited to choose from available materials, children are encouraged to choose a role and cast others, including their parent(s), in other roles, then to play out the evolving story. Often, emotionally fragile children will choose to be "heroes" while casting others as "villains" or helpers. The adult may ask (in a whisper): *How do you want me to be? Shall I be nasty or nice?* or *What should I say/do next?* and follow the child's directions. In this way, the child learns mastery of self.

Non-verbal communication

Preparation is crucial. To help children become more aware of their bodies, try the warm-up exercises (Techniques CD, No. 75) to prepare the voice and body for role play. If we feel trusted we are more likely to trust. Consensus needs to be reached in advance on safety, for example, signals for "fight" scenes. Such interactions invite greater mutuality between parent and child.

Exploring character

A useful way to explore role is to physically practise the stance and attitude that a character may assume. As we try out the pose, we feel a change in our body. Experiencing this physical change helps us to recognise and project associated attitudes and feelings. The reactions of others to the physical image we project serve to inform us how to continue to play this role effectively. Each person can be interviewed in role as their chosen character.

Sculpting

Characters can be sculpted as a means of exploring connections. The child is invited to place each member of the family group in relation to the next and bend them to a particular shape or image. Toys, dolls or models can be arranged in a "sculpt", from which the separate elements may be combined to make a story. Cassons (2004, p.7) proposes sculpting to be effective because 'it combines pattern making, spatial awareness, symbolism, non verbal expression and embodiment', and thus connects the emotional knowledge of the right brain with the analytic ability of the left.

Exploring character

Others, as the "audience", ask questions and from the character's response, convey the impact the character has on them. It can also be useful to compare fictional roles of authority figures such as police officers, doctors and teachers, encountered in real life.

Using specific drama-therapeutic techniques

Doubling

Doubling replicates early attachment interactions. An adult may *double* for the child, in role as the protagonist (key player). All of the following strategies can be effective.

- Repeat the child's phrases. This allows you to discretely check that you have heard the child correctly (Bannister, 1997).
- Speak on behalf of the child *as if* you are the child. Ask, *Can I be you for a minute?* and on gaining permission, say, *I wonder what they want me to do? I'm scared I won't be very good and everyone will laugh at me.* Check with the child as to whether you have got this right (Hughes, 1998).
- Speak for the child in role. For example, you can exhibit their fears and worries by saying, *I don't know if I can trust this person* and asking *How will I know?*
- You might show how hard it would have been for a young child to influence or alter the outcome of events.
- Demonstrate alternative courses of action to illustrate how bullies should be treated and victims protected from them.

Modelling

As with doubling, the purpose of modelling is to question unhelpful assumptions held on the basis of previous experience and to offer alternative responses and outcomes. We adults can model what *should be*, by dramatically exposing *what shouldn't*. Young and emotionally delayed children assume their perception to be the only one so it can worry them when adults do not share their view. Foster carers and adoptive parents need to challenge the unhelpful assumption that rejection is deserved in order to enable children to "rewrite" their earlier experience. In play as a witch or vampire, the adult might say how hard it is to be hated and enquire how to be "nice" and respectful.

Exaggeration

Heightening the expression of feelings is a valuable facet of drama which, like mirroring, replicates early experience in which mothers magnify their baby's emotions. A parent might take the role of "servant" to complain of horrid treatment by the "king" and demand a reason. If asked to act as a bully, saying in a theatrical aside, *I'm not used to being so nasty; it's hard for me* conveys that oppressive behaviour is undesirable. Demonstrating how it feels to be bullied by cowering invites reflection on its impact. Parents and carers can use awareness of their own feelings to interpret those transferred by the child. Labelling these feelings through the privacy of story helps parents to become more attuned to their children while giving practice at desired and helpful responses.

Sharing roles

Sometimes, children take oppressive roles to retain control. It also helps them to gain mastery over habitual feelings of powerlessness. However, being repeatedly stuck in the same parts can be wearing. You can avoid this trap by sharing roles, saying *I'm bored with being horrid* and suggesting *Shall we swap?* so that both gain other perspectives.

Keeping safe

It is important for adults to avoid potential collusion with previously abusive experience. For instance, if a child demands adults close their eyes for too long or insist on darkness 'as it's night time', the adult(s) is advised to acknowledge but not indulge the child's request. Instead, it is better to clarify the need for everyone to feel safe.

Three wishes

In the context of the story, children may be granted three wishes (to help them identify their deepest longings and desires, or to work out how to change in order to keep friends). The child might grant three wishes to their parent's or carer's character, which enables the parent to guess at what the child most desires. Acknowledging their desires can release children, helping them to grieve their loss and adjust to their new situation. Three wishes convey a message of empowerment and hope that protects us from falling into apathy, despair or depression (Goleman, 1996) and helps us plan for the future.

Ritual and ceremony

Ritual carries a message of order, continuity and predictability. Even when dealing with change, rituals can connect new events to previous ones, drawing on tradition and the experience of past generations. They enable children to predict what comes next and to know what is expected of them, so helping to restructure the brain. Having a regular time and space to play is of critical importance for children with little experience of routines that give a sense of control and reassurance. Ideally, these accompany life history work, such as use of candle ceremonies (see No. 26, Techniques CD) to mark the child's new identity as an adopted person. Sroufe *et al* (1996) found shared subjective experience to be one of the most important aspects of relationship and psychological development.

Concluding the session

At the conclusion of each session, we need to de-role and reflect on arising feelings, guidance for which is given at the end of this chapter. Having a record of enacted play scenes facilitates reflection and placing it in a folder of children's scripts and stories (ideally with illustrations and photos of child in role) enhances their self-esteem. Each time children read the story they created will consolidate their learning.

Drama in practice

The previous section looked at the mechanics of practice. The following case examples are used to illustrate that practice in detail. (See Techniques CD for more ideas.)

Acting out the past

There are numerous contributors to the development of dramatherapy, from theatre and therapy. Of particular relevance to work with children was Stone (1971 cited in Payne, 1993), who noticed that in dramatic play, the child obtained a reflected view of himself from other perspectives that were different but related both to him and the role. These influences strongly resonate with the task of involving children and parents in dramatising children's life history both fictionally and in a literal sense, as observed in the intensely emotional experience, described as follows.

Rehana

Rehana, age 11, asked to revisit her life history, so as to understand more clearly why, having been moved for the fifth time, she was placed for adoption. We devised a list of key moments from her past life. She chose to play the part of her birth mother.

Her adoptive parent, cast as *teacher,* acted dismissive and unsympathetic. Seeing the confusion on Rehana's face, I asked if this portrayal was accurate. Rehana said her teacher had known about their mother's infirmity and taken them to school for weeks. She recalled that her mother had rarely moved, spoken or smiled. Invited to show us, Rehana lay on the sofa and over several minutes (which felt like hours) demonstrated her mother's moving in excruciating pain. It enabled Rahena to connect with the sense of hopelessness and despair, in a mother who had paid her minimum attention.

Dramatising events from her history allowed Rehana's "observing self" to reframe the pattern whereby she blamed herself for having been rejected. Drama proved a gentle way of developing tolerance for emotion and self-exposure. Though inherently painful for this avoidant child, the drama also allowed for moments of hilarity in the course of costume changes and recall of funny as well as sad memories.

Daniel

Daniel, now 12, had been removed from his birth family at age five and placed for adoption two years later. The referral was prompted by school exclusions resulting from his immature behaviour. His adoptive parents complained that Daniel was too easily led and that he ruined their attempts to give him a good time.

Daniel's birth parents had been addicted to alcohol. His birth father had been extremely violent to the mother, who had visited him in prison in defiance of her promises to keep the children safe. Daniel's fierce loyalty to his birth mother led his adoptive parents to fear that he would trace his birth family if he knew where to find them. We decided to dramatise his life history. On reading the history, Daniel was thrilled to view himself as brave and heroic and loved dressing up to improvise it but still held fantasies of his mother as a victim who had received insufficient help.

At the beginning of the play, Daniel giggled a lot, causing his adoptive mother to worry that he wasn't taking any of it seriously. Yet children and young people need to laugh in order to relax and build trust to prepare to address their painful experiences.

During the play we stopped regularly to check the written life history for accuracy of information requested by Daniel, such as dates, how old he had been at particular junctures, and to record each of his recollections of the events we were portraying.

In scene 6, Daniel (*as doctor*) had been shocked to realise that his birth mother's treatment had to be delayed due to her inebriation. The (*therapist as*) birth mother had reacted by being alternately rude and pleading for the doctor's mercy. Abruptly, the "doctor" told her she was wasting his time as no one could help her unless she made an effort to stop drinking. She protested pathetically: *You're being cruel. I can't help it!* Daniel (*doctor*) said: *You've made your decision. Now you must live with it.*

We explored how hard it had been for the children to have parents unable to look after themselves, let alone their children. Daniel recalled his baby brother being sick from sour milk in dirty bottles. Surmising his mother had been too drunk to even wash out her baby's bottles, he expressed disgust. However, in the course of analysing how she had turned out this way, Daniel accepted that her problems had started in childhood and continued to affect her capacity to take responsibility for herself or her children, or indeed to have any kind of satisfying relationships in adulthood.

Daniel's play

At hospital, the birth mother (*therapist*) gives birth to Daniel. Nurse (*adoptive mum*) hands the baby to birth mother who names him. The scene switches to court, where the social worker (*adoptive mum*) asks the judge (*Daniel*) for a care order and is refused. A police officer (*Daniel*) takes a call from the birth grandmother who alleges that the birth dad broke her window. Birth dad (*Daniel*) threatens her, so a few days later, she retracts her statement. The police officer attends fights between the parents.

In the next scene the birth mum *(therapist)* is drunk when the social worker *(adoptive mum)* calls at the grandparents' home and agrees to children being cared for by them.

The family move house. The social worker notes improvements but worries how they will cope with an older son who has been thrown out of his foster placement. Birth mum, heavily pregnant with her seventh child, insists she'll have her son back.

In Scene 6, the birth mum arrives at hospital, drunk, with a broken arm. The doctor *(Daniel)* is advised by the nurse *(adoptive mum)* that he can't give the anaesthetic required to set her arm due to the patient's intoxication. A few weeks later, Daniel, aged five, comes downstairs to find doors hanging off hinges or missing from the kitchen cupboards. His birth dad promises to fix them. A few days later, the birth mum tells a social worker *(adoptive mum)* of her partner hitting and spitting, and that the children had hidden, terrified. The social worker *(Daniel)* visits the grandparents, who are drunk. Police arrive and remove the children to foster care.

From here on, Daniel became far more affectionate towards his adoptive parents and began to take responsibility for his actions. His family moved to another area, which also helped to give him a fresh start. Daniel settled well into his new school where he was reassessed and placed in higher ability groups. Soon he began to win merits. He joined army cadets, took up cricket and within weeks was voted team captain.

Changing the outcome

In the course of processing their experience, finding out how it was, children often like to explore how it should have been. They may change the endings of events to suit their needs, using (fictional) means to gain power over experiences of oppression.

Nina

Eleven-year-old Nina had been placed for adoption, as the oldest of six children, following neglect and abuse in her birth family. Her parents had kept moving town and changing names to escape recognition by the authorities. Invited to focus on happier memories led a resistant Nina to describing how her life had really been. She had been relied on to attend to siblings waking at night, hungry or with wet beds. She remembered her father playing uncomfortable tickling games and telling him to stop.

She recalled frequent screaming, door slamming and no one taking notice of her mum. The anger wrought by these memories initially had Nina regressing to earlier traumatised expression of her fear, resulting in violent tantrums when asked to get ready for bed. In spiralling anxiety, she worried, *If I can't play my game now, I may never play again, so, perhaps I will never be fed either and then I'll die!*

We decided to improvise Nina's life history to enable her to realise how courageous she had been. Nina chose to open the play with a scene from her mother's childhood, taking the part of her *mother* until later scenes when she acted as herself. She directed seventeen scenes, from which key moments are drawn below.

Nina's play

In Scenes 9 and 10, Dad *(played by adoptive mum)* kept threatening Mum *(Nina)*, who escaped with the children to a refuge where he found them and repeated his threats.

By Scene 12, Mum having decided that she had seen enough of Dad's ill temper, announced her plan for revenge. She "poisoned" his food and placed a "bomb" in his lap while he lay "asleep". Puzzled, Nina's adoptive mum asked if this was "real". Nina explained, *No – it's what should have happened!* She decided that the bomb would not actually kill him just wound him enough to cause 'pain for the rest of his life'.

Nina discovered that there are situations in life when choices are limited but are still there to be made. This helped her to realise that she was able to make choices for herself, so would not have to go through the rest of her life as a victim. Nina processed early memories by enacting her own stories of creatures that suffered adversity. She found new ways to manage relationships.

Exploring life history through metaphor

Younger children are naturally more responsive to the metaphor of fiction than to literal explanations of their life history. As with the dramas we previously described, for this approach, a selection of clothes, inviting fantasy (a magic wand, witch's hat) as well as reality (police helmet and handcuffs), a few coins, bags, play dough to make pretend food will stimulate children's imagination. Often, a bag of items is enough to encourage them to engage in play and direct the adults around them.

Rosie

From infancy, Rosie had experienced neglect, violence and many changes of care, her mother's mental ill-health prompting frequent admission to hospital. Removed to foster care at two years of age, Rosie was then placed at age four with an adoptive family without understanding why she was moving again. To her it felt like kidnap. Failing to understand why Rosie was so demanding, her adoptive mother became so insecure and depressed that within three months, Rosie had returned to her previous foster carers but exhibited far more disturbed behaviour.

At the age of eight, Rosie moved to a long-term foster placement. A natural thespian, Rosie skilfully directed her foster carer and the therapist brought in to help. Here, she felt freer to dramatically explore confusing and frightening events in her earlier life. Rosie expressed her fear of restriction (such as car seatbelts) but used play to practise ways of getting on with her new family and coping with sibling rivalry, with good results. She progressed at school, an environment in which she previously struggled.

Rosie's play

Many of Rosie's plays explored her persistent fear of kidnap. In one of her dramas, she directed the kidnapper *(therapist)* to arrive during the night and announce, *I'm your real mum. Come with me.* The caring mother *(foster carer)* searched for and found her missing child. The next night, the kidnapper took the kind mother away. The child wakes to find her kind mother had been locked up. The kidnapper told her, *If I can't have you, I'm not going to let you have your new mum.* The kind mother expressed despair, whereupon the kidnapper 'fell asleep' *(therapist herein creating the opportunity for the mother to be rescued)*. The kind mother and brave child imprison the kidnapper, commenting, *Now you know how it feels to be locked up!* Eventually, contriving to transform the kidnapper into a "kind granny", Rosie fondly observed, *It's like having two mums being nice to you.*

In the following drama, a girl and her best friend were repeatedly kidnapped and found to be severely injured; however, *(Rosie advised that)* their injuries would magically heal once they had received enough hugs and cuddles from their kind mum.

By joining in the play, modelling kindness and empathy, Rosie's foster carer made an important contribution towards enabling Rosie to process her fear-inducing memories.

Young children who haven't yet learned the reasons for rules still believe "right" and "wrong" to be that which is permitted or prohibited by parental figures, as frequently evidenced in Rosie's play which projected the child as "wrong" and parent as "right".

Mick

Mick, aged seven, was adopted when he was three years old. He struggled to express his feelings. Aware of a void in his memory of his pre-verbal years and plagued by vampires in his dreams, Mick explored his fears through drama.

Mick's play

Casting himself as a "vampire", his adoptive mother as a "baddie" and therapist as a "friend" who would save him, Mick decreed the baddie had only lost a few of his ten lives. On his adoptive mother's face he placed a series of masks and directed her to remove one each time she was meant to evolve as someone else. When the last one had been taken off, Mick bashed the mask to pieces so that it could no longer 'see, hear, speak, touch, taste, smell or feel anything'. Its hold over Mick had now "died".

We held a ceremony to celebrate the loss of its power, acknowledging Mick's immense courage and his mother's impressive capacity for holding all these fears. Having his fears validated enabled Mick to appreciate that his new adoptive mother understood his fears, was able to contain them and was now keeping him safe.

Using fictional settings to demonstrate real experience

When children become confused about the past, a useful way to help them is to employ everyday settings such as the supermarket, school, park, surgery or police station, fictionally, to demonstrate contrasting manners and attitudes. In this way, we can show and explain the different ways that parents can behave with their children and, within the story, give children the power to decide what should happen next.

Luke

Luke, now five, was removed at two-and-a-half years from his birth family after sustaining several head injuries, neglect and witnessing violence between his learning-disabled parents who had been in care and suffered mental health problems. After two years in foster care, Luke was placed in his adoptive family. Six months on, his behaviour had become increasingly challenging. As his birth parents' emotional availability had been unpredictable, Luke lived in a state of acute anxiety. He hit out wildly without apparent provocation, could be affectionate yet was very controlling. Therapeutic work began with small toy figures for playing scenes on a "life map".

It soon became apparent that lacking (verbal) recall of his early life had left Luke confused. He told his adoptive mother that the story played on his life map was actually about someone else. Therefore, the aim of the following scene was to illustrate how parents (such as his) treat their baby when they have no role model.

Luke's play

Luke helped to set up a supermarket scene, with a play till and groceries. He chose to be the cashier, serving customers. The first customer *(his adoptive parent)* modelled appropriate manners. A second customer, Lola *(therapist)*, was an irritable, tired and drunk mother, who crashed her way to the till, knocking over the display. When the cashier complained, the mother protested defensively, *Well, I couldn't help it could I? You're just having a go at me!* Stuffing a biscuit into the mouth of her young baby *(doll)*, she complained that since he kept crying, he must hate her. Advised that the baby needed milk and cuddles, Lola threw the baby *(doll)* at the cashier, shrieking, *You have him then, see if I care. I'm off to the pub!* The police were called and Luke as "cashier" was left reflecting to the first customer (his adoptive mother), *This baby needs a kind mummy like you, to look after him properly.*

Luke became fascinated by this mother's anti-social behaviour and chose to perform variations of the play several times over the following weeks. The drama brought home to him just how vulnerable he had been in his birth mother's care. He saw that (even though her options had been limited), she had made choices when she had abandoned him without ensuring that he was safe. The repeated dramatic processing of his experience reduced the impact of his painful memories. Luke started to attach more securely to his adoptive parents and to sustain friendships.

Using dramatic play to address specific emotions

Fear

Drama is a potentially explosive medium that requires immense sensitivity from the involved adults. Children's fragile self-esteem is easily harmed by sarcasm and unkind teasing because they tend to believe the negative things said to them and about them. Oppenheim and Goldsmith (2007) advise that, to heal and flourish, children need parents to give more positive than negative messages. Joe, age 11, revealed strong emotions in the course of exploring his terrifying nightmares.

Joe's play

Bertie had a horrible dream in which the hooded monster, Zarlac, kidnapped him, took him to a dungeon and made him do evil deeds. The stairs zig-zagged, getting you lost so you thought you were always going round in circles... After a very long time, Bertie was rescued by his *(foster)* mum and big sister. They helped him to destroy Zarlac, using ingenious methods that took the power out of Zarlac's eyes.

This play was successful because Joe's carer engaged in the drama to the extent of expressing her child's fear, while remaining sufficiently distanced to enable Joe to access the help and use his own creativity to destroy the "monster" representing his abuser. After a few weeks, Joe's nightmares had ceased. If his carer had been less receptive, Joe may have continued to perceive adults as untrustworthy.

Powerful negative feelings are just as important as positive feelings as they help us realise that something needs to change. Drama provides a "container" for violent emotions since in fiction, anything can happen. Moreover, fiction provides privacy to explore feelings that may otherwise be too painful to confront, the truth becoming apparent due to its containment within the story (Jennings, 1992).

For traumatised children, the starting point is to address their fear state. Using instruments such as drums and percussion, the child can be invited to make a sound, and thus discharge pent-up energy. The adult follows the child's beat. As the child's tension reduces, so will the tempo. The child may then experiment at making sounds to match feelings – *Let's guess which feeling you're playing*. This can turn into a concert of feelings, each taking turns to lead. It can develop into a drama in which the instruments are used to echo the feelings experienced in play.

Anger

Anger is often a cover for feelings of powerlessness, mockery, or unfairness. While righteous anger fuels energy to address injustice, anger can be destructive and if unacknowledged, can lead to the child having a sense of interminable disappointment and ultimately, depression. The following story was acted by Sonia, age seven, who became intensely frustrated while waiting for adoptive parents to be identified.

Sonia's play

Once there was a puppet that was very angry. The puppet didn't know why it was angry. It just was. It didn't like people being kind because that made it feel crosser than ever. One day someone tried to make friends but the puppet poo'd on her stuff. *Oh dear!* said her friend. *You must be feeling cross! I wonder, what might help?* Well, it turned out to be the puppet's birthday! *Shall we have a party?* asked the puppet's friend. She gave the puppet a present and the puppet said, *Thank you!*

They ate sausages, jelly and ice cream, and a special iced cake decorated with the puppet's photo. They played musical chairs and pass the parcel. The puppet enjoyed the party but later was still cross and sat on her friend's stuff to "poo".

The puppet's action of excreting on her friend's stuff, revealed the child's anger, masking her fear of rejection. Sonia acted on a belief that 'if I do nasty things, people will go away, which proves I am unworthy of their attention'. Her mother, having experienced a chaotic abusive childhood, had been frightened and frightening. Sonia had spent many hours watching for her return from the pub, never knowing who she would bring home that night. In foster care, Sonia found it hard to sustain her outward happy-go-lucky persona. She displayed strategies of Avoidant Attachment (Type A), craving yet fearing closeness, anticipating rejection. This puppet play helped her to recognise that she rejected people before they could reject her, and to experiment with other ways to interact. Sonia later made a successful transition to adoption.

Loss

Sometimes, children's loss leaves them feeling so anxious, that they reject offers to engage in playful activity. The child in the following excerpt believed he was too naughty to deserve any such kindness, a fear he expressed as *Peter Pan* (on a pretend telephone).

Philip's play

Peter Pan phoned Wendy *(therapist)* to advise her of two boys who had been very naughty. Sounding very anxious, he declared they didn't deserve any fun, explaining, 'The boys can't be happy'. Wendy empathised with how horrid it is to have such cross feelings and advised that having fun makes you happy. She invited them to join her on an adventure to see if they liked it. Peter Pan accepted the offer and "battled" with Captain Hook *(brother)*. They took turns to "die" and be 'revived' by Tinkerbelle's *(adoptive mother)* magic dust. Captain Hook chose to turn "good".

The family climbed into a boat, killed "sharks" and rescued friends by hurling 'horrible creatures into the sea in a net loaded with stones', then enjoyed an exotic picnic.

The family united in fighting off intruders, laughing and enjoying each other's company, while the children especially loved rocking in a boat on stormy seas. The play stimulated their imagination, for example, the invention of 'sausage and candy floss trees'.

Trickery and disguise

Children in care frequently complain of having felt tricked so rely on adults acting as role models to be authentic in portraying their own feelings and to notice if something doesn't feel right. In role as "witch", ask *What do I need that will help people to like me?* Children can make a chart of desirable qualities. They often suggest 'wear nicer clothes' (a less threatening appearance being a viable starting point), 'say please and thank you' and 'help with jobs'. From using fictional context to realise desirable characteristics, children think more confidently: 'Now I know what is required of me!'

Jimmy

Having idealised his birth mother, Jimmy cast his adoptive mother and therapist in supporting roles, to dramatise aspects of his earlier life. The following vignette illustrates his inversion of parental role. A child "trained to be a soldier" he blamed himself for his birth parent's failure to care for him. Solving problems, fictionally, helped Jimmy to resolve his own lack of confidence and gain a sense of self-worth.

Jimmy's play

Jimmy's hero encountered 'two sad little men who turned out to be children trained to be soldiers'. The hero recognised that his forthcoming journey would be 'dangerous'. As Julius Caesar, he used a combination of trickery and disguise to resolve problems. In one drama, Caesar disguised himself as a monkey, to distract guards, then as a dog, he chewed prison bars trying to help his Princess escape. Finally, as a vampire, he shocked the offending Pirate, and won the ensuing swordfight. Though exultant, Jimmy confessed he didn't believe in happy endings as, usually, people 'got on each other's nerves', thus diminished his efforts. Reminded that in story 'anything can happen', he acted a scene in which he had the Princess *(representing his learning disabled birth mother)* safely cared for by characters bearing his adoptive parents' names.

Addressing specific issues

Improvisation is a useful means to address specific difficulties and practice life skills. When problems feel insurmountable, feelings run high and traumatised children are easily alarmed. The way we invite change is to provide an experience that is carefully prepared and managed so that, within a fictional context, each participant can explore a variety of attitudes and be helped to recognise which ones are helpful and which are not. However, we strongly advise specialised professional training in the use of such techniques.

In role, as in ordinary life, children may persistently deny need of help or protection, perhaps too afraid or too unaware to admit to vulnerability. The following excerpt is from a drama devised to explore the impact of helpful versus unhelpful attitudes.

The adoptive parents in the family concerned had found it especially difficult to cope with their daughter's refusal to ask for help. Aged nine but at least two years delayed in her development, the child was easily intimidated by her parents' impatience. The intention of the play was not to dominate, but to provide a (safely fictive) experience of how it feels to encounter unpredictable behaviour from someone who seems too scary to challenge.

Intimidation

Choosing the part of Ratty, the child proposed the play open with the creatures sleeping in the forest. They were woken by Bear. The therapist took the role of Hawk, projecting exaggeratedly haughty and bullying attitudes. In swooping on Ratty, Hawk annoyed those who felt protective of her. Ratty appeared bemused, anxious to please and excited by so much attention. Owl (social worker) warned Ratty who ran nervously round in circles. As Bear, the adoptive mother was horrified by Hawk's rigid defence of his behaviour, hence her closing remark: *There's no point in talking when one of us won't even try to change!*

The drama served to heighten awareness of mutual responsibility and led to fruitful discussion on the ways we affect one another by our behaviour and attitudes.

WISE OWL: (social worker) HAUGHTY HAWK: (therapist)

RATTY: (child) GRUMPY BEAR: (adoptive mum)

The animals were asleep in the forest. GRUMPY BEAR rang the bell. They woke and stretched. HAWK announced 'I'm hungry!' and promptly swooped after RATTY who ran squeaking round the forest. HAWK stretched out his claw to trip the squealing RATTY.

BEAR *(roars)*: Oi! Leave Ratty alone!

HAWK: Just who do you think you are? *(wafting his magnificent plumage)*

WISE OWL: I'm calling a meeting!' *(pleading)* Hawk, I wish you wouldn't hunt Ratty. Can't you find some other food?

HAWK: Well, the forest is a bit short of mice and right now I fancy a bit of Rat.

BEAR: Hawk should be shot. Let's find a gun and shoot him!

RATTY: I don't think that would be right.

WISE OWL: No, we shouldn't be resorting to violence. We're all part of the same Community. We should be trying to help each other.

BEAR: But poor Ratty was scared! You were, weren't you Ratty?

RATTY: No, not really. *(sounding timid, anxious to please)*

Ratty didn't want to make Hawk cross with her. She liked pleasing people. Hawk snorted rudely and swooped after Ratty again. Ratty ran round the forest, alarmed.

OWL: *(shouting, sounding horrified)* Stop!' *Hawk stopped.*

HAWK: *(puffing his chest)* Just having a bit of fun! Is the meeting over now?

BEAR: It's over. There's no point in talking when one of us won't even try to change!

Lying

The following play was devised to give the adoptive parent an opportunity to act as errant teenager and experience how it felt to be free of parental responsibility. The Princess was invited to challenge the Queen's authority. It was hoped that her 11-year-old would gain from realising decisions that parents have to make in order to protect their children.

Wild Princess

Scene 1: The Palace (phone rings)

GRIZELDA: Hi Mirabelle, you coming out? I've got some nice men lined up for us!

MIRABELLE: Yeah, right – sounds great! I'll tell Mum! Mum, I'm going out tonight. What time can I stay out till?

QUEEN: Well, I don't know. 9 o'clock? You are only 12 years old!

MIRABELLE: Get real. You are just so embarrassing! I'm not coming back before 12!

QUEEN: That's not on and you know it! (*lots of bargaining takes place until eventually...*)

QUEEN: Right you can stop out till 10.30. I'll send a coach and horse to collect you.

MIRABELLE: You're joking! (*phone rings*) Hi Griz, mum says I've to be back at 10.30!

GRIZELDA: Tell her you can sleep over at mine.

MIRABELLE: Mum, Griz says I can sleep at hers!

QUEEN: We don't know her family darling. No, you have to be back at 10.30!

(*Lots more arguing but Mirabelle eventually agrees. Inspecting Mirabelle, Queen discovers she's hiding a very short miniskirt under her clothes.*)

QUEEN: You're not going out in that young lady. Obviously I can't trust you! You can forget going out! (*Mirabelle storms off, banging and crashing*) And don't go trashing your room either! (*phone rings*) Hello Grizelda. Mirabelle's grounded! She tried to sneak out in a skirt that's way too short.

GRIZELDA: (*lying*) That was my skirt, I asked her to bring it back.

QUEEN: Do you think I was born yesterday? I know the tricks you kids get up to!

GRIZELDA: You're just having a go at me!

QUEEN: I don't want Mirabelle out too late. You're only 12. Sleep here if you like.

GRIZELDA: Thanks. Promise we won't be late if you let her come out.

QUEEN: Alright, but I'm sending the coach and horses for you both at 10.30.

The adoptive mother thoroughly enjoyed herself behaving as irresponsibly as her brief permitted! In playing the part of Queen, the child had a much tougher time and realised that each time she allowed Mirabelle too much freedom, she was behaving in the way her birth mother had with her older sister. The child could see why the Princess kept lying, but expressed her desire for greater freedom and spending power. Her adoptive mum agreed to her child's requests to spend her pocket money on the phone she wanted.

Taking without permission

In the setting of a (fictional) supermarket, a variety of issues can be presented by the customers. The following excerpt illustrates work with Helen, age 13, who had been taking make up and money from adoptive parents, without permission. She cast her adoptive mother as supervisor, later exchanging roles to act as a teenager with attitude.

In role as cashier, Helen was confronted with the need to assert her authority, to prevent the theft of goods. Then, acting as the shoplifter apprehended by the police, she experienced the consequences of being caught and shamed. Helen decided that most people who get caught would not repeat the crime. Her adoptive mother enjoyed acting as a deceitful customer set on outwitting the cashier, and recognised how easy it was to be caught in the sheer excitement of risky behaviour. Realising Helen's need of her attention, she allowed her daughter to experiment with her (adoptive mother's) make up. The thefts curtailed and Helen began to negotiate for her privileges in advance.

Carly

One day, the cashier *(Helen)* was serving various customers. A single mother *(therapist)* slipped a tin of baked beans into her bag, assuming no one was looking. The cashier called the supervisor. On being confronted the single mother cried, *How will I feed my family now?* The supervisor said she would call the police. They decided she could have another chance as she agreed to return the goods.

An old lady *(adoptive mother)* entered the shop, slipped some ketchup into her bag and hurried to pay for other items. Observing this, the cashier called the supervisor, who disbelieving, replied, *You were trained to stop shoplifting, not to accuse old ladies!* But the cashier produced the ketchup from the lady's bag so the supervisor called the police. The old lady pleaded, *My son is a vicar. I'll never live it down!* The supervisor said, *Oh, he won't need to know!* The police decided not to press charges.

A teenager *(Helen)* stole things but at first, no one saw her. A second time, she was caught in the act. Her mum shouted, *Why did you let yourself get caught?* The police officer responded: *That's hardly the right attitude!* The mother said, *What do you know? I never had any choice! I stole or starved!* and let her daughter go into care. Helen decreed the moral of the story was: *You need respect, loyalty, kindness, trust, patience, understanding and talking to make relationships work.*

De-roling

"De-roling" is the process of shedding role(s), and is essential to help children disengage from the vested power of fictitious characters so that they resume their usual personality and way of being. The simplest way to de-role is to invite each person to state their real name and confirm that they are no longer the character for example: *I am Joan. I'm not the supervisor in this shop!* Follow-up discussion helps to make sense of the action which has just taken place. Children and parents are invited to share the feelings they experienced during the play. Here are some of the questions that can be asked during this process.

Debriefing

- Ask everyone: *How did that feel for you?*
- Ask the child: *Tell me what happened.* If the child can't remember all the sequences, the adults may prompt the child with their own recollections.
- Ask each in turn: *Did the other characters act as you expected?*
- Ask the child first: *What would you have liked to be different?*

- Ask each in turn: *What do you need from the others?*
- Ask each person: *What advice would you give your character?*
- Invite the child to provide a "moral" or message to the story, perhaps decide what they would like to happen next.
- Agree who will make a written record of the drama that took place.
- The following session can begin with reading the record as a lead in to discussing how it helped, how successfully adjustments have been made.

Measuring the effects of dramatic play

- What themes (or dichotomies such as good *v* evil) were prevalent in the play?
- What patterns of interaction might indicate a particular attachment style?
- How did the child make you feel (included, excluded or pushed around)?
- Does the child seek frequent reassurance from their parent?
- Does the child appear wary of displaying feelings?
- Was there secrecy or deception?
- Was the child able to/willing to share (such as sharing "food" with her doll)?
- Does the child use the available materials? If so, are they used as intended?
- Does the content of the play consist mainly of risk or ritual?
- Is the child especially vigilant? Can s/he explain/rationalise his/her fears?
- Is the child easily distracted? What held his or her attention for longest?
- Does the child willingly involve others or show preference for solitary play?
- Does the child initiate ideas? Or does s/he lack confidence to use own ideas?
- Was the child able to create a sequence of events?
- Did the child resist, or attempt a structure with a 'beginning middle and end'?
- How were objects handled (with sensitivity, respect, disregard or cruelty)?
- How confidently are intentions communicated verbally and non-verbally?
- What evidence is there of emotional reciprocity between characters?
- Was the child able/willing to give advice?
- Were characters able to resolve problems? How?
- How did involved adults relate to child? Did they concede power?
- Were parents playful? Did they show integrity, warmth, were they helpful?

Conclusion

In providing valuable opportunity for fun, laughter and joy, drama is an effective vehicle for children to explore their experience both literally and metaphorically, Drama offers children an opportunity to 'walk their story' so that from replaying sequences, past memories become less painful; fictional contexts allow the child to accept or reject connection to his or her own experience. The techniques used in drama replicate healthy mother–infant relationships. Young children respond especially well to sensory materials while puppets are useful in providing a focus that facilitates emotional communication. Children's self-esteem is enhanced by finding the answers in play, to predicaments on which their characters are consulted.

Summary

- Children have a right to know why they were removed from their birth parents, especially since many blame themselves for their rejection.
- Children depend on substitute parents to support them emotionally.
- Life history work needs to include positive as well as negative memories.
- The longer information is withheld the less easily children will trust adults.
- The more complex the problem, the greater the need to understand the source of difficulties and to support foster carers and adoptive parents.
- Children and parents benefit from parents' inclusion in life history work.
- Children need age-appropriate explanations to address their divided loyalties, fear of abandonment and their feelings of powerlessness and confusion.
- The history can be improvised or scripted as a series of brief "snapshots" of the actual events or it can be represented in metaphor.
- Some children choose to change the outcome to 'what should have happened' as a means of putting right the wrongs they endured.
- Fictional settings are useful to address specific problems.
- Powerful negative feelings are important to acknowledge and work through.
- Non-verbal signals are effective for safety and enhancing mutuality.
- Rituals help to restructure the brain and assist with processing memories.
- Recording the play consolidates learning.
- Evaluation is an essential part of the process for determining future need.

Chapter 9
Therapeutic stories

Introduction

The previous chapter explored the use of dramatic play in therapeutic work with fostered or adopted children, as a means to understand the source of their difficulties and thus identify the reasons for fearful reactions, and to help them to make new attachments. In the same context, we now focus on the value of story-telling illustrated by four specific stories devised and written by Joan Moore.

How stories help us to learn

Learning is the matching of new data to knowledge we already store in our memory (Perry and Pollard, 1998), primarily through the five senses. The psychobiology of healing shows that stories help us to recognise the patterns that rearrange the chemical as well as the mental and emotional levels at which we function. This is because we absorb stories both unconsciously and consciously. As in the case of Rosie (Chapter 8), who used the notion of being kidnapped as a metaphor for the fear induced by multiple moves to different families, stories are an ideal way to effect change as they use metaphors that connect physical sensation (sensori-motor experience) with understanding (cognition) and affect (the outward expression of feeling).

Metaphor originates from the Greek words *meta* and *phora* meaning 'to carry across' (Cox and Thielgard, 1987). A metaphor is a kind of symbolisation, bridging our inner and outer worlds, effectively linking left and right brain activity. It allows us to connect with others so that we share their feelings at a deeper level. For example, when a friend tells us they have "fallen in love" we can appreciate that they may be experiencing life as a "bed of roses". There are pages of metaphors accessible on the internet, in categories relating to the body, food, life, feelings and relationships.

Metaphor helps:

- when an individual is "stuck" – we know how it feels to "wade through mud";
- to revive memories by mediating between associated connections;
- to provide a representation of relationship patterns;
- to build a new reality by connecting the past to a potentially altered future;
- to distance a person from the emotional content of painful feelings;
- to explore the taboo, permit expression such as revenge, yet gives privacy so that we become more closely acquainted with our feelings and limitations.

Reminding us of earlier relationships

It is often unnecessary to comment and link story to reality. In fact, to do so may reduce its therapeutic value, especially for emotionally fragile children who are more responsive to the privacy of fiction and may resent connections to reality being made too explicit. Stories, drama, art and movement are vehicles for metaphor.

In drama, we experiment with roles to practise other ways of being while in art, inner feelings are outwardly projected on paper, canvas and through sculpture. Movement, for example, rocking and stroking, provides metaphors that help us to remember the meaning we attached to our earliest experiences. Children who have not experienced the rhythmic engagement and disengagement in a healthy infant–mother relationship may grow up to feel "spineless", too weak to cope under pressure (Meekums, 2002). Fright makes our bodies react as if to "jump out of our skin"; we aspire to be close to someone yet at times we "need space" and conflict can lead us to "lock horns". Stories and metaphors invite choice to maintain existing patterns or to create new ones. Bettelheim (1982) promoted the use of fairytales to help children to resolve crises in the process of learning to manage their feelings and relationships.

Story-telling to facilitate attachment

In ancient lore, Neptune is the Roman god of water, later linked with Poseidon, Greek god of the sea. Water is often associated with the flow of feeling we describe as "emotion". At times we may be carried away in a "sea of emotion" and experience "tides of feeling" that "ebb and flow". Our planet has more oceans than land, hence water may be chosen to represent all the loving and "good" in the world, its quantity being so great, it can absorb and dispose of the "bad". I use NEPTUNE as a mnemonic to summarise the value of stories in work with fostered/adopted children.

Telling stories:

Normalises events (through hearing of difficulties encountered by others).

Empowers us to believe we can solve problems, thus "redraw" the map.

Provides enrichment from the shared understanding that ultimately heals.

Teaches us that change happens anyway, to encourage us out of feeling stuck.

Understanding other perspectives gives insight into what is causing blockage.

Nourishes our wealth of wisdom from engaging with the story, then observing.

Experience is gained on multiple levels, including five senses, memory and emotion.

Inspiration

Children gain inspiration from hearing stories that illustrate the resolution of problems with which they identify. In picturing the setting and quandaries, they recognise the characters' feelings and understand their motivation, which helps them to see their own way forward. By dramatising these physical and feeling states, we experience the connection between them. For instance, in play, the repetition of storms might symbolise domestic violence during which, to the child witnessing, it felt as if "the sky crackled with anger". Play and drama offer a chance to try things out and make decisions by discovering what others think. A primary goal in facilitating attachment is mutual understanding. Through story-telling we can show what it "feels like", how it was for us, and share feelings, fears, fantasy and fun.

The Techniques CD contains instructions for engaging children in storytelling and on exploring themes contained in a selection of familiar children's fairy tales (see, for example, Nos. 52, 65, 70 and 82).

Addressing specific themes

The rest of this chapter features four stories which address themes that typically arise for children removed from their families, such as loss and loneliness, anger, feelings of fear, exhaustion, rejection, abandonment, being overlooked and the sense of not belonging.

Each story is followed by discussion points. The stories are brief, to encourage children who find it hard to concentrate. When complex feelings are raised, it may be more helpful to listen to the child telling you what they want you to hear than to continue reading the story. Children's feelings are easily bruised or buried. Their memories can be so painful to hear that, without consciously realising, we may discourage them in order to protect ourselves. Sensitivity on the storyteller's part is of critical importance. If you are unsure of how to make connections between fiction and real life in a way that will be heard as empathic, it is best to allow children to assimilate the message without sensing that they must "own" any connection to their particular situation. Otherwise it may be experienced by a child as patronising or highly embarrassing, as though they are somehow "wrong" and in need of correction.

Using the story

- Create a scene from the story, using clay or playdough.
- Paint the scenery or a picture of the scene and characters.
- Cardboard tubes can be used to make puppets to enact the story.
- Masks can be made from paper plates or balloons pre-coated in paper mâché.
- Bed sheets or curtains create scenery, for example, blue for sea, red for fire.
- Act the story: even two people can adopt several roles between them.
- Changing headwear for each character clarifies which role you are playing and serves to distinguish fiction from reality. It's fun to dress up!
- For the story, *How Wind learned to blow gently*, a sun headdress can be made from strips of yellow card stapled to a card headband.
- After enactment, it is important to derole. State clearly, *I am not [character's name] any more, I am [your own name]*.
- It may be helpful to talk about arising feelings, observing how characters addressed their dilemmas. Ask what helped and what was unhelpful.
- Encourage story-telling enthusiasts to join a drama group, so that they gain more confidence. (See Chapter 8 for further ideas.)

Knowing the source of children's difficulties helps us to understand their behaviour. Children who have been abused, abandoned and suffered sustained loss cannot be unaffected by their experience and easily plunge into shame when sensing they are being blamed or admonished. Many children may benefit from learning new methods to manage relationships. However, the most effective way to achieve this is via the adults modelling respect for the child so that the child gains self-respect.

Story 1: *How Wind learned to blow gently*

Once upon a time, in a land far away, at the foot of a mountain, lay a village where the people lived happily until one day, inside the mountain, there was a fire. Suddenly, a volcano erupted. Masses of lava poured down the mountainside into the valley and burned the children who were playing and had been taken by surprise. The volcano kept erupting, as though enjoying its power. Children wept. People worried and prayed. Wind heard them praying. She was upset about the children getting burned and wished she could help but when she blew, her breezes only made their pain worse! Also, Wind felt a bit jealous of all the attention people were giving to the volcano.

Finally, the volcano burned itself out. All that was left was a deep hole in the mountain. People warned the children to stay away from the hole. Wind felt crosser than ever! What power this volcano had, even after it had expired! The people carried on praying to keep their children safe from it. They rebuilt their houses using even stronger materials.

Time went by. Wind felt bitter towards the volcano. It seemed to Wind that no one noticed her any more. She felt so mad she furled herself into a tight ball and hovered over the hole in the mountain until she slid into the hole, then burst into a tornado – which is a mighty strong wind that can do a lot of damage. The tornado spiralled up into the sky, making a massive black cloud that covered the sun. The world went dark. No one could see a thing. Children lay shaking with fear. The tornado was so strong! Some of the shelters were blown apart, causing terror and chaos. Cattle escaped, stampeding across the land. The people needed their animals for food. Now they didn't know what to do!

Sun worried. Try as she might to peep through, she was hidden behind the giant black cloud and didn't know what to do. Wind just kept getting carried away, exultant yet terrified of her power. Sun begged Neptune, god of the sea, to make the waves rise up and stop Wind. But the giant waves frightened the children too!

Luckily, moisture from the waves rose into the air, causing rain to fall. The rain dampened Wind's spirits. Finally she stopped spinning. The tornado was over. Sun came out and dried the land. The people basked in the sun, enjoying its warmth. The children played and began to have fun again. 'You see,' said Sun to Wind, 'extremes of climate don't help anyone.' Wind felt very ashamed and lay still. Sun continued, 'We need you Wind! Your strong breezes are the best thing to dry out the land after the rain. Besides, the children burn from my hot rays, so right now, a gentle breeze will do nicely. We all have a purpose.'

'What about the volcano?' asked Wind, 'What purpose did that serve?'

'There are always some mysteries,' explained Sun. 'At least the village houses are built more strongly now, so the children will be safer.' Wind wafted gentle breezes and the people of the land lived in peace for many years.

Discussion

- The volcano exploding was terrifying for the people and their children. How do children keep safe in such frightening situations? They have to be brave. Wind was upset when the children were burned as she couldn't help them. Feeling powerless is very frustrating and upsetting.
- Wind didn't like the volcano having so much power. It made her jealous!
- Sometimes our feelings can be so big, they carry us away so we can't stop. It can stop us noticing other people's feelings. Can you think of an example?
- Sun gave Wind some good advice. What do you think children can do?

Commentary

Volcanoes, earthquakes and tornados are earth-shattering events that serve as metaphors for the experience of domestic violence. It is truly terrifying for children to witness violence of a scale that leads to severe injury between parents on whom they depend for safety and survival. Natural disasters portrayed fictionally help children who are self-blaming to see that what happened was not their fault.

In the story, Wind did not create the volcanic eruption that caused the children to be burned, even though she turned herself into a tornado. This can lead to a discussion of the impact that domestic violence has had on the child and on their brothers and sisters.

Often, one child is favoured while another is the family scapegoat, a situation likely to cause intense rivalry. By taking a range of different parts, children can practise putting across different viewpoints and compare the effectiveness of various solutions.

They may see how much the story translates to the real-life situations they have encountered. However, until a child volunteers her or his thoughts about this, it is more helpful to respect their privacy and focus on how characters felt in the story.

Story 2: *Robbie Rabbit takes the lead*

Once upon a time, a rabbit called Robbie lived in the woods among lots of woodland creatures. One day, Robbie Rabbit started going to Forest School. She didn't like it when the others looked in her direction. To Robbie, it felt like being inspected and it made her feel weird. Robbie wanted to be like the others. She learned to copy them so they would like her. Robbie saw Sally Squirrel dart up a tree. Robbie tried to run up the tree herself but slipped and fell. 'Ouch!' screeched Robbie. 'Dear me,' said Mummy Rabbit. 'You're so muddy we can't see your pretty tail. What happened?'

As Robbie told her about her accident, Mummy Rabbit asked, 'Why did Sally Squirrel go up the tree in school lessons anyway?' Robbie didn't know but the next day, she found out that Sally Squirrel didn't like learning her spellings so ran up the tree when lessons started! Robbie Rabbit liked learning and didn't mind spelling words like "carrot" or "grass" or even "farmer"! Robbie liked the challenge but still wanted to be like the others. It seemed like the best way to fit in.

One day, Woody Woodpecker kept tapping at a tree so hard his beak snapped. Woody was taken to the Animal Sanctuary to have his beak fixed. Robbie noticed everyone being kind to Woody, so she copied him. But Robbie's nose was much softer and soon bled. 'Silly creature!' scolded the teacher and sent Robbie home to her burrow. When Mummy Rabbit heard what happened, she said, 'Why don't you show them how fast you can learn? Instead of copying those silly creatures, let them copy you!' And do you know, that's exactly what Robbie did!

When the otters dared everyone to dive into the rapids, Robbie knew it was a silly and dangerous thing to do. 'No. I'll race you up the hill instead!' she said. Most of the others copied Robbie who soon had lots of friends. They told her, 'We don't like stupid dares!' When anyone suggested pranks to get out of school, Robbie would say, 'You make yourself look silly if you want. I'm not going to!' The teachers began to realise that Robbie was a very smart rabbit indeed. They gave her the special job of helping slower ones learn to read signs like "No entry" or "Danger!" The parent animals were pleased to see Robbie playing with their youngsters, knowing they would be safe as Robbie knew the rules and wouldn't play silly dangerous games. Thrilled, Mummy Rabbit said, 'I'M SO PROUD OF YOU!' Robbie became much happier having so many friends.

Discussion

- Robbie doesn't like people looking at her. She feels self-conscious. Do you mind when people look at you? How does it make you feel?
- Robbie copies other animals because she wants to be like them. But it gets her into difficulties. Often children get into trouble from copying each other.

- Why did Sally Squirrel escape up a tree? Was it a good idea for Robbie to copy her? What else do you think Robbie could have done?
- Woody enjoyed being made a fuss of. Is that why Robbie copied him?
- How does Robbie know when it's wise not to copy other creatures?
- Does this apply to children? How will you decide when not to copy others?
- Could you invite children to follow you? What can you say or do when they dare you to do something that is not allowed or will get you into trouble?
- What activities do you like best that could involve other children? How will you ask them? Shall we practise how to ask others to do things you want?

Commentary

Children who have experienced severe neglect and trauma in their first three years tend to have difficulties relating to peers. They want to be like them, be accepted and not stand out, but may not have developed "theory of mind" and be much less aware that other people do not automatically think and feel about everything the same way they do.

Socially, these children "miscue". They also interpret messages literally. For instance, on request, to 'pull your socks up' they may literally pull up their socks, not recognising the symbolic meaning of the phrase. Such literal interpretation is one of the traits of Asperger's Syndrome, for which there is a specialist assessment. However, many neglected children who exhibit such problems do not necessarily attract such a diagnosis. They often cope by imitating the actions and following other children.

The story of Robbie Rabbit addresses dilemmas regularly faced by such children that, as a result, lead them into trouble. In this story, the rabbit tries to emulate other creatures and in the process makes several unfortunate mistakes, but eventually begins to protect herself. She learns how to recognise dangers in order to keep safe; also, how to make friends by inviting the others to join in with her.

The story can be used as a guide for children who fail to understand the unwritten social rules and consequently struggle to gain acceptance into informal social groups.

Story 3: *How Eddie Eagle made friends*

A baby eagle was found in a rocky crevice by some parent eagles while they were searching for material to build their nest. The baby eagle had been abandoned and his wing was broken. 'Poor baby bird!' the big eagles cried, 'We'll look after you.' They named him Eddie. He could feel their warmth and hear how much they cared about him, so he settled quickly into this new eyrie. As a baby bird, Eddie had been very brave, surviving all kinds of danger. Sometimes he felt tiny and frightened. Other times he felt very powerful. Mummy and Daddy Eagle continued to be kind, showing him how to hunt for food and build a nest, as they loved their little bird.

As he grew bigger, Eddie had to learn rules he didn't always understand. He got cross when he saw the other birds breaking rules that he was trying to keep. One day, Eddie saw some vultures swoop over a rock and hang by their claws from a precipice. 'Hey!' shouted Eddie. 'THAT'S NOT ALLOWED!' The vultures flew to Eddie, flapping their wings across his eyes. They were cross with him for interfering in their play. 'MIND YOUR OWN BUSINESS!' they screamed. Eddie was scared.

Mummy Eagle heard the commotion and quickly herded Eddie home. She soothed his ruffled feathers, explaining, 'You were cross because you thought they were being naughty,' Eddie nodded. 'But they're bigger than you' said Mummy Eagle, explaining. 'Vultures can hang from cliff edges. It's best to let grown-ups deal with the big birds!' She stroked Eddie's feathers until he felt better.

The next day at Bird School, Eddie looked for someone to play with. The other birds gathered at a creek catching worms. 'Oi!' yelled Eddie. 'Come over here!' The teacher heard Eddie yelling and told him off. 'That's not very nice,' she said, sounding strict. But Eddie didn't understand why. Later he told Mummy Eagle about it. 'All you wanted was a friend to play with!' she said. 'It's lonely being all by yourself, isn't it?' Eddie nodded. 'Perhaps tomorrow you can ask the birds if you can join in their game. It's always better to ask the others what they would like to do rather than tell them,' said Mummy Eagle. Now he knew what to do, Eddie felt better.

It was another sunny day. The birds fluttered round a new little robin. Eddie noticed the robin looking a bit nervous. He waited until the others started playing a game. Then Eddie went up to the robin and asked her if she would like to play. The robin said she would but felt scared as the other birds were so much bigger than her. Eddie said, 'Don't worry, I'll look after you.' Eddie and Robin became great friends and Eddie stopped feeling lonely. The other birds saw him being kind, so they invited him to join in their games. Mummy Eagle reminded Eddie to ask nicely so he practised. The other birds liked it when Eddie was polite and friendly. They admired his flying skills and loved hearing his stories. Eddie became very glad to have so many good friends!

Discussion

- Eddie was abandoned by his first parents then found by some kind eagles. That happens to children too. I wonder why Eddie had to be so brave.
- Can you remember having adventures? Do you want to tell me about them?
- I wonder how Eddie felt in his new home. There must have been lots of new smells and different things to see, hear and touch. What was your first home like? Can you remember how it was?
- Eddie's new parents teach him lots of things. How do your parents help you?
- What are your favourite activities?
- The vultures scream at Eddie, terrifying him. It's horrid to be screamed at!
- Eddie was cross with the vultures when they seemed not to obey the rules. Do you find it annoying when people don't obey rules? Which rules?
- The vultures are bigger birds. In this story they're like teenagers, doing risky things. There are different rules for different age groups. Do you know why? Younger children need more safety. Teenagers are getting ready to be grown ups. So the rules are different for them.
- Eddie's classmates don't come when he calls them. Why, do you think?
- Mother Eagle knows Eddie needs a friend. She reminds him to ask, instead of tell others what to do. Is that useful advice for children to follow?
- What might help you remember this advice? Shall I tie a silky ribbon in your pocket that you can feel, to remind you of me when you go out to play?
- Are there any new children in your class whom you can help to look after?

Commentary

The story of Eddie Eagle was written for children who find it difficult to make friends, the aim being to demonstrate ways to accommodate to the rest of the group. Often, children who had inadequate care miss learning "cause and effect", so they fail to understand the impact their behaviour can have on others. Due to their emotional immaturity, such children can appear to be very bossy in play situations because they have not learned a more helpful model of how to relate to or "be" with others. They haven't learned to share and cannot understand why everyone doesn't do as they want them to. Many neglected children have to learn to meet their own needs in the absence of reliable care from their birth parents. Due to not having experienced nurturing, safe, parental authority, they become self-reliant and learn to treat everyone as peers, regardless of age or status.

The story illustrates what happens to Eddie Eagle when he gets out of his depth by trying to tell the bigger vultures that they must obey the rules he has learned. Eddie also tries to tell his own peers to 'come over here!' They ignore him because they resent his bossy tone of voice and resist being told what to do by him. As a result,

Eddie feels rejected and lonely. Luckily, Mother Eagle kindly guides him in how to manage his relationships more successfully. Shored up by her love, Eddie makes friends with a nervous robin. Friendships grow, illustrating the social progression that can result when children experience sufficient empathy, support and guidance from caring adults.

Story 4: *Mika Moth's escape*

Once upon a time, deep in the forest, there lived a pretty moth called Mika. She had several sisters. In this forest were many dangers for delicate moths to watch out for.

One day, Mummy Moth met a large hairy spider. Spider noticed she had lovely spots and said, 'You are beautiful!' Mummy Moth liked to hear Spider saying such nice things to her. It gave her a lovely fluttery feeling inside.

Spider persuaded Mummy Moth to visit his web. 'Bring your babies too,' he said.

The moths went to his web but Mika didn't like it. The web was sticky and clung to her. Spider wanted Mummy Moth to look after him and if she didn't do as he asked, he turned nasty. Spider even warned them he would pull their legs off if Mummy Moth didn't obey him. The Moths were scared of Spider. But each time they tried to escape, a piece of the web stuck to their back so Spider was able to find them again.

Mummy Moth felt sad and frightened. The only way to make Spider happy was to give him the sap from a plant that grew nearby but this plant was poisonous. When the effects wore off, Spider became nastier than ever. Mummy Moth drank the sap too as she wanted to feel happy like Spider was at first. Spider and Mummy Moth slept so long in the day, they were awake through the night when Spider would keep coming to Mika and her sisters while they were trying to sleep. They didn't like it and wished he would leave them alone. They felt scared.

The young moths began to plan their escape. While Spider was asleep they made friends with a beetle. Beetle said, 'Come to me when Spider is nasty. I will keep you out of his sight.' But Spider found them and Beetle didn't know where else they could go. By this time, Mika's beautiful colours had begun to fade and she didn't feel like herself any more. She cried and cried.

A passing butterfly heard Mika's cries and asked her what the matter was. When she heard Mika's story, the butterfly flew off to tell Wise Owl who said, 'This won't do! These little moths must be properly looked after.' He sent some dragonflies to take the moths to a safe meadow where some kindly butterflies looked after them. 'Don't worry, we'll keep you under our wings,' they said. They praised Mika for being so brave.

Soon Mika's beautiful colours grew back to their former glory. Dragonfly visited and taught her how to fly so she could make more friends and feel safer. Mika was much happier living with the butterflies, though sometimes she felt sad when she thought about Mummy Moth. She hoped Mummy Moth was alright, but wished she could have looked after them better and kept them safer.

Discussion

- Mika Moth lived in a forest full of dangers. Do you think she worried about these dangers? Which do you think worried her most?
- Mika's mummy met a spider who was nice to her at first but soon frightened the moths. It's wrong to frighten anyone, especially little ones who are not able to protect themselves. What should Mummy Moth do? How could Mika and her sisters keep safe?
- Mummy Moth drinks the sap that made her too sleepy to care for her children. Sometimes humans take pills or drink stuff that makes them poorly. I wonder how children look after themselves when their parents are not able to.
- Are children able to guess when their mum is too ill to look after them? How?
- The moths are especially scared of Spider at night time. He was very creepy! Children need to be safe. They need their sleep too. Sometimes it's hard for them to get away from people they don't trust. Who should they ask for help?

Commentary

The story of Mika Moth addresses the threat and reality of sexual abuse, and 'the sap making them too sleepy' opens discussion about parental alcohol and drug misuse resulting in lack of care or safety for the children. This story needs to be used with immense sensitivity, particularly if a child whom you suspect has been abused has not made any disclosures. Direct questioning of the child needs to be avoided. However, it must also be made clear to the child that any information that indicates children are unsafe has to be acted on, in order to protect other children from harm.

The key message to get across is that children need protection and have a right to be safe. Many children live in families where the boundaries of play and comfort-seeking are blurred, all too often as a consequence of their own parents' experiences in childhood. If children have been unprotected, they do not always know what is "unsafe" and may seek stimulation in ways that are unhealthy and potentially harmful. If young children display affection in an overtly sexualised manner, they can be shown how to enjoy warm attention by sitting beside the parent rather than on their lap. It is the task of adoptive parents and foster carers to educate their children in self-care and protection, to demonstrate respect for privacy, whilst providing nurturing care and affection. Story-telling that includes sensory and physical play will excite the child's senses, redirecting their need for stimulation into ways that are healthy.

Conclusion

This model describes the use of stories in a way that provides a multi-sensory experience, which enables us to connect with each other at a deeper level than by merely talking. It is the sensory experience combined with enduring patience and the sincere interest of carers that helps children to feel safer to attach more securely to their new parents.

Summary

- In stories, we recognise the patterns that affect emotional functioning.
- Metaphor enables us to connect physical and feeling states.
- Children build a new reality by connecting the past and future through story.
- Fiction provides the distance to allow pain to be confronted more safely.
- Sensory experience in play serves to replicate healthy mother–infant bonding.
- The experience of fictional characters can help us to view things differently.
- Stories addressing themes such as loneliness can show new ways forward.
- In role as a fictional character, adults can model respect for children, to encourage them to learn self-respect.
- Stories can demonstrate the social rules and expectations, illustrating how to make friends by showing concern for others, without being didactic.
- Children's need for protection and safety can be made clear in order to help them to learn how to protect themselves.

Conclusion

It is easy to condemn the evil doer, so much harder to understand him.

(attributed to Dostoevsky)

Much has been written to help social workers, foster carers and adoptive parents but we hope that the ideas and concepts in this handbook will work for the reader in new ways. We find that when parents and carers are helped to understand the sources of their children's problems, they find more resources within themselves to work towards effective resolution. Social workers have often declared lack of confidence to engage in direct work with children so we hope that, within this book, they will discover windows of opportunity and feel inspired. We have sought to explain human behaviour and its attendant influences, and hope the connections between each of the disciplines have been made clear enough to enable involved practitioners and caregivers to make more informed assessments and support children through transition to permanence.

Let us consider what we have learned from such broad sources of information. Certainly, the recent decade of neurobiological research has confirmed the relevance of John Bowlby's theory of attachment – that humans are essentially social creatures, dependent on being in relationships to survive and to co-exist. We find that attachment, initially at least, is not culturally determined; rather, it is a universal phenomenon, especially during the first year when infants instinctively attach to their primary caregivers in order to survive. Developments in neuroscience have shown us the remarkable plasticity of young children's brains, which makes them so receptive to quality care yet just as vulnerable to damage, as seen in the upsetting effects on babies of the still faces of depressed mothers, influencing the formation of early pre-verbal memory, with lasting repercussions. Such research clarifies infants' physical and psychological needs for comfort, guiding us to the importance of supplementing the early "attachment dance" for those whose early needs were not met, and who instead suffered the trauma of neglect and abuse that becomes further compounded when children have repeated moves within care.

We find the resulting patterns of aggression and repression to be mainly fear based and propose that, in the process of planning care solutions for children and young people, the task of "matching" them with substitute parents will be enhanced by practitioners gaining more comprehensive understanding of attachment patterns, for example, to enable them to assess individual bias towards cognitive or emotional judgements. This will direct intervention to focus on specific need so, as Crittenden (2008) advises, people inclined to repress or exclude affect (Type A) can be helped to recognise and validate feelings, thus expanding their repertoire of responses, while those too caught up with their own anxiety (Type C) can be guided to take in the "whole picture" in order to regulate feeling states that influence their responses.

Children in public care are especially vulnerable, yet their views, as reported in research (McLeod, 2008), are not always sought or adequately represented. Like all of us, children want to enjoy life and to feel that they belong, yet those who, as a consequence of neglect, are delayed in functioning make continuous demands on caregivers. As with babies, the urgency to calm them tends to take precedence over everything else, so that substitute parents can feel subsumed and overwhelmed. Neglected, abused children need responses that alleviate the stress in their nervous system so that they can access new information, in order to learn to self-calm. The aim of intervention, then, is to enable these children to seek and receive the comfort and protection they need and also feel freer to explore their environment flexibly.

So often, in referring to a child's self-harming and dangerous actions, carers and professionals say things like, 'You've got to tell her, she can't carry on like that!' Of course, we can advise children until we are blue in the face, but such verbal input is unlikely to change patterns that are neurologically imprinted by early experience. We have found that, through the process of enacting their life history, children discover for themselves the reasons for these embedded patterns. From exploring various predicaments in play, they practise new ways of being and begin to realise their capacity for change. Without scientific evidence or randomised control trials we can only speculate that it is the repetition of explanations, combined with sensory experiences in the context of a consistent warm, attuned relationship, in which spontaneity occurs within play situations, which influences the biochemistry and restructure of the child's brain, in replicating missed nurture and anesthetising the effects of trauma.

Through imaginative and sensory play, we observe children learning new ways to self-soothe, methods they can call on to distract themselves in other situations which provoke uncomfortable feelings of shame, embarrassment or fear. It is important to be able to set these feelings aside in order to survive day-to-day life. Those unable to do so continue to be highly aroused and either aggravate people around them or refuse to talk about their feelings but stay "churned up". Either extreme leads to depression. Increased, maladaptive functioning may, in time, attract diagnoses of mental illness.

The research we have referred to throughout this work clearly shows that such emotional disturbance stems from regulatory problems, conditioned during the earliest years of life by inadequate or dangerous parenting practices, albeit that the more severe problems are also compounded by "co-morbidity" – other related factors that make the task of diagnosis and treatment so much more complicated and challenging.

The ever-popular programmes of cognitive behaviour therapy are mainly organised around verbal (conscious) communication on the assumption that we consciously choose to act in particular ways, when the reverse is generally the case for traumatised children whose unconscious all too often governs their responses. Therefore, we encourage parents and practitioners involved in making assessments to observe the child's somatic (non-verbal) expression rather than to rely solely on verbal language.

We find that many substitute parents show increased empathy on appreciating their foster/ adoptive child's stage of grieving and being helped to recognise when they are operating developmentally at a younger emotional age and stage. In the course of our attempts to normalise experience, adoptive parents express relief on being advised of research findings (e.g. Triseliotis *et al*, 1997; Rushton, 2003) that the majority of adopted children grow up to be well-adjusted adults. If social workers can use the monthly hour allocated to them to work with each child on their caseload, implementing reflective listening skills – perhaps with a "third object" – most children will feel emotionally held through the process of change; they will arrive in a substitute home using feeling words to ask for needs to be met and as a result, be more likely to receive appropriate responses. In our experience, the hurts felt by most parents and children heal once they feel heard. If significant difficulties continue, then receiving focused therapeutic support helps enormously, enabling the child's brain to grow new connections. Dramatic play has, for some adoptive families, been effective even with quite traumatised children. In physically dramatising the story, children explore what happened, compare their experience to what should have happened, and discover what can still happen to enhance their future. Of course, it is hard to prove which part of these interventions is most effective, yet children's stories tell us much about the process. Therapy provides a bridge from misfortune and despair to hope for a better future.

If we want to change the past we need to know what we want, in order to create a more desired future. Empathy helps us to be less judgemental, invoking a desire to "resolve" and "reframe" rather than "blame and shame". We hope that improved understanding resulting from this knowledge base will lead to heightened empathy. Yet, while it is incumbent on professionals to find ways to support the most vulnerable children in our society, research indicates that parents who fail to care for or protect their children often do so for reasons they don't understand. Rising figures for prescription drugs to treat depression and increased concerns about violent behaviour in school and on the streets indicate mounting stress in our western society. If we want to reduce stress levels, the solution has to start with the care of infants. Developments in neuroscience clearly show a need to prioritise relationships, for instance, by creating policies in health, education and allied social services that allow time to attend to feelings.

However, to prevent repetition of maladaptive patterns, less fortunate mothers need role models from whom they can learn how to entertain and cope with their babies. To respond to the causes rather than symptoms of society's ills requires change in our infrastructures. For example, if housing estates were designed to invite greater cohesion, it might help reduce the isolation problems of single parents. If infants in pushchairs face their mothers, more communication can result. Health surgeries might influence infant care by showing films of how the brain develops, with babies and mothers enjoying rewarding and reciprocal interactions. Freely available leaflets illustrating ways for parents to entertain babies and children could stimulate interest and learning. Patients have reported gaining relief from stress by reading displays of poetry and hearing soothing music in the waiting rooms of mental health clinics. Creative therapies are increasingly evidenced to be more effective than medication, for instance, to treat depression, being ultimately cheaper and achieving swifter results.

If we achieve little else, we hope the range of ideas in this book will inspire social workers to engage in direct work with the children in their care, and that foster and adoptive parents will use the information to engage in play with their children to enhance relationships and lead to greater security, self-esteem and mutual pleasure.

Appendix 1
Listening skills

In order to ascertain how children see their world, we need to help them express their wishes and feelings. This also helps to bring to attention any developmental delay. Time is often limited for such assessments in relation to court work; using the various techniques described here will help social workers make more informed assessments.

Use PACE:

P – playfulness

A – acceptance

C – curiosity

E – empathy

Equals LOVE

(Dan Hughes, 2000)

Listening with empathy

Use empathetic listening so the child feels heard. Empathetic listening in this context is rather like being a sports commentator noticing or "tracking" what is happening. This means simply noting what the 'child' is saying and doing. The child will tell you or show you their meaning if they can. The adult reflects the feeling expressed by the child, saying for example, *So you were really sad about that!* In this way the child feels heard. We feel as we feel and children need their feelings to be accepted. The aim is to observe themes and patterns from what we see and hear, without imposing our values or judgements.

As the child plays with the toys, comment on the action, for example: *The red car is following the green car. Oh! The car crashed!* (heightening tone as you say this). The child might say, *The man's dead,* and you might respond: *Poor man!* (lowering your voice to show sadness).

Repeat what you heard the child say. The child might qualify it. Then ask, *What happened next?* Children will often elaborate. Say, *Wow, what a story!* so the child feels heard without being led.

Use of transference and counter-transference

In listening to children it is important to be aware of how we are feeling in their company. How you the adult feels can mirror how the child feels. (This is known as "transference".) These feelings will inform you how the child has experienced previous relationships with caregivers. On recognising how they are affected by the child, parents and professionals also see how their reaction ("counter-transference") can impact on the child. These two terms are explained in Chapter 5 of the Handbook on play and communication (see ideas for parents under 'healing and feeling'). All reflective listening is therapeutic, although this is not a therapy as such.

Additional listening skills

Parents and carers can use the listening skills described above and the healing and feeling play ideas below as a way to soothe their children and return them to a peaceful state from which to explore the world and learn to understand their feelings.

- When a child seeks ATTENTION in a way that you find irritating, you may feel ANNOYED ➔ if at that point you can take time to think about how you are feeling you will probably become aware that the child's behaviour is about his or her need for attention. Once you are aware of this, you can try the following approaches: play with them, do something soothing using sensory materials (e.g. using warm water, bubbles or warm play-dough; give older children or young people some fur fabric or a soft toy to stroke; play with clay or cook pizza or cakes. This kind of nurturing activity enables the child to gain affirmation from those with whom they are sharing it.
- When the child enters a POWER contest, you may feel ANGRY ➔ In these circumstances, adoptive parents and carers need to set boundaries and try to stay in their own space (see calming visualisation for parents under Chapter 4, Grief and Loss).
- When the child seeks REVENGE, the adult may feel VERY HURT ➔ It is important for carers and adoptive parents to remember that the child is likely to be seeking revenge for the past, rather than against them. Stay in a safe place but don't move out of sight. Allow the child time to express their frustration. Acknowledge hurt without making judgements. Afterwards, adults can reassure children by giving them a cuddle, using soothing language and encouragement.
- When the child shows INADEQUACY, the adult may feel HOPELESS or HELPLESS ➔ Return to the earlier developmental stage being displayed by the child. Reassure and encourage the child by reviewing a past achievement, move or change so that the same strategies he or she has already achieved can be used to overcome the present inadequacy. For example, if you ask the child to lay the table but they refuse, give the child a puzzle or activity for a younger child. When the child completes it, praise him or her for remembering how to do it, as a reminder of their competency, and then suggest they lay the table.
- When the older child seeks APPROVAL of FRIENDS and peers, adults may feel WORRIED or ANXIOUS ➔The child needs reassurance and approval for the simplest things that they are achieving daily. Using reflective listening, play the Counters game (see Handbook, Chapter 4) to encourage the child's self-esteem and to demonstrate your empathy with their worries.

Appendix 2
Preparing for a direct work session

Preparation: techniques for social workers

What do I need to start?

Before meeting a child, as a social worker you will need to read all the information available and create a "flow chart" of the child's previous moves, noting the impact of these losses, moves or changes. This knowledge is essential to make sense of what the child tells you through play.

Children find it most encouraging when they experience their social worker as a non-threatening reflective listener, who pays close attention by paraphrasing their words using 'active listening skills', as described in Appendix 1.

Choosing a venue

You will need to decide where the assessment is taking place, ideally somewhere safe and quiet. If the venue is away from the child's home or school, a safe person (carer/parent) needs to transport the child. If sessions take place at home the child may initially need the adoptive parent or foster carer with whom they feel safe to be present. After the first time, children (if old enough) can be seen alone. Children can be given a box or folder in which to store their pictures, stories, and photos. It is very useful for social workers to have their own small toy bag (see list in Techniques); the contents can be arranged on a play mat to form a boundary in which play rules apply.

Preparing the child

Children need to know how many times you are coming for these special playtimes, which need to be named as you go: *'This is the first play time, this is the second'* and so forth. Calculating how much time is given to this part of the assessment is important in order to avoid making unrealistic promises. Keep to the date and times of sessions as the children will become anxious if they are let down and then won't trust social workers.

During the penultimate session the child can be reminded:

As next time is our last special playing time, is there anything else you want to tell or show me? How shall we end this time together? Shall I bring cakes or would you like to play a game?

Introducing yourself and why you are here

You could explain your role as follows:

My name is ... My job is to come to see you and play or talk to you about what might be worrying you or making you feel muddled, so that I can tell the people who are making up their minds about how to help you and your family know what you think and feel. I cannot keep secrets about you not being safe or about people hurting you, so only tell me what you feel comfortable sharing. Little secrets like where you hide your teddy/makeup are OK, but it's important that you are safe.

There is a special person called a judge, a bit like a wise old owl, who listens to the grown-ups and decides what would be best for the children but first, she or he needs to know what the children think. That's why I have come to find out.

With *younger children* you can use a puppet or toy to introduce yourself and explain why you have come. If possible, come down to the child's level, smile and using a warm tone of voice, say *My name is ... this is my friend Tortoise. He's very shy*. Withdraw the head into the body of the puppet to show how he is feeling and say, for example, *'Can you show Tortoise your toys (or pretty shoes)?'* The child will soon want a go, so takes the puppet. Then you can address the puppet (as a third object): *Oh Tortoise, Jo has really pretty shoes!* and so on. This takes the focus off the children who are then able to project their feelings on to the puppet, about what is happening to them in their everyday life. The puppet can accompany the social worker on visits to children who will see them as child friendly. If you continue with another technique, first, explain the above rules and let the child find their own level. Join in by listening reflectively.

A substance like "silly putty" is useful when making introductions to *older children*. Model it by moving it calmly in your own hands and then share it with the young person as you chat, much as you would offer a piece off gum. As they manipulate the putty, it calms them via the sensory experience. The putty bounces, can be used to make animals or people, and is excellent for 3D eco-maps for assessment purposes. A pile of magnets for adolescents to fiddle with is useful in removing the need for eye contact. Activities such as computer games, jewellery making or making clay chess-type figures to represent family members that can be squashed if a young person is feeling very tense are all also effective ways to get to know young people.

Setting boundaries

Children are reassured by the stating of safety rules, for example:

The toys stay on the mat or in this room. You can do almost anything on the mat or in the room. If there's something you may not do [like breaking toys, hurting, hitting or throwing things], I'll let you know.

If they test the boundaries after having been given time to follow the rules of play, explain: *I said I would let you know if there is something you may not do. That is something you may not do but you can do almost anything else.* This will prevent children from escalating matters. If a child persists in doing something dangerous after a further warning, the session needs to end. You can explain that you will come back for the next session and pack the toys away. If limits are conveyed in a clear but friendly manner, children very much enjoy having an adult's undivided attention and are generally keen to keep the rules in order to ensure this. If they are reluctant to engage or just very angry that their parents are insisting they are seen by you, using scribble drawings, clay or musical instruments will help to defuse the strong feelings and enable the child to express their wishes and feelings.

If children persist in doing something dangerous, you can warn them again and count down from ten, giving plenty of time between each number. If the child carries on not co-operating, you need to tell them that the session has ended for today. You should explain that you will pack the toys away, and come back for the next session at the same time. If limits are conveyed in a clear but friendly tone, it is rare to have to end a session owing to rules having been exceeded.

During the session

Children who are allowed to explore the playroom or mat without being directed will find their own level, if the adult uses reflective listening skills. You may obtain all the information and wishes and feelings required for court without resort to techniques, but they can be useful especially when time is short. We can introduce these by saying, *Let's play one of your games, then one of mine and finish with yours!*

In assessment sessions with children, social workers may need to record their observations as they go along, in which case you need to explain to children why you are writing., for instance: *I want to tell the judge exactly what you said* or *I am writing your story because it is so interesting.* Later, giving children a typed copy of their story, ideally with a picture inserted, is validating and can reassure them.

Some useful phrases

- *Can you tell Teddy why you were sad?*
- The adult talks to Teddy saying, *Teddy, John seems sad. Do you think he could tell you how he is feeling?*
- Take your eye contact away from the child so she or he can tell Teddy something without feeling inhibited.

Forms of questioning

- 'What' and 'How' questions are most useful.
- 'Why' is less effective since the child is unlikely to know the answer.
- 'Where' could cause children to feel pressure if they think social workers are trying to prise information from them.

In social work, we have to be *very* careful not to lead the child via questions or games. Be sure to use open-ended questions, i.e. not those that lead to a 'yes' or 'no' answer. It is also important to avoid directing children to answer in a particular way.

Prompting expansion

Explain that you can invite a child to expand on a point by using enquiry such as, *I am wondering if you would like to choose ...?*

If a child is playing with dolls or animals you could say: *Can you show and tell me how the story went?* Then, if they are stuck, ask: *What happened next?* If the story then stops, say: *Wow, what a story! Thank you for sharing that with me.*

Reflecting feelings

This can be done by saying, for example:

- *Ouch! Ouch!* if Teddy gets hurt
- *You did enjoy that,* upping your tone of voice, *How did you feel?*
- *It seems you're finding this really painful,* offering a cuddly toy to hug.

In noticing a child's play, show sincere interest by using phrases such as:

- *Really?*
- *I see!*
- *That's interesting*
- *That's fun.*
- *Oh, how sad.*
- *Would you like to tell me about it?*
- *Can you tell me what else happened?*

Endings

It is important to give a child a five-minute warning that a play session or interview is about to end. You could ask: *'We have five minutes left, so can you think of an ending to this game or story?'* Another tactic to read a story featuring the issues being explored (see Chapter 9 and Resources in Techniques CD). Children can be given a sticker as a positive way to end when they have accepted the rules.

When coming to the end of a series of sessions the child needs plenty of time to realise their social worker is parting for good. Being told at least three sessions in advance will allow them time to express anger and control part of the "goodbyes". (They may never have had this choice before.) For the final session the social worker can say:

As next time is our last special play times, is there anything else you want to tell or show me? How shall we end this time together? Shall I bring a cake or would you like us to play a game of your choosing?

On finishing, the child will need to be told what information will be shared with the adults, including the judge. You will need to reflect what the child has told you even if your conclusion about the child's safety differs from the child's. Information sharing needs to be gentle but honest. It often comes as a great relief to children when adults take responsibility for their not being safe or nurtured.

Bibliography

Adcock M. and White R. (1998) *Significant Harm*, Croydon: Significant Publications

Ainsworth M. (1978) *Patterns of Attachment: A psychological study of the strange situation*, Hillsdale, NJ: Lawrence Erlbaum Associates

Ainsworth M. (1989) 'Attachments beyond infancy', *American Psychologist*, 44:4, pp.709–16

Aldgate J., Jones D., Rose W. and Jeffrey C. (2006) *The Developing World of the Child*, London: Jessica Kingsley Publishers

Axline V. (1967) *Dibs, in Search of Self*, Harmondsworth: Penguin

Axline V. (1987) *Play Therapy*, New York: Ballantyne Books

BAAF (1984) *In Touch with Children Training Course*, London: BAAF

Bailey S. (2006) 'Adolescence and beyond', in Aldgate J., Jones D., Rose W. and Jeffrey C. (eds), *The Developing World of the Child*, London: Jessica Kingsley Publishers, pp.208–225

Bannister A. (1997) *The Healing Drama: Psychodrama and dramatherapy with abused children*, London: Free Association Books

Baron-Cohen S. (1995) *Mindblindness – An essay in autism and theory of mind*, London: The MIT Press

Bentovim A. (1998) 'Significant harm in context', in Adcock M., White R. and Hollows A. (eds.) *Significant Harm*, Croydon: Significant Publications, pp.57–89

Bergman N., Anderson G., Moore E. and Hepworth J. (2003) 'Early skin to skin contact for mothers and their healthy newborn infants', *Cochrane Library*, April 2003, Oxford

Bettelheim B. (1982) *The Uses of Enchantment: The meaning and importance of fairy tales*, Harmondsworth: Penguin

Bettelheim B. (1997) *A Good Enough Parent*, London: Thames & Hudson

Black D. (1990) 'What do children want from parents?' *Adoption & Fostering*, 14:1, pp.43–50

Bowlby J. (1973) *Attachment and Loss: Separation anxiety and Anger: Vol II*, London: Hogarth Press

Bowlby J. (1979) *The Making and Breaking of Affectional Bonds*, London: Tavistock Publications

Bowlby J. (1988) *A Secure Base*, London: Routledge

Bratton S. and Landreth G. (2006) *Child Parent Relationship Therapy: Training manual of the Play Therapy Association of South Arizona*, New York, NY: Routledge

Brocklesby E., Le Vaillant J., McCormick A., Mandelli D. and Mather M. (2009) 'Substance misuse in pregnancy: an unrecognised and misdiagnosed problem for a child', *Seen and Heard*, 19:1, pp.22–32

Broomhall C. (2003) *The Eternal Child*, London: Ebury Press

Burnell A. and Vaughan J. (2008) 'Remembering never to forget and forgetting never to remember', in Luckock B. and Lefevre M. (eds) *Direct Work: Social work with children and young people in care*, London: BAAF, Chapter 15, pp.223–233

Cairns K. and Fursland E. (2007) *Safer Caring: A training programme*, London: BAAF

Camis J. (2001) *My Life and Me*, London: BAAF

Carlson E. (1997) *Trauma Assessment: A clinician's guide*, New York, NY: Guilford Press

Cassons, J. (2004) 'Sculpting', *The Prompt*, Newsletter of the British Association of Dramatherapy, Summer edition, pp.7–11

Chambers Dictionary (2001) Edinburgh: Chambers

Cleaver H. (2006) 'The influence of parenting and other family relationships', in Aldgate J., Jones D., Rose W. and Jeffrey C. (2006) *The Developing World of the Child*, London: Jessica Kingsley Publishers, pp.122–140

Cole M. and Cole S. R. (1996) *The Development of Children* (third edition), New York, NY: W.H. Freeman

Corrigan M. and Floud C. (1990) 'A framework for direct work with children in care', Practice brief, *Adoption & Fostering*, 14:2, pp.28–32

Cox M. and Thielgaard A. (1987) *Mutative Metaphors in Psychotherapy: The Aeolian mode*, Leicester: Leicester University Press

Crittenden P. (2008) *Raising Parents: Attachment, parenting and child safety*, Uffculme, Devon: Willan Publishing

Crittenden P. and Claussen A. (eds.) (2003) *The Organization of Attachment Relationships: Maturation, culture and context*, Cambridge, MA: Cambridge University Press

Damasio A.R. (1998) 'Emotion in the perspective of an integrated nervous system', *Brain Research Reviews*, 26, pp.83–86

DCSF (Department for Children, Schools and Families) (2003) *Every Child Matters*, London: HMSO

DCSF (2009) *The Protection of Children in England: Action plan in response to Lord Laming*, London: DCSF

Department for Education and Skills (DfES) (2000) *Raising Skills, Improving Life Chances*, White Paper, London: HMSO

DfES (2006) *Working Together to Safeguard Children: A guide to inter-agency working to safeguard and promote the welfare of children*, London: The Stationery Office

DfES (2007) *Care Matters: Time for change*, Green Paper, London: DfES

DfES (2009) *Care Matters: Time for change*, White Paper, London: DfES

Department of Health (2000) *Framework of Assessment for Children in Need and their Families*, London: HMSO

Department of Health (2004) *National Service Framework for Children, Young People and Maternal Services*

Dostoyevsky, (1821–1881) www.tomstrong.org/quotes/q.D.html-

Dozier M., Stovall K. C., Albus K. E. and Bates B. (2001) 'Attachment for infants in foster care: the role of caregiver state of mind', *Child Development*, 72, pp.1467–77

Ekman P. (1992) 'Facial expressions of emotion, new findings, new questions', *Psychological Science*, 3, pp.34–88

Erikson E. (1950*) Childhood and Society*, New York, NY: Norton

Fahlberg V. (1994) *A Child's Journey through Placement*, London: BAAF

Fein G.G. (1987) 'Pretend play: creativity and consciousness', in Gorlitz P. and Wohlwill J. (eds.) *Curiosity, Imagination and Play*, Hillsdale, NJ: Lawrence Erlbaum Associates

Fisher E.P. (1992) 'The impact of play on development: a meta analysis', *Play and Culture*, 5, pp.159–81

Fonagy P. and Bateman A. W. (2008) 'Comorbid anti-social and borderline personality disorders: mentalisation-based treatment', *Journal of Clinical Psychology*, 64, pp.181–94

Fonagy P., Target M. and Shmueli-Goetz Y. (2003) 'Attachment representation in pre-school children: the development of the Child Attachment Interview (CAI)', *Journal of Child Psychotherapy*, 29:2, pp.171–186

Forbes H. and Post B. (2006) *Beyond Consequences, Logic and Control: A love based approach to helping attachment challenged children with severe behaviours*, Boulder, CO: Beyond Consequences Institute

Fraiberg V. (2008) *The Magic Years*, London: Scribner

Freud A. (1965) *Normality and Pathology in Childhood, Assessment of Development*, New York, NY: International Universities Press

Freud A. (1966) *The Ego and the Mechanisms of Defence*, New York, NY: International Universities Press Inc.

Freud S. (1925) 'The Unconscious', in *Collected Papers*, London: Hogarth

Gardini S, Cloninger CR, Venneri A (2009) 'Individual differences in personality traits reflect structural variance in specific brain regions', *Brain Research Bulletin*, 79, pp.265–70

Gerhardt S. (2004) *Why Love Matters: How love shapes the baby's brain*, Hove: Brunner Routledge

Gilligan R. (1997), 'Beyond permanence? The importance of resilience in child placement practice and planning', *Adoption & Fostering*, 21:1, pp.12–19

Gilligan R (2009) *Promoting Resilience: A resource guide on working with children in the care system* (second edition), London: BAAF

Goleman D. (1996) *Emotional Intelligence*, London, Bloomsbury

Goodall J. (1990) *Through a Window: Thirty years with the chimpanzees of Gombe*, London: Weidenfeld & Nicholson

Griffin J. and Tyrrel I. (2003) *Human Givens*, Chalvington, UK, The Human Givens Publishing Co.

Hartley L.P. (1953) *The Go Between*, London: Hamish Hamilton

Heinicke C.M. and Westheimer I. (1966) *Brief Separations*, International Universities Press

Howe D. (2005) *Child Abuse and Neglect: Attachment, Development and Intervention*, London: Palgrave Macmillan

Hughes D. (1998) *Building the Bonds of Attachment: Awakening love in deeply troubled children*, New Jersey: Jason Aronson Inc.

Hughes D. (2003) 'Psychological intervention for the spectrum of attachment disorders and intrafamilial trauma', *Attachment & Human Development*, 5, pp.271–79

Isaacs S. (1930) cited in Courtney, R. *Drama and Feeling: An aesthetic theory*, Canada: McGill-Queen University Press

James J. (2007) 'Life story work: a biographical account of identity therapy?', *Seen and Heard*, 17:2, pp.32–41

Jennings S. (1992) *Dramatherapy with Families, Groups and Individuals: Waiting in the wings*, London: Jessica Kingsley Publishers

Jewett C. (1984) *Helping Children Cope with Separation and Loss*, London: Batsford

Jung C. (1953) *Personality Types*, London: Routledge

Kane P. (2004), *The Play Ethic*, Rochdale: BNPB

Katz L., Spoonemore N. and Robinson C. (1994) *Concurrent Planning*, Washington, DC: McMillan Publishing Co.

Kelly G. (1953) 'A cognitive theory of personality', in Hjelle L. and Ziegler D. (1992) *Personality Theories, Basic Assumptions, Research and Applications*, New York: McGraw-Hill

Klein M. (1975) *Envy and Gratitude and Other Works: 1946–1963*, London: Hogarth Press

Kohlberg L. (1984) *The Psychology of Moral Development Vol 2*, San Francisco, CA: Harper and Row

Kubler-Ross E. (1969) *On Death and Dying*, London: Routledge

Lahad M. (1992) 'Storymaking in assessment: method for coping with stress', in Jennings S. (ed.) *Dramatherapy Theory and Practice II*, London: Routledge

Laming, Lord (2003) *The Protection of Children in England: A progress report*, London: The Stationery Office

Landreth G. (ed.) (2001) *Innovations in Play Therapy: Issues, process and special populations*, Hove: Brunner-Routledge

Le Doux J. (1998) *The Emotional Brain: The Mysterious underpinnings of emotional life*, London: Phoenix

Lefevre M. (2008) 'Communicating and engaging with children and young people in care through play and the creative arts', in Lucock B. and Lefevre M. (eds.) *Direct Work: Social work with young people in care*, London: BAAF, Chapter 8, pp.130–150

Luckock B., Lefevre M. and Orr D., with Tanner K., Jones M. and Marchant R. (2006) *Knowledge Review: Teaching, learning and assessing communication skills with children in social work education'*, London: Routledge

Luckock B. Stevens P. and Young J. (2008) 'Living through the experience: the social worker as the trusted ally and champion of young people in care', in Lucock B. and Lefevre M. (eds.) *Direct Work: Social work with young people in care*, London: BAAF, Chapter 1, pp.1–16

McIntee J. (1992) *Trauma: the psychological process*, cited in Archer C. (1999) *Next Steps in Parenting the Child who Hurts: Tykes and Teens*, London: Jessica Kingsley Publishers

McLeod A. (2008), *Listening to Children: A practitioner's guide*, London: Jessica Kingsley Publishers

Main M. and Goldwyn R. (1984) *Adult Attachment: Scoring and classification system*, Unpublished manuscript, Berkeley, CA: University of California

Main M. and Hesse E. (1990) 'Parent unresolved traumatic experiences are related to infant disorganized attachment status: Is frightened or frightening parental behaviour the linking mechanism?' in Greenberg M. Cicchetti D. and Cummings E. (eds.) *Attachment in the Preschool years: Theory, research and intervention*, Chicago, IL: University of Chicago Press, pp.126–139

Marsh P. (1968 or 1988?) *Eye to Eye: How people interact*, Topsfield, MA: Salem House Publishing

Maslow A. (1943) 'A humanistic theory of personality', cited in Hjelle L. and Ziegler D. (1976) *Personality Theories: Basic assumptions, research and applications*, New York: McGraw Hill

Meekums B. (2002) *Dance Movement Therapy: A creative psychotherapeutic approach*, London: Sage Publications

Mehrabian A. (1972) cited in Carton J. Kessler E and Pape C. (1999) 'Nonverbal decoding skills and relationship well-being in adults', *Journal of Nonverbal Behaviour*, 23:1, pp.91–100

Moore J. (2006) 'Theatre of Attachment: using drama to facilitate attachment in adoption, *Adoption & Fostering*, 30:2, pp.64–73

Moore J. (2009) 'The Theatre of Attachment: dramatherapy with adoptive and foster families', in Jennings S. (ed.) *Dramatherapy and Social Theatre*, London: Routledge

Moore J. and Peacock F. (2007) 'A sensory approach to assessing and obtaining the views of children delayed in development', *Seen & Heard*, 17:4; pp.25–37

Morrison M. (2007) *Talking about Adoption to your Adopted Child*, London: BAAF

Oaklander V. (1978) *Windows to Our Children*, Utah: Real People Press

Oppenheim D. and Goldsmith D. (2007) *Attachment Theory in Clinical work with Children: Bridging the gap between theory and practice*, New York: Guilford Press

Pallett C., Blackeby K., Yule W., Weissman R. and Scott S. (2008) *Managing Difficult Behaviour: A handbook for foster carers of under-12s*, London: BAAF

Passingham R. (2008) *What is Special about the Human Brain?*, Oxford: Oxford University Press

Perry B. (2002) 'Childhood experience and the expression of genetic potential: what childhood neglect tells us about nature and nurture', *Brain and Mind*, 3, pp.79–100

Perry B. (2008) *The Traumatised Child: Healing brain, mind and body*, Conference Paper, Child Mental Health Centre, London: 14 June 2008

Perry B., Anda R., Felitti V., Bremner D., Walker J., Whitfield C., Dube S. and Giles W. (2006) 'The enduring effects of abuse and related adverse experiences in childhood: a convergence of evidence from neurobiology and epidemiology', *Eur Arch Psychiatry Clinic of Neuroscience* 256, pp.174–86

Perry B. and Pollard R. (1998) 'Homeostasis, stress, trauma and adaptation: a neurodevelopmental view of childhood trauma', *Child and Adolescent Psychiatric Clinics of North America*, 7:1, pp.22–46

Perry B. and Szalavitz M. (2008) *The Boy who was Raised as a Dog and Other Stories from a Child Psychiatrist's Notebook: What traumatized children can teach us about loss, love and healing*, New York: Basic Books

Piaget J. (1952) *The Origins of Intelligence in Children*, New York: International Universities Press

Piaget J. and Inhelder B. (1969) *The Psychology of the Child*, London: Routledge & Kegan Paul

Plummer D. (2004) *Helping Children to Build Self-esteem*, London: Jessica Kingsley Publishers

Prior V. and Glaser D. (2006) *Understanding Attachment and Attachment Disorders: Theory, evidence and practice*, London: Jessica Kingsley Publishers

Pullman P. (2004) 'Opinion', *Guardian Education*, 30 March, p.27, cited in Aldgate *et al* (2006) *The Developing World of the Child*, London: Jessica Kingsley Publishers

Robertson J. (1953) 'A two-year-old goes to hospital', University Park, PA: Penn State Audio Visual Services

Rogers C. (1961) *On Becoming a Person: A therapist's view of psychotherapy*, London: Bowden

Rose R. and Philpot T. (2005) *Life Story Work*, London: Jessica Kingsley Publishers

Ruch G. (2008) 'Developing "containing contexts" for the promotion of effective direct work: the challenge for organisations', in Luckock B. and Lefevre M. (eds.) *Direct Work: Social work with young people in care*, London: BAAF, Chapter 21, pp.295–306

Rushton A. (2003) *The Adoption of Looked After Children: A scoping review of research*, London: Social Care Institute for Excellence/Policy Press

Rushton A. and Monck E. (2009) *Enhancing Adoptive Parenting: A test of effectiveness*, London: BAAF

Russ S. (2004) *Play in Child Development and Psychotherapy: Toward empirically supported practice*, New York: Lawrence Erlbaum Associates

Russ S. and Cooperberg M. (2002) 'Play as a predictor of creativity, coping and depression in adolescence', in Russ S. (2004) *Play in Child Development and Psychotherapy: Toward empirically supported practice*, New York: Lawrence Erlbaum Associates

Russ S., Robins D. and Christiano B. (1999) 'Pretend play: longitudinal prediction of creativity and affect in fantasy in children', *Creativity Research Journal*, 12, pp.129–39

Russ S. and Schafer E. (2002) *Affect in Play Emotional Memories and Divergent thinking*, in Russ and Cooperberg (2004), as above

Rutter M. (1985) 'Resilience in the face of adversity: protective factors and resistance to psychiatric disorders', *British Journal of Psychiatry*, 147, pp.589–611

Rutter M. (ed.) (1996) *Genetics of Criminal and Anti-social Behaviour in Childhood*, Chichester: John Wiley & Sons

Rutter M. (1999) 'Resilience concepts and findings: implications for family therapy', *Journal of Family Therapy*, 21, pp.119–44

Rutter M. and the English and Romanian Adoptees study team (2009) *Policy and Practice Implications from the English-Romanian Adoption Study: Forty five key questions*, London: BAAF

Rutter M. and Rutter M. (1993) *Developing Minds: Challenge and continuity across the life span*, Harmondsworth: Penguin

Ryan T. and Walker R. (2007) *Life Story Work: A practical guide to helping children understand their past*, London: BAAF

Satir V. (1972) *Peoplemaking*, London: Souvenir Press

Sayers A. and Roach R. (2011) *Child Appreciation Days*, London: BAAF

Schaefer C. (2003) *The Foundations of Play Therapy*, Chichester: John Wiley & Sons

Schofield G. (1998) 'Inner and outer worlds: a psychosocial framework for child and family social work', *Child & Family Social Work*, 3:1, pp.57–67

Schofield G. (2005) 'The voice of the child in family placement decision-making', *Adoption & Fostering*, 29:1, pp.29–44

Schofield G. (2008) 'Providing a secure base – an attachment perspective', in Luckock B. and Lefevre M. (eds.) *Direct Work: Social work with children and young people in care*, London: BAAF, Chapter 3, pp.43–57

Schofield G. and Beek M. (2006) *Attachment Handbook for Foster Care and Adoption*, London: BAAF

Schore A. (2006) *Affect Dysregulation and Disorders of the Self*, London: Norton

Seligman M. (1995) 'The optimistic child', cited in Goleman D. (1996) *Emotional Intelligence*, London: Bloomsbury

Selwyn, J., del Tufo S. and Frazer L. (2009) 'It's a Piece of Cake? An evaluation of an adopter training programme', *Adoption & Fostering*, 33:1, pp.30–43

Selwyn J., Sturgess W., Quinton D. and Baxter C. (2006) *Costs and Outcomes of Non-infant Adoptions*, London: BAAF

Shah S. and Argent H. (2006) *Life Story Work: What it is and what it means*, London: BAAF

Siegel D. (1999) *The Developing Mind*, New York, NY: Guilford Press

Siegel D. (2001) 'Toward an interpersonal neurobiology of the developing mind: attachment, relationships, "mindsight" and neural integration', *Infant Mental Health Journal*, 22:1–2, pp.67–94

Simmonds J. (2008) 'Foreword: Direct work with children – delusion or reality?', in Luckock B. and Lefevre M. (eds.) *Direct Work: Social work with young people in care*, London: BAAF, pp.xiii–xxvi

Slade P. (1954) *Child Drama*, London: Norton

Sroufe A., Cooper R. and De Hart G. (1996) *Child Development: Its nature and course* (third edition), London: McGraw Hill

Stanislavski C. (1988) *An Actor Prepares*, London: Methuen

Stephenson O. (1998) *Neglected Children: Issues and dilemmas*, Oxford: Blackwell

Stern D. (1985) *The Interpersonal World of the Infant*, New York, NY: Basic Books

Stern D. (1998) *The Diary of a Baby: What your child sees, feels and experiences*, New York, NY: Basic Books

Stone G. (1993) cited by Jones P., in Payne H., *Handbook of Inquiry into the Arts Therapies: One river, many currents*, London: Jessica Kingsley Publishers

Stringer B. (2008) *Communication through Play*, London: BAAF

Sunderland M. (1998) *Draw on Your Emotions*, Oxon: Winslow Press

Sunderland M. (2003) *Helping Children with Loss*, Bicester: Speechmark

Sunderland M. (2007) *The Neuroscience of Attachment*, Conference Paper, Bedford, UK, 31 March

Sunderland M. and Englehart P. (2005) *Managing Anger*, Bicester: Speechmark

Tangney J. P. and Dearing R. L. (2002) *Shame and Guilt*, New York, NY: Guilford Press

Teicher M. H., Samson J. A., Polcari A. and McGreenery C. E. (2006) 'Sticks, stones and hurtful words: relative effects of various forms of childhood maltreatment', *American Journal of Psychiatry*, 163:6, pp.993–1000

Triseliotis J., Shireman J. and Hundleby M. (1997) *Adoption: Theory, practice and research*, London: Cassell

van der Kolk B. (2007) 'Developmental trauma disorder: towards a rational diagnosis for children with complex trauma histories', *Psychiatric Annals*, 35:5, pp.401–08

van der Kolk B., McFarlane A. and Weisaeth L. (eds) (2007) *Traumatic Stress: The effects of overwhelming experience on mind, body and society*, New York, NY: Guilford Press

Vanfleet R. (2004) *Filial Therapy: Strengthening parent–child relationships through play* (second edition), Sarasota, FL: Professional Resource Press

van Gennep A. (1987) *The Rites of Passage*, London: Routledge

van IJzendoorn M. H. (1996) in Grossmann K. E., Grossmann K. and Waters E. (eds.) (2006) *Attachment from Infancy to Adulthood: The major longitudinal studies*, New York, NY: Guilford Press van Velsen C. (1997) 'Theoretical models of post-traumatic stress disorder: psychoanalytical models', in Black D., Newman M., Harris-Hendricks J. and Mezey G. (eds) *Psychological Trauma: A developmental approach*, London: Gaskell, pp.61–63

Vygostsky L. (1962) *Thought and Language*, Cambridge, M.A.: M.I.T. Press

Vygotsky L. (1967) *Imagination and Creativity in Childhood*, Moscow: Prosvescheniye (original work published in 1930)

Walker J. (2008) 'The use of attachment theory in adoption and fostering', *Adoption & Fostering*, 32:1, pp.49–57

Waller D. (2008) *What Do You Feel?*, Emotional learning cards, London: Iniva

West J. (1996) *Child Centred Play Therapy* (second edition), London: Hodder Arnold

Westheimer (1966)

Willett J. (1977) *The Theatre of Bertolt Brecht*, London: Methuen

Winnicott C. (1986) 'Face to face with children', in BAAF, *Working with Children*, Practice Series 13, London: BAAF, pp.38–48

Winnicott D. (1962) 'The theory of parent–infant relationships', Papers, *International Journal of Psychoanalysis*, 41, pp.571–98

Winnicott D. (1971) *Playing and Reality*, New York, NY: Basic Books

Winnicott D. (1988) *Human Nature*, London: Free Association Books

Winston's Wish Charity (2000) *Muddles, Puddles and Sunshine: Your activity book to help when someone has died*, Stroud: Hawthorn Press

Wolfs R. (2008) *Adoption Conversations: What, when and how to tell*, London: BAAF

Wolpert L. (1990) *Malignant Sadness: The anatomy of depression*, London: Faber & Faber

Useful books and resources

Below is a small selection of children's books and other resources used by the authors.

Adoption (also useful for attachment)

Foxton J. (2002) *Nutmeg Gets Cross* and *Nutmeg Gets Adopted*, London: BAAF

Orritt B. (1990) *Going into Care*, London: The Children's Society

Thom M. and Macliver C. (1986) *Bruce's Story*, London: The Children's Society

Voake C. (2003) *Ginger Finds a Home*, London: Walker Books

Anger and rage

Bang M. (1999) *When Sophie Gets Angry – Really, really angry...*, London: Scholastic

McCarthy D. (2007) *If You Turned into a Monster* and *Speaking about the Unspeakable*, London: Jessica Kingsley Publishers

Moss D. (1989) *The Hyperactive Turtle*, Bethesda, MD: Woodbine House

Oram H. (1982) *Angry Arthur*, London: Red Fox

Pallett C., Blackeby K., Yule W., Weissman R. and Scott S. (2008) *Managing Difficult Behaviour: A handbook for foster carers of the under 12s*, London: BAAF

Richardson J. (1989) *The Bad Mood Bear*, London: Red Fox

Sunderland M. (2000) *A Nifflenoo called Nevermind: A story for children who bottle up their feelings*, Bicester: Speechmark

Sunderland M. (2003) *How Hattie Hated Kindness*, Bicester: Speechmark

Whitehouse E. and Pudney W. (1987) *A Volcano in my Tummy*, London: New Society Publishers (helping children to handle anger)

Attachment

Bedford D. and Chapman J. (2001) *Big Bear Little Bear*, London: Little Tiger Press

Bell M. (2008) *Elfa and the Box of Memories*, London: BAAF

Burningham J. (1963) *Borka: The adventures of a goose with no feathers*, London: Little Greats

Daly N. (1995) *My Dad*, New York: Margaret K. McElderry Books (also useful for attachment and domestic harm fuelled by alcohol)

Gliori D. (1999) *No Matter What*, London: Bloomsbury

Inkpen M. (1997) *Everyone Hide from Wibbly Pig*, London: Hodder

Ironside V. (2004) *The Huge Bag of Worries*, London: Hodder (also useful for fear)

Jensen V.A. and Haller D.W. (1977) *What's That?* London: Collins

Lupton H. and Fatus S. (2001) *The Story Tree*, Oxford: Barefoot Books

Rosen M. and Oxenbury H. (1989) *We're Going on a Bear Hunt*, London: Walker Books

Seeney J. (2007) *Morris and the Bundle of Worries*, London: BAAF

Sendak M. (1963) *Where the Wild Things Are*, London: Red Fox

Shannon D. (1998) *No, David!*, London: Scholastic

Sunderland M. (2000) *The Frog who Longed for the Moon to Smile: A story for children who yearn for someone they love*, Oxon: Wimslow Press

Sunderland M. (2009) *Draw on Your Emotions*, London: Speechmark

Vanni G.B. and Siff L.A. (2005) *Love*, Edinburgh: Canongate

Waller D. (2008) *What do you Feel?* Emotional learning cards, London: Iniva

Williams M. (1992) *The Velveteen Rabbit*, London: Egmont

Bodily functions

Gomi T. (2004) *Everybody Poos*, London: Frances Lincoln Children's Books

Muller B. (2007) *Farley Farts*, New York: North South Books

Roberts D. (2003) *Dirty Bertie*, London: Little Tiger Press

Bullying

Baumgart K. (2003) *Laura's Secret*, London: Little Tiger Press

Goffe T. (1991) *Bully for You*, Swindon: Child's Play International Ltd

Sunderland M. (2000) *A Wibble called Bipley and a Few Honks: A story for children who have hardened their hearts or become bullies*, Oxon: Wimslow Press

Court preparation

Bray N. (1989) *Susie and the Wise Hedgehog go to Court*, London: Porksmere

NSPCC (1993) *The Child Witness Pack: Helping children to cope*, London: NSPCC

Direct work

Beckerleg T. (2008) *Fun with Messy Play: Ideas and activities for children with special needs*, London: Jessica Kingsley Publishers

Kerr J. (1993) *Mog the Forgetful Cat*, London: Picture Lions

Luckcock B. and Lefevre M. (eds.) (2008) *Direct Work: Social work with children and young people in care*, London: BAAF

Mason M. (1989) *Nothing Special*, London: Working Press (also useful for identity)

Plummer D. (2007) *Helping Children to Build Self-Esteem: A photocopiable activities book*, London: Jessica Kingsley Publishers

Plummer D. (2008) *Social Skills Games for Children*, London: Jessica Kingsley Publishers (particularly useful for attachment work)

Romaine M., with Turley T. and Tuckey N. (2007) *Preparing Children for Permanence: A guide to undertaking direct work for social workers, foster carers and adoptive parents*, London: BAAF

Stewart J. (2000) *Me and My Mammoth*, Basingstoke: Macmillan

Stower A. (2005) *Slam*, Dorking: Templar Publishing

Striker K. (1984) *The Anti Colouring Book*, London: Hippo Books

Stringer B. (2009) *Communicating through Play*, London: BAAF

Sunderland M. (2000) *Using Story Telling as a Therapeutic Tool with Children*, Bicester: Winslow

Sunderland M. (2000–2003) Stories and guidebooks on specific themes, Chesterfield: Winslow

> *A Nifflenoo called Nevermind,* a story for children who bottle up their feelings
>
> *Willy and the Wobbly House,* a story for children who are anxious or obsessional
>
> *A Pea Called Mildred,* a story to help children pursue their hopes and dreams
>
> *The Frog who Longed for the Moon to Smile,* to help children with grief
>
> *The Day the Sea Went Out and Never Came Back,* helping children with loss
>
> *Ruby and the Rubbish Bin,* helping children with low-self esteem
>
> *How Hattie Hated Kindness,* helping children locked in rage or hate
>
> *Teenie Weenie in a Too Big World,* helping children with fear and/or disability
>
> *A Wibble called Bipley and a Few Honks,* for children who have hardened their hearts or become bullies

Divorce and separation

Sanford D. (1985) *Please Come Home: A child's book about divorce*, Hong Kong: Multnomah (also useful for attachment, loss and domestic and other types of harm)

Domestic violence

Edwards N. (2005) *Talking about Domestic Violence*, London: Chrysalis Children's Books

Foxon J. (2007) *Spark Learns to Fly*, London: BAAF

Eating and food

Stickland P. and Stickland H. (1994) *Dinosaur Roar*, London: Penguin (particularly useful for attachment and neglect)

Exploration

Agard J. (1981) *Dig Away Two-Hole Tim*, London: Hodder (also useful for identity and attachment)

Brown E. (2002) *Handa's Hen*, London: Walker Books (also useful for loss)

Fear

Angelou M. (1993) *Life Doesn't Frighten Me*, New York, NY: Harry N. Abrams

Bourgeois P. (1987) *Franklin in the Dark*, London: Scholastic

Cooper H. (2008) *The Bear under the Stairs*, London: Picture Corgi Books (also useful for attachment)

Donaldson J. and Scheffler A. (1999) *The Gruffalo*, Basingstoke: Macmillan (also useful for attachment)

Huebner D. (2005) *What to Do When You Worry Too Much: A kids' guide to overcoming anxiety*, Washington, D.C.: Magination Press

Stimsom J. (1996) *Worried Arthur*, London: Ladybird (useful for attachment)

Waddell M. and Firth B. (1990) *Can't You Sleep Little Bear?* London: Walker Books (also useful for attachment)

Grief and loss

Cattanach A. (2008) *Malpas the Dragon*, London: Jessica Kingsley Publishers

Foxon J. (from 2000) *Nutmeg* series, London: BAAF

Jewett C. (1995) *Helping Children with Separation and Loss*, London: BAAF/Batsford

Kerr J. (2002) *Goodbye Mog*, London: HarperCollins

Krementz J. (1988) *How it Feels when a Parent Dies*, New York, NY: A. Knopf

Mellonie B. (1998) *Lifetimes*, London: Banham

Winston's Wish, *Muddles, Puddles and Sunshine*, Stroud: Hawthorn Press

Identity, diversity and self-esteem

Butler J. (2001) *Whose Baby Am I?*, London: Puffin

Cooke T. (1996) *So Much*, London: Walker Books

Green L. (1983) *No-one Loved Horace Until ...*, Deeping: Minimax Books (also useful for attachment)

Griffiths J (2007) *Picnic in the Park*, London: BAAF

Hedderwick M. (1997) *Katie Morag and the Two Grandmothers*, London: Red Fox

Hoffman M. and Littlewood K. (2002) *The Colour of Home*, London: Frances Lincoln Children's Books

McCormick W. (1999) *The Night you were Born*, London: Orchard Picture Books

Parnell P. (2005) *And Tango Makes Three*, London: Simon & Schuster

Parr T. (2001) *It's Okay to Be Different*, London: Little Brown

Storer A. (2001) *The Mole who Needed Glasses*, London: Tesco

Same-gender parents

Argent H. (2007) *Josh and Jaz Have Three Mums*, London: BAAF

Merchant E. (2010) *Dad David, Baba Chris and Me*, London: BAAF

Newman L. (1989) *Heather has Two Mummies*, Northampton: In Other Words Publishing (also useful for attachment)

Newman L. (1991) *The Belinda's Bouquet*, London: G.M.P. Publishers

Valentine J. (2004) *One Dad, Two Dads, Brown Dads, Blue Dads*, Boston, MA: Alyson Books

School

Willis J. and Ross T. (2003) *I Hate School*, London: Andersen Press

Separations

Amos J. *Divorce, Death, Hospital* and *Moving*, Series, London: Cherrytree Books

Seeney J. (2007) *Morris and the Bundle of Worries*, London: BAAF

Stickney D. (1982) *Water Bugs and Dragonflies: Explaining death to children*, London: Mowbray

Varley S. (1994) *Badger's Parting Gifts*, London: Picture Lions

White L. (2007) *Ethan: What happened to my baby brother?* Melbourne, Australia: Brolga Publishing

Sex education

Blank J. (1982) *The Play Book for Kids about Sex*, London: Sheba Feminist Publishers

Cole B. (1995) *Mummy Laid an Egg*, London: Red Fox

Meredith S. (1998) *Growing up: Adolescence, body changes and sex*, London: Usborne

Sexual harm

Freeman L. and Deach C. (1982) *It's My Body: A book to teach young children how to resist uncomfortable touch,* USA : Parenting Press Inc

Gil E. (1986) *I Told My Secret: A book for kids who are abused,* Walnut Creek, USA: Launch Press

Hessell J. (1988) *I'm Glad I Told Mum: A parent's and child's guide to coping with sexual abuse,* Auckland, NZ: Beaverbrooks

Hindman J. (1992) *A Very Touching Book for Little People and for Big People,* Ontario, Canada: Alexandra Associates

Hotto N. (1987) *Tom Doesn't Visit us Anymore,* Ontario, Canada: The Women's Press

Morgan L. (1986) *Katie's Yukky Problem: A story about bad touching,* Auckland, NZ: Papers Inc

Rouf K. (1989) *Secrets,* London: The Children's Society

Siblings

Simon F. (2000) *Don't be Horrid Henry,* London: Orion Books

Sleep

Ross T. (2005) *I Don't Want to go to Bed,* London: HarperCollins

Terminal or life-threatening illness

Center for Attitudinal Healing (1978) *There is a Rainbow Behind Every Dark Cloud,* Berkeley, CA: Celestial Arts

Center for Attitudinal Healing (1982) *Straight from the Siblings: Another look at the rainbow,* Berkeley, CA: Celestial Arts

Kohlenberg S. (1993) *Sammy's Mommy has Cancer,* Washington, DC: Magination

Krisher T. (1992) *Kathy's Hats: A story of hope,* Morton Grove, IL: Albert Whitman & Co.

Links to other services and resources

www.baaf.org.uk

www.nspcc.org.uk

www.actionforchildren.org.uk

www.kidscape.org.uk